The Practitioner Inquiry Series

Marilyn Cochran-Smith and Susan L. Lytle, SERIES EDITORS

ADVISORY BOARD: JoBeth Allen, Rebecca Barr, Judy Buchanan, Robert Fecho,
Susan Florio-Ruane, Sarah Freedman, Karen Gallas, Andrew Gitlin,
Dixie Goswami, Peter Grimmett, Gloria Ladson-Billings,
Sarah Michaels, Susan Noffke, Marsha Pincus, Marty Rutherford,
Lynne Strieb, Carol Tateishi, Diane Waff, Ken Zeichner

Narrative Inquiry in Practice:
Advancing the Knowledge of Teaching
  NONA LYONS &
  VICKI KUBLER LaBOSKEY, Editors

Learning from Teacher Research
  JOHN LOUGHRAN, IAN MITCHELL, &
  JUDIE MITCHELL, Editors

Writing to Make a Difference:
Classroom Projects for Community Change
  CHRIS BENSON &
  SCOTT CHRISTIAN with
  DIXIE GOSWAMI &
  WALTER H. GOOCH, Editors

Starting Strong: A Different Look at
Children, Schools, and Standards
  PATRICIA F. CARINI

Because of the Kids: Facing Racial and
Cultural Differences in Schools
  JENNIFER E. OBIDAH &
  KAREN MANHEIM TEEL

Ethical Issues in Practitioner Research
  JANE ZENI, Editor

Action, Talk, and Text: Learning and
Teaching Through Inquiry
  GORDON WELLS, Editor

Teaching Mathematics to the New Standards:
Relearning the Dance
  RUTH M. HEATON

Teacher Narrative as Critical Inquiry:
Rewriting the Script
  JOY S. RITCHIE &
  DAVID E. WILSON

From Another Angle:
Children's Strengths and School Standards
  MARGARET HIMLEY with
  PATRICIA F. CARINI, Editors

Unplayed Tapes: A Personal History of
Collaborative Teacher Research
  STEPHEN M. FISHMAN &
  LUCILLE McCARTHY

Inside City Schools: Investigating Literacy in
the Multicultural Classroom
  SARAH WARSHAUER FREEDMAN,
  ELIZABETH RADIN SIMONS,
  JULIE SHALHOPE KALNIN, ALEX
  CASARENO, & the M-CLASS TEAMS

Class Actions: Teaching for Social Justice in
Elementary and Middle School
  JoBETH ALLEN, Editor

Teacher/Mentor:
A Dialogue for Collaborative Learning
  PEG GRAHAM, SALLY HUDSON-ROSS,
  CHANDRA ADKINS,
  PATTI McWHORTER, &
  JENNIFER McDUFFIE STEWART, Eds.

Teaching Other People's Children: Literacy
and Learning in a Bilingual Classroom
  CYNTHIA BALLENGER

Teaching, Multimedia, and Mathematics:
Investigations of Real Practice
  MAGDALENE LAMPERT &
  DEBORAH LOEWENBERG BALL

Tensions of Teaching:
Beyond Tips to Critical Reflection
  JUDITH M. NEWMAN

John Dewey and the Challenge of
Classroom Practice
  STEPHEN M. FISHMAN &
  LUCILLE McCARTHY

"Sometimes I Can Be Anything": Power,
Gender, and Identity in a Primary Classroom
  KAREN GALLAS

Learning in Small Moments:
Life in an Urban Classroom
  DANIEL R. MEIER

Interpreting Teacher Practice:
Two Continuing Stories
  RENATE SCHULZ

Creating Democratic Classrooms:
The Struggle to Integrate Theory and Practice
  LANDON E. BEYER, Editor

Narrative Inquiry in Practice

ADVANCING THE KNOWLEDGE
OF TEACHING

Edited by Nona Lyons and Vicki Kubler LaBoskey

TEACHERS
COLLEGE
PRESS

Teachers College, Columbia University
New York and London

Published by Teachers College Press, 1234 Amsterdam Avenue, New York, NY 10027

Chapter 12 reprinted with editorial changes from *Teaching and Teacher Education*, Vol. 15, Frances O'Connell Rust, "Professional Conversations: New Teachers Explore Teaching Through Conversation, Story, and Narrative," pp. 367–380, Copyright 1999, with permission from Elsevier Science.

Library of Congress Cataloging-in-Publication Data

Narrative inquiry in practice : advancing the knowledge of teaching / edited by Nona Lyons and Vicki Kubler LaBoskey.
    p. cm. — (Practitioner inquiry series)
    Includes bibliographical references and index.
    ISBN 0-8077-4247-3 (pbk. : alk. paper) — ISBN 0-8077-4248-1 (cloth : alk. paper)
    1. Education—Research—Methodology. 2. Narration (Rhetoric) 3. Storytelling.
I. Lyons, Nona. II. LaBoskey, Vicki Kubler. III. Series.

    LB1028 .N253 2002
    370'.7'2—dc21   2002019430

ISBN 0-8077-4247-3 (paper)
ISBN 0-8077-4248-1 (cloth)

Printed on acid-free paper
Manufactured in the United States of America

09 08 07 06 05 04 03 02   8 7 6   5 4 3 2 1

Contents

Preface   vii

Introduction   1

1 Why Narrative Inquiry or Exemplars for
   a Scholarship of Teaching?   11

   Nona Lyons and Vicki Kubler LaBoskey

PART I: Uncovering Narrative Teaching Practices: A Sampler

2 Stories as a Way of Learning Both Practical
   and Reflective Orientations   31

   Vicki Kubler LaBoskey

3 Narratives That Teach: Learning About Teaching from
   the Stories Teachers Tell   48

   Anna Ershler Richert

4 Out of Despair: Reconceptualizing Teaching
   Through Narrative Practice   63

   Rebecca Akin

5 Teaching Through Relationships and Stories   76

   Nancy M. Cardwell

6 The Personal Self in a Public Story: The Portfolio
   Presentation Narrative   87

   Nona Lyons

7 Using Narrative Teaching Portfolios for Self-Study   101

   Vicky Anderson-Patton and Elisabeth Bass

8 The Development of Teachers' Narrative Authority
   in Knowledge Communities: A Narrative Approach
   to Teacher Learning   115

   Cheryl J. Craig and Margaret R. Olson

**PART II: Embedding and Extending Inquiry Through Narrative
   Research Practices**

9 Three Narrative Teaching Practices—One Narrative
   Teaching Exercise   133

   D. Jean Clandinin, F. Michael Connelly, and Elaine Chan

10 Action Research as Border Crossing:
    Stories from the Classroom   146

    Anne Rath

11 Narrative Research in Teacher Education: New Questions,
    New Practices   160

    Helen Freidus

12 Professional Conversations: New Teachers Explore
    Teaching Through Conversation, Story, and Narrative   173

    Frances O'Connell Rust

13 In Conclusion: An Invitation   189

    Vicki Kubler LaBoskey and Nona Lyons

About the Editors and the Contributors   201

Index   205

Preface

> My argument is that until we find ways of publicly displaying, examining, archiving, and referencing teaching as a form of scholarship and investigation, our pedagogical knowledge and know-how will never serve us as scholars in the ways our research does. The archival functions of research scaffold our frailties of memory, and we need something comparable for the scholarship of teaching.
>
> —Lee Shulman, *The Course Portfolio*

When Ernest Boyer published his landmark book, *Scholarship Reconsidered*, he argued that colleges and universities need "new forms of scholarship" beyond the traditional model—what he called the scholarship of discovery. He identified three new forms, including the scholarship of teaching, a scholarship that would contribute to a knowledge of teaching and transform and extend it. Boyer's work launched a series of investigations into college teaching.

Sponsored by the Carnegie Foundation and the American Association for Higher Education (AAHE), the new research took up a set of pressing questions: What is the evidence of a scholarship of teaching? How can it be inquired into, documented, represented? If such an idea is to be considered seriously, Donald Schön suggested, action research by practitioners would be needed and would have to produce knowledge that is valid, according to criteria of appropriate rigor. A fundamental feature for a new scholarship of teaching was, then, the notion of active inquiry into it by practitioners themselves. But how? This book takes up this important question and suggests narrative as a candidate mode of inquiry to address it.

For an activity to be considered as scholarship, Lee Shulman (1998) suggests at least three key characteristics: it should be public, susceptible to critical review and evaluation, and accessible for exchange and use by other members of one's scholarly community. Yet, Shulman argues, these are generally absent for teaching. In this book we present one model for achieving these ends: what we call exemplars of inquiry—teaching and research practices made public and accessible for peer review, testing, and evaluation. Chapter authors have tried out these practices. We invite others to do the same, to extend this work, and contribute to building a usable knowledge of teaching.

The intellectual roots of this project for us are found in several sources. Our long-term research on teaching portfolios first directed our attention to narrative and its possibilities. Portfolios became the means of documenting and representing the story of learning a portfolio maker was constructing, the place where stories could be housed and the evidence of teaching and learning presented. But the portfolio represents something more: It is a mode of inquiry. The evidence it presents and the story it tells result from an investigation, an interrogation into some surprising encounter, some puzzle about teaching or learning—what Dewey called a doubt, a perplexity. Through a portfolio, that investigation can be made public and open to scrutiny.

Interviews with students about the portfolio process proved a rich avenue for understanding what students themselves found in a portfolio work, the sometimes hard-earned insights uncovered. Here, narrative storylines were an essential feature.

For each of us there are other roots of this work. Vicki LaBoskey finds narrative closely tied to her interest in fostering self-study. Nona Lyons connects narrative to research interviewing she began as a doctoral student and has continued for nearly two decades. Eliot Mishler alerted us to the significance of the interactive nature of research interviewing, to how unlike a survey questionnaire it was, and to its story qualities—and how to pay attention to and not dismiss them.

Then the groundbreaking work of Jerome Bruner cast the entire project in a new perspective. He argued that narrative was more than simply telling a story. It was a way of knowing as powerful as scientific knowing but different from it. Although there is a long tradition of narrative in education, Bruner's work confirmed that narrative inquiry could be an important and legitimate way of knowing—could advance a knowledge of teaching. Ernest Boyer argued, too, for this enterprise—for expanding the forms of scholarly work of the academy, and especially for advancing a scholarship of teaching. But it was equally clear that such a scholarship needed to be seen as having validity.

Eliot Mishler's ideas about exemplars and their validity proved immensely useful. His consultations with us at one of our Portfolio Conferences helped us to frame a way of validating narrative practices. Donald Schön's questions about the epistemologies embedded within the culture of institutions alerted us to the significance and politics of institutional epistemologies, to what can or cannot support the tasks of narrative inquirers. It is a critical dimension, aligned with the work of William Perry and Mary Belenky and Blythe Clinchy and their colleagues.

In bringing this project to publication, we are grateful to Carol Collins of Teachers College Press and to her colleagues for their excellent assistance. We appreciate, too, the very astute comments of the reviewers of our original book proposal. We want to acknowledge the important contribution of Jane Attanucci, who read and commented on the manuscript at a crucial point, and, of Joan Moon, who gave us critical editorial support. We especially thank our students, our colleagues, and our own mentors: Maxine Greene, who has celebrated narrative and the imagination as ways of knowing, particularly of the little known, the likely marginalized; Lee Shulman, who has steadfastly and eloquently promoted a knowledge of teaching; Blythe Clinchy and Mary Belenky, who advanced our knowledge through their own important work on ways of knowing; Nel Noddings and Carol Gilligan for revelations as to the centrality of caring relationships and communications in education; and Jean Clandinin and Michael Connelly, who went before, crafting narrative inquiry into a significant research mode for studying experience in education. They helped us stay the course. As always, we thank Robert Lyons and Pete, Sara, and Jeff LaBoskey for their moral support, constancy, and understanding.

Introduction

Long before we envisioned a book on narrative knowing or considered narrative practices as potential exemplars, models for investigating teaching practice, we were engaged in conversations around our own teaching and research. Seeking an alternative to the then standard mode of teacher assessment, namely objective tests, which, in our view, cannot capture the often messy, unpredictable complexities of teaching practice, we began in the early 1990s asking our teacher interns to construct a teaching portfolio. Students were to document and present evidence of their learning about teaching, their students' learning, and their development and performance as beginning professionals. We experimented with portfolios and followed our students into their early years of teaching. Each January, we came together with other teachers and teacher-educators to share our work at the Portfolio Conference one of us convened at the Harvard-Radcliffe Cronkhite Graduate Center in Cambridge, Massachusetts. We watched with keen interest as the newly constituted National Board for Professional Teaching Standards began requiring experienced teachers to prepare a teaching portfolio as part of their application for board certification.

As we gathered our own compelling evidence of the certain benefits of portfolio processes, especially to foster a teacher's reflective inquiry into his or her own practice, puzzles emerged. They eventually led us to the discovery of how narrative is implicated in portfolio work and, by extension, in other teaching practices. We came to see that narrative was not simply storytelling, but could be a mode of inquiry, a way of knowing, knowing about teaching. Then, when Ernest Boyer (1990) argued compellingly for a new "scholarship of teaching" and Donald Schön (1995) declared that it had to engage practitioners—teachers themselves—in their own action research, larger political and epistemological questions came into view. The classic argument between teachers rooted in the contexts of their inquiries versus impartial, detached university researchers emerged. Could a knowledge of teaching created by practitioners really count? To whom? By what criteria? With what validity? When Schön warned that becoming involved with a new scholarship of teaching "meant becoming involved in an epistemological battle," coming up against the entrenched model of "technical rationality" of the research university, we came to understand the urgent need for a new epistemology. That is a view of knowledge that did not privilege standard research-based theory and techniques, but could foster attention to "practical competence"; support teachers to claim the legitimacy of their own investigations; and generate a knowledge of practice, complementary to other research yet testably valid—if there was to be a dynamic, new scholarship of teaching (Schön, 1995). How did we come to see these interconnections and why do we believe narrative inquiry is a significant way to address them?

NARRATIVE: A SCAFFOLD AND A MODE OF INQUIRY

Early on, we identified narrative in the storymaking and storytelling elements of a portfolio process. It was patently evident in the construction of the story of a teacher as a beginning professional, as he or she gathered evidence and reflected on learning about teaching and learning—the essential elements of a teaching portfolio. But, we wondered, what meaning did storying one's experience of learning have to a storyteller? What connection was there to becoming a reflective practitioner, a clear goal of our portfolio work? (LaBoskey, 1994; Lyons, 1998). When we discovered—as did the National Board for Professional Teaching Standards—that not all new or experienced teachers easily engage in reflection or distinguish among description, analysis, and reflection, we interviewed our own students, taped their portfolio discussions, and pondered their responses and our own practices.

We reviewed how we were scaffolding the portfolio process, reexamining the first exercises we used to introduce reflection. ("Please bring in an entry you would include in a teaching portfolio: Be prepared to tell why you might include this evidence, and what, on reflection, it is you have learned about teaching and learning from it.") We found narrative there. We began to see that teachers' conversations about teaching or learning, essential to portfolio making, were in fact narratives that captured discourses of meaning and interpretation. Conversations became texts to examine and hold up to scrutiny for teachers themselves. The narratives that portfolio makers fashioned to present their portfolios in public next caught our attention. One of us began a study of them, asking students what meaning they found in these narrative creations.

All of these efforts brought us to new realizations: how narrative could at once be a way to scaffold and organize portfolio evidence *and* a method of inquiry. As inquiry, narrative involved an intentional reflective process, the actions of a group of learners interrogating their learning, constructing and telling the story of its meaning, and predicting how this knowledge might be used in the future. We came to see that narrative was fundamentally an activity of mind, a way of gathering up knowledge of practice, simply, a way of knowing, and of knowing that one knew. A portfolio could be a unique medium both of narrative inquiry and the means to document and represent the evidence of the process (Lyons, 2001). While these discoveries about narrative came about through our own portfolio work, others were making similar ones through different routes.

Running parallel to this work, even predating it, was a dramatic eruption of interest in narrative in the social sciences—what some call the interpretive turn (Hiley, Bohman, & Shusterman, 1991; Rabinow & Sullivan, 1987). As early as 1981 Mitchell noted, "There is an aura of intellectual excitement and discovery" about the study of narrative which "has now become a positive source of insight for all branches of human and natural science" (Mitchell, 1981, p. ix). In education, attention to narrative, long focused on its ancient role as a likely medium for carrying a message, something to be conveyed and learned, now shifted to it as a means to capture the situatedness, the contexts, and the complexities of human action in teaching and learning. Narrative was more than a story, a teller, or a text.

Then, in 1986, Jerome Bruner's startling assertion that narrative is a way of knowing confirmed this. Bruner argued that although narrative is complementary to traditional scientific knowing, it is also different from it. One mode cannot be reduced to the other. Bruner's work brought claims and counterclaims for narrative knowing in teaching. It connected current arguments with ones most ancient: explanation was not interpretation or meaning (Bruner, 1986; see also Bernstein, 1983; Hiley, Bohman, & Shusterman, 1991). By the 1990s the standards of positivism that had dominated the social sciences in the 20th century no longer remained unchallenged. There was not one framework but many. In education, a parallel shift occurred. The process-product paradigm of standard research on teaching and learning was turned on its head. Teaching is about the construction of knowledge and meaning by individuals, not simply the transmission of information.

Discussions about narrative in teaching accelerated, as they did in literary criticism, history, psychology, philosophy, feminist theory and the law—to name a few fields. In education, Michael Connelly and Jean Clandinin (1990) continued their careful explorations of narrative as a mode of inquiry, as other researchers and teachers documented their experiences (Carter, 1993; Elbaz, 1983; Gudmundsdottir, 1981; Witherell & Noddings, 1991). Narrative seemed a fundamental phenomenon, a "primary act of mind," Barbara Hardy (1977) argued, as had W.J.T. Mitchell (1981) and Alasdair MacIntyre (1984). Narrative discourse was not just a "manner of speaking, but foundational to learning as a whole" (McEwan & Egan, 1995, p. xi). Philosopher Martha Nussbaum advanced Aristotle's argument for an education of students that would foster through narrative the development of an imaginative knowledge of possibilities, "not for something that has happened, but the kind of thing that might happen," an essential capacity for developing citizens of the world (Nussbaum, 1997, p. 86).

In teaching, narrative forms continued to expand. They became embedded in the professional experiences of beginning and master teachers alike, as well as researchers (Casey, 1995). It became commonplace for practitioners meeting in groups to examine a case study, an autobiography, or a play. Their perceived power to convey subtleties and complexities of contexts, cultures, and the meanings of people who interact in learning made these narrative forms attractive. Research on cognition bolsters the claims of the importance of contexts and collaborative processes of learning. It shifts attention from the minds of individuals to the interacting social and physical contexts of participants in learning, to the thinking they do together, the tools they use, and products they create in constructing knowledge and meaning—all elements of a narrative process (Putnam & Borko, 2000).

PERSISTENT QUESTIONS ABOUT NARRATIVE KNOWING IN TEACHING

Yet, in spite of the interest, arguments, and ample theoretical groundings for them, stubborn questions remain about narrative for educators, as well as for other social scientists: Precisely how is narrative defined? How is it used in actual teaching practices? What constitutes a narrative teaching practice? And, Can the claims for narrative as a way of knowing in teaching be warranted? How?

In education, we believe these questions have a special salience. They have persisted throughout the history of teaching as a profession, in spite of the accelerated efforts by teachers and teacher-educators to engage in action research and other inquiries into teaching (Clandinin & Connelly, 1995; Cochran-Smith & Lytle, 1999; Lampert, 2000; Lytle & Cochran-Smith, 1992). They are linked to a clearly problematic past and the power politics of knowledge claims in the professions. As Grant and Murray (1999) document, what counts as teacher knowledge has consistently been challenged in the history of teaching as a profession, in contrast to the role knowledge claims play in justifying other professions, such as medicine or the law.

"What the public believes about the knowledge base of a profession does affect the power, status, and economic rewards of its practitioners. While several professions have succeeded in cloaking its [*sic*] work in perceptions of great worth, the public has been less willing to believe any comparable saga about teachers" (Grant & Murray, 1999, p. 7). Such is the case today. Perhaps, as Schön bluntly suggests, this resistance is tied to research universities and their commitment, for the most part, to a particular epistemology, a view of knowledge "that fosters selective inattention to practical competence" (Schön, 1983, p. vii).

But Ernest Boyer's publication of *Scholarship Reconsidered* (1990) brought a bold suggestion and a challenge to advance a new knowledge of practice. Arguing that colleges and universities urgently needed new forms of scholarship to go beyond the traditional model, what he called the scholarship of discovery, Boyer identified three new forms: a *scholarship of integration* to make connections across disciplines; *a scholarship of application* to address consequential problems of people and institutions; and a *scholarship of teaching* that would not only contribute to knowledge but transform and extend it. Donald Schön immediately saw the implications: These new forms of scholarship lie much closer to practice and are "inimical to the conditions of control and distance that are essential to technical rationality of the epistemology of the university." Problems of practice are usually ill-formed and actors in the practice situation undeniably interested—a dramatic contrast to the conception of practice as technical rationality, characterized as the application of theory to problems of objective, disinterested practitioners. Needed for a new scholarship of teaching would be inquiries into teaching by practitioners themselves, forms of action research that would in turn produce knowledge that is testably valid and create new claims to knowledge that "must lend themselves to intellectual debate. . . ."(Schön, 1995, pp. 27–34).

In this book, we take up these issues. We present a set of narrative teaching and research practices that function as inquiries into teaching and learning; *and*, a method for testing their validity through forums of discussion and debate. Drawing on actual practices of teachers, teacher-educators, and researchers, this book offers a sampler of narrative practices for use in diverse settings of inquiry with preservice and in-service teachers, with new and with master practitioners, with elementary and secondary teachers, and with researchers. A set of narrative practices is presented in detail. The knowledge teachers uncover is described for each practice. These narrative practices, primarily the fruits of teacher and researcher inquiries, useful for building a scholarship of teaching, are presented as a set of what we call *candidate exemplars*.

VALIDITY AS THE SOCIAL CONSTRUCTION
OF TRUSTWORTHINESS

The exemplar idea and its method of validation were first put forward by Eliot Mishler for inquiry-based research. Mishler argues that certain research practices that serve as potential models for how a practice works are and can be validated, but not by traditional experimental methods (Kuhn, 1962/1970; Mishler, 1990). For, rather than relying for their assessment on an investigator's strict use of standard procedures, these researchers rely on their own understanding of the actual situations of practice in a field of inquiry. Exemplars—models of how a practice works—are tested, but through a process Mishler calls *validation*. Validation here refers to trustworthiness; that is, to the degree to which other practitioners or researchers turn to, rely or will rely on, and *use* the concepts, methods, and inferences of a practice as the basis for their own theorizing, research, or practice (Mishler, 1990, p. 419). In this book, we adopt the ideas of an exemplar and its validation and apply them to narrative teaching and research practices.

As editors, we find the idea of exemplars and the process of validation persuasive. We believe that the process is one of the ways that teachers, teacher-educators, and researchers do in fact revise and refine their practices: by trying them out. In this way, the validity of claims can be tested through discussion by those who have themselves tried a practice: the knowledge of practice is warranted through a process of social construction. Indeed, the set of narrative practices presented in this book has in part been produced through this process. Of the 15 authors of this book, 9 have participated in the annual January Portfolio Conference at least once; many have regularly participated since its inception in 1994, sharing their narrative practices, trying others, and attesting to their trustworthiness.

Here we define narrative practices preliminarily, as intentional, reflective human actions, in which teachers and their students, or researchers and their colleagues, interrogate their teaching or research practices to construct meaning, interpretation, and knowledge of some aspect of teaching or learning through the creation of narrative(s).

But this collection of practices, while considered at best practices of the contributors, is not to be thought of as unproblematic. Indeed, that is the purpose of this book: to offer them as candidate exemplars, making them available for interrogation and potential testing by a larger teaching and research community. All chapter authors address the following: What is the practice, the evidence of its usefulness, and issues or potential issues that may be problematic.

Some related issues concerning narrative are not fully addressed here. Current research on narrative and its myriad methodologies are only selectively reviewed (Mishler, 1995). As the chapter authors indicate, they themselves represent different narrative methodologies. Nor does this book examine all narrative teaching or research practices. It focuses on those practices usually taking place with groups of participants. Emphasis is on the narrative practice, its features, how it works, how it might benefit others, and what might possibly be problematic. Discussion of the connection of this work to related issues of epistemology is addressed in Chapter 1. Implications of narrative inquiry for a scholarship of teaching are outlined there.

This book, then, addresses teachers, teacher-educators, the educational research community, school reformers, educational philosophers, and those generally interested in narrative practices and their validity for the education of professionals, whether in the fields of education or other social science disciplines, but especially for building a scholarship of teaching.

OVERVIEW OF THE BOOK

Chapter 1 discusses narrative inquiry as a way of knowing in teaching, elaborating a conceptual framework for defining narrative practices and for considering narrative teaching and research practices as ways of knowing and potential exemplars. It presents a set of such exemplars, and offers a method for validating them through rigorous intellectual discussion and debate, arguing that narrative practices provide a way to publicly interrogate, examine, and display the scholarship of teaching. Finally, it connects narrative knowing in teaching to contemporary, political issues of epistemology, to teaching as a profession, and to the need to develop a new epistemology for a scholarship of teaching.

Part I presents a sampler of seven distinct narrative practices for teaching and teacher education. Each chapter describes the problem addressed and how it is approached. In Chapter 2, Vicki LaBoskey documents her own discovery of the logic of a narrative mode of knowing as she struggles to revise a teaching assignment that asks her teacher interns to observe different classroom teachers and answer the question, Are these classrooms similar or different on how "setting the tone" for the year was addressed? In what ways? Why? Students then write and share a story of a compelling issue they find in their observations. Chapter 3 and Chapter 4 may be thought of as companion pieces. In Chapter 3, Anna Richert describes her work with experienced teachers in urban settings and how texts these teachers create over a schoolyear foster their ability to reflect on their efforts to create classrooms with equitable pedagogies. Richert believes that these narrative accounts can "stop the action" of real live classrooms long enough for teachers to create texts and, through them, to examine their day-to-day work in schools. In Chapter 4 Rebecca Akin—a participant in one of Richert's courses—suggests how creating narratives as a means of interrogating her own practice is transformative, helping her to reconceptualize herself as a teacher. Nancy Cardwell in Chapter 5 examines the power and the potential limitations of personal life history narratives that experienced teachers create and use to foster trusting relationships with their urban students and to offer them alternative models of dealing with difficult life situations that they encounter sometimes.

Chapters 6 and 7 bear a relationship to one another. In Chapter 6, Nona Lyons explores the narratives that portfolio makers create for public presentations of their portfolios, placing them within a larger portfolio assessment system and then looking specifically at the presentation narrative as a special intentional reflective inquiry. In Chapter 7, Vicky Anderson-Patton and Lis Bass, using the portfolio idea as outlined by Lyons, share their experiences as they engage in a collaborative self-study and consider how to use narrative within a portfolio process to document their own learning. Simultaneously they encourage and support portfolio development by their student teachers. In Chapter 8, Cheryl Craig and Margaret Olson review a set of narrative practices they use—Craig in attempting to establish knowledge communities with teachers, and Olson to validate multiple perspectives on cultural diversities.

Part II takes up narrative research practices. Designating a set of narrative practices as research practices has come to us to seem in some ways arbitrary. For narrative as a mode of inquiry always serves an investigative function. However, the narrative practices presented here are ones specifically directed to systematic research: In Chapter 9 Jean Clandinin, Michael Connelly, and Elaine Chan describe the process of introducing students to thinking narratively as these students begin planning their doctoral research; Anne Rath in Chapter 10 examines how to shepherd a diverse group of classroom teachers in Ireland in action research projects in their own school settings; and in Chapter 11 Helen Freidus finds in researching the implementation of a literacy project how focus interviews became reflective texts for collaborative learning for both teachers and researchers. Frances Rust (Chapter 12) uncovers how conversations beyond teacher-education classrooms can become narratives that sustain dialogue in the professional learning of practicing teachers struggling in tough urban environments through their first years of teaching.

In sum, the teaching and research practices surveyed in these chapters address significant puzzles and problems of teaching and learning, describe the contexts in which these practices took shape, and outline the functions that narrative serves along with some of their consequences—

one model of narrative analysis shared by other researchers (Mishler, 1995).

In the final chapter, Vicki LaBoskey and Nona Lyons return again to narrative as a mode of knowing and revisit the exemplar idea. They take up the work of several teacher-educators/researchers who have been testing three of the practices, and report on their results. They link these explorations to the new scholarship of teaching that Ernest Boyer outlined. A critical task for an emerging scholarship of teaching is how to interrogate, document, and represent a scholarship of teaching. As the American Association for Higher Education suggests, an activity designated as scholarship needs three things: it should be public, susceptible to critical review and evaluation, and accessible for exchange and use by other members of one's community (Shulman, 1998). We believe narrative exemplars meet these requirements. This book promises to advance a scholarship of teaching and elaborates how that is possible.

We suggest that the teaching and research practices presented here offer important insights and some cautions: about narrative inquiry as a reflective way of knowing in teaching; about its contribution to the slow revolution as teachers claim their right to name the knowledge of practice; and about the sobering political dimensions surrounding the knowledge of teaching. The book closes with a challenge: to extend this work and create a powerful, new, compelling scholarship of teaching.

REFERENCES

Bernstein, R. (1983). *Beyond objectivism and relativism: Science, hermeneutics, and praxis*. Philadelphia: University of Pennsylvania Press.

Boyer, E. (1990). *Scholarship reconsidered*. Princeton, NJ: Carnegie Foundation for the Advancement of Teaching.

Bruner, J. (1986). *Actual minds, possible worlds*. Cambridge, MA: Harvard University Press.

Carter, K. (1993). The place of story in the study of teaching and teacher education. *Educational Researcher*, 22(1), 5–18.

Casey, K. (1995). The new narrative research in education. In M. Apple (Ed.), *Review of Research in Education* (vol. 21; pp. 211–254). Washington, DC: American Educational Research Association.

Clandinin, J., & Connelly, M. (1995). *Teachers professional knowledge landscapes: Secret, sacred, and cover stories*. New York: Teachers College Press.

Cochran-Smith, M., & Lytle, S. (1999, October). The teacher research movement: A decade later. *Educational Researcher*, 15–25.

Connelly, M., & Clandinin, J. (1990). Stories of experience and narrative inquiry. *Educational Researcher* 19(5), 2–14.

Elbaz, F. (1983). *Teacher thinking: A study of practical knowledge*. London: Croom Helm.

Grant, G., & Murray, C. (1999). *Teaching in America: The slow revolution*. Cambridge, MA: Harvard University Press.

Gudmundsdottir, S. (1981). Story-maker, story-teller: Narrative structures in curriculum. *Journal of Curriculum Studies, 23*, 207–218.

Hardy, B. (1977). Narrative as a primary act of mind. In M. Meek, A. Warlow, & G. Barton (Eds.), *The Cool Web*. London: Bodley Head.

Hiley, D. R., Bohman, J., & Shusterman, R. (1991). *The Interpretive Turn: Philosophy, Science, Culture*. Ithaca, NY: Cornell University Press.

Kuhn, T. S. (1962/1970). *The structure of scientific revolution*. Chicago: University of Chicago Press.

Lampert, M. (2000). Knowing teaching: The intersection of research on teaching and qualitative research. *Harvard Educational Review, 70*(1), 86–99.

LaBoskey, V. K. (1994). *Development of reflective practice: A study of preservice teachers*. New York: Teachers College Press.

Lyons, N. (1998). *With portfolio in hand: Validating the new teacher professionalism*. New York: Teachers College Press.

Lyons, N. (2001). *Interrogating, documenting, and representing the scholarship of teaching, I & II*. Unpublished manuscript, University College Cork, Ireland.

Lytle, S., & Cochran-Smith, M. (1992). Teacher research as a way of knowing. *Harvard Educational Review, 62*(4), 447–474.

MacIntyre, A. (1984). *After virtue: A study in moral theory*. (2nd Ed.). Notre Dame, IN: University of Notre Dame Press.

McEwan, H., & Egan, K. (1995). *Narrative in teaching, learning, and research*. New York: Teachers College Press.

Mishler, E. (1990). Validation in inquiry-guided research: The role of exemplars in narrative studies. *Harvard Educational Review, 60*, 415–442.

Mishler, E. (1995). Models of narrative analysis: A typology. *Journal of Narrative and Life History, 5*(2), 87–123.

Mitchell, W. T. J. (1981). *On narrative*. Chicago: University of Chicago Press.

Nussbaum, M. (1997). *Cultivating humanity: A classical defense of reform in liberal education*. Cambridge, MA: Harvard University Press.

Putnam, R. T., & Borko, H. (2000). What do new views of knowledge and thinking have to say about research on teacher learning? *Educational Researcher, 29*(1), 4–15.

Rabinow, P., & Sullivan, W. (1987). *Interpretive social science: A second look*. Berkeley: University of California Press.

Schön, D. (1983). *The reflective practitioner: How professionals think in action*. New York: Basic Books.

Schön, D. (1995, November/December). The new scholarship requires a new epistemology. *Change, 27*(6), 26–34.

Shulman, L. (1998). *The course portfolio*. Washington, DC: American Association for Higher Education.

Witherell, C., & Noddings, N. (Eds.). (1991). *Stories lives tell: Narrative and dialogue in education*. New York: Teachers College Press.

CHAPTER 1

Why Narrative Inquiry or Exemplars for a Scholarship of Teaching?

NONA LYONS AND VICKI KUBLER LaBOSKEY

We open this chapter with two vignettes, brief scenes of teachers deliberately engaged in thinking through a puzzle of their practice by creating a narrative of it and, simultaneously, uncovering aspects of their own construction of knowledge. Here, narrative is a mode of inquiry, a way of knowing. While some question the validity of narrative knowing in teaching, we argue for a new approach, what Eliot Mishler terms validity as a process of validation: by determining the trustworthiness of a given practice. We describe how certain narrative practices can serve as exemplars, models of inquiry for others to try in their own settings. The purpose is not to replicate but rather to extend these investigations to new settings. In this discussion, we outline a conceptual framework for this book and link the validity of narrative practices to three interconnected contexts: the present urgency to expand alternative approaches to validity for research on teaching; the slow revolution now at work as teachers do claim authority to investigate and name the knowledge of practice; and the need for a new, robust epistemology, a view of knowledge with attention to practice in support of developing a valid scholarship of teaching. Here we ask: What is the role of narrative in the construction of teachers' knowledge, and in learning to teach? How should this knowledge be judged or validated?

TWO VIGNETTES

It was a dialogue that could have been overheard in any kindergarten classroom. But it took place in Vivian Paley's classroom. And it puzzled her:

"He did that on purpose! You knocked my tower down on purpose!" Fred grabs Wally's leg and begins to cry.

Wally pushes Fred away. "I'm a dinosaur. I'm smashing the city."

"You didn't ask. You have to ask." The tears have stopped.

"Dinosaurs don't ask."(Paley, 1981, p. 8)

When Vivian Paley is puzzled or troubled by a child's behavior and how she might respond to it, she becomes especially attentive to the child's fantasy play. She will bring her tape recorder to a doll corner or the sacred story rug, tape the stories the child tells and, later, other children's conversations that flow from acting it out. Paley will listen again to these stories as she transcribes the tape, refining her understanding of what may be going on for the child, observing the sense other children make of the scene, thinking about what her response has been, what it will be on the following morning, and how she will share it with her colleagues. Paley frequently writes down these stories of her practice and her thinking and theorizing about them. In her books, Paley charts her changing understandings about the meaning of play, story, and fantasy in the lives of children and in her own teaching. In *The Boy Who Would Be a Helicopter*, Paley writes:

> Amazingly, children are born knowing how to put every thought and feeling into story form. If they worry about being lost, they become the parents who search; if angry, they find a hot hippopotamus to impose his will upon the world. . . . It is play, of course, but it is also story in action, just as storytelling is play put into narrative form. The distinctions are important to me because this story playing and storytelling have become the curriculum of any classroom in which I am the teacher. Somewhere in each fantasy is a lesson that promises to lead me to questions and commentary, allowing me to glimpse the universal themes that bind together individual urgencies. (1990, p. 4)

We begin with Vivian Paley because we believe that Paley, a passionate proponent of narrative, demonstrates that, just as storytelling and fantasy are "nothing less than Truth and Life to children," so too are they to effective teachers. Storying an experience, an imperative for Paley, can be a way for teachers to construct meaning and preserve what it is they know and how they think, and rethink their craft, capturing those illuminations discovered in the midst of classroom life and tested and refined over time. It is a way of making teachers' knowledge conscious and public, and open to scrutiny. Paley, an inveterate interrogator of teaching practice over the course of a long career, provides a model of the teacher as inquirer, engaged in a narrative teaching practice that is a way of knowing—what we want to describe and identify as a narrative exemplar. In a recent book,

Paley acknowledges the effect of her interrogations: "Midway into my teaching career I extended my kindergarten to a full-day program to have more time for stories. It marked the beginning of a new way of teaching for me" (Paley, 2001, p. 5).

Now a second vignette, this one of a teacher just entering the profession but who, like Paley, uses narrative as a way to understand and rethink her practice. As a student teacher, Emma Rich finds herself in an impoverished, rural New England community teaching mathematics to high school students termed by their school as "challenged." The term triggers a remembrance of an earlier experience, one Emma now links to the ninth graders before her. She describes these events in a portfolio entry called "The Automechanics" (Lyons, 2000). It tells of her experience working for an auto repair shop to set up a computer program when, unexpectedly, she is asked to cover for a Parts Department vacationer and finds herself "challenged":

> "I need a PCV for a '94 Dodge Spirit," a voice called. I stocked the last of the transmission fluid on the shelf, wearily pulled myself up to a standing position, wiped my hands on my jeans and looked up into the grease-streaked face of one of the auto technicians. Meanwhile another technician is on the phone, while a woman stands at the customer counter waiting for me to look up bike racks. How did I, who cannot tell an oil can from a fuel tank, find myself in this predicament?
>
> The general manager and owner felt I would be perfect for the Parts Department summer replacement since they use a computer system for inventory. They forgot one small detail: the fact that I knew nothing about parts or cars. I was truly technically challenged.
>
> I panicked every time one of the technicians asked for parts. One technician remarked that I looked like a "deer caught in the headlights." Around me, technicians would talk about jobs and what tests they would do to determine what part of the car needed to be fixed or replaced. They amazed me with how much they knew. These are the people who had failed classes in high school and whom teachers had deemed unintelligent, who were in the lower tracks. Here I was, a graduate of an Ivy League school and a former high school valedictorian, feeling incompetent . . . this wasn't the information that was necessary in this world.
>
> Then, I realized how awful it feels not to know what is going on when everyone around you does and I could understand the fright some of my students might feel in my math classes. Even

though I know that I am an intelligent person, I seriously called my intelligence into question.

I realize how much more our society values only certain intelligences. The technicians are considered to be skilled technicians but few would call them brilliant. I disagree. I am amazed by the ability of technicians to problem-solve based on listening to an engine, feeling a part, land-looking at parts. Many can transfer their knowledge to fixing computers, VCRs, etc. They analyze complex problems using their sense and convey their body of knowledge with their hands.

It is my goal to gear my lessons to as many intelligences as possible such that all of my students can feel intelligent and confident in their abilities.

Through this vignette, we sense the shame and frustration of Emma Rich and those technicians as students. But we see, too, the teacher coming to a new understanding. These challenged students suddenly appear in a different guise, in their strengths, their knowledge, and their abilities. Through a reflective narrative, the teacher fashions a new perception, a new meaning. As philosopher Martha Nussbaum suggests, narrative reaches us in part through the imagination, helps us to imagine, to see more finely, and respond to possibilities and vicissitudes of others' lives; and engages us in deliberative, ethical considerations that make possible new perceptions (Nussbaum, 1990, 1997). Storying the person contextualizes him or her, makes that person present to us in all his or her humanity.

But this kind of deliberation does something more: it can direct or redirect a teacher's actual practices. In the vignettes presented here, each of the teacher storymakers forges new knowledge, meanings, and understandings of their students and their ways of knowing; of refining or recasting theories of teaching and learning, such as the role of story in the lives of children or multiple intelligences; of new perceptions of others, especially students; and of ethical values—all revealed through a reflective narrative inquiry.

These teachers reveal an attitude John Dewey saw as necessary to engaging in reflective inquiry, that is, intellectual responsibility. For Dewey, to be intellectually responsible is to consider "the consequences of a projected step, to be willing to adopt these consequences"; the irresponsible "do not ask for the meaning of what they learn, in the sense of what difference it makes to the rest of their beliefs and their actions" (Dewey, 1933/ 1998, pp. 32–33). These teachers have.

THE CLAIMS OF NARRATIVE KNOWING IN TEACHING

Although it is a commonplace that teachers frequently and almost naturally turn to story to communicate their classroom experiences and their knowledge of teaching, it is just as likely that in doing so they have been easily dismissed and often demeaned. At least two issues have proven problematic: that a teacher is an inside inquirer, not the detached, objective observer of standard experimental science; and whether the knowledge narrative inquiry produces should be considered as knowledge at all. But in 1984, when Jerome Bruner addressed the American Psychological Association (APA) and asserted baldly that there are two modes of thought or cognitive functioning, the traditional logical-scientific and a narrative mode, he at once transformed the argument.

Bruner contended that although the two modes of knowing are complementary, neither is reducible to the other. Each provides a distinctive way of ordering experience, of constructing reality. The logical-scientific (or "paradigmatic") mode is centered around the narrow epistemological question of *how* to know the truth; "the narrative, around the broader and more inclusive question of the *meaning* of experience" (Bruner, 1986, pp. 11–13, citing Rorty). One seeks explications context free and universal, and the other context sensitive and particular.

While Bruner's work paralleled the unprecedented shift of interest in narrative and interpretation in several social science disciplines, it especially caught the attention of educators who were making use of narrative in their own research and practice. Narrative as story seemed especially useful to capture the situated complexities of teachers' work and classroom practice, often messy, uncertain, and unpredictable.

But narrative promises more than action vignettes. As Bruner contends, narrative operates by constructing two landscapes simultaneously, two planes, one of action and one of consciousness, that is, of *"what those acting know, think, or feel"*(quoted in APA, 1984; emphasis added). "Story," Mitchell similarly claims, "is a mode of knowledge emerging from action . . ." (Mitchell, 1981, p. x). Philosopher Alasdair MacIntyre suggests that all human actions are enacted narratives. "It is because . . . we understand our own lives in terms of narratives that narrative is appropriate for understanding . . . others" (MacIntyre, 1984, pp. 211–212).

As narrative research in teaching proliferated into the 1990s, claims for narrative knowing through story, especially teacher stories of their practice, seemed insistent. But even as this work advanced, new cautions about narrative, especially about the danger of what was to count as knowledge, again emerged.

Kathy Carter queried, "Was every insight a teacher had to be elevated to knowledge" (Carter, 1993). Others argued that it does not follow that everything a teacher believes or is willing to act on merits the label "knowledge." Carter went on to say: "For those of us telling stories in our work, we will not serve the community well if we sanctify storytelling work and build an epistemology on it to the point that we substitute one paradigmatic domination for another without challenging the domination itself" (Carter, 1993, p. 220). In 1994, in an extensive review of "Knowledge in Research on Teaching," Fenstermacher used Bruner's labels to capture what he termed two types of knowledge about teaching: "Formal knowledge fits the paradigmatic mode; practical knowledge the narrative mode" (Fenstermacher, 1994, p. 35).

Yet, he also questioned: "Is it possible to be engaged as a scientist in the study of human action and make contributions to both formal and practical knowledge . . . ? At issue here is whether there are systematic and dependable ways to go about discovering the practical knowledge that underlies human action?" Fenstermacher went on to raise a larger question about practical knowledge and its validity and, by implication, that of narrative: "There is much merit in believing that teachers know a great deal and in seeking to learn what they know, but that merit is corrupted and demeaned when it is implied that this knowledge is not subject to justification or cannot or should not be justified." The challenge for teacher knowledge research "is not simply one of showing us that those teachers, think, believe, or have opinions, but that they know. And even more important, that they know that they know" (Fenstermacher, 1994, p. 36).

Responding to Fenstermacher, Clandinin and Connelly (1996), innovators in explicating and exploring narrative inquiry to study teachers' work and experience, challenged his dichotomous formulation. They argued that teachers indeed know what they know. But the knowledge teachers hold will always be qualified by "it depends,"—it depends on the knowledge contexts in which teachers function, on the situations of those involved, and on the politics of what counts for knowledge (Cochran-Smith & Lytle, 1999; Pendlebury, 1995). Cochran-Smith and Lytle (1999), longstanding advocates of teacher research, see Fenstermacher's critique in a harsher political light. They reject the formal/practical dualism. To them it detracts from and limits a view of the real complexities of teaching and learning. Further, they see it as an example of what has happened so often "when new voices and modes of discourse, like certain versions of teacher research, push their way into existing conversations about ways of knowing. Those located squarely inside the dominant epistemological and methodological paradigms use established terms, conventions, standards, and definitions to evaluate and essentially dismiss, alternative ones" (1999,

p. 23). Clearly, claim Anderson and Herr (1999), "the formal/practical knowledge debate is about more than research epistemology and methodology; it is about the very nature of educational practice itself." Such claims are not unfounded.

THE KNOWLEDGE OF TEACHING: A CONTESTED DOMAIN

In teaching, the knowledge claims of teachers have long been contested. As sociologists Gerald Grant and Christine Murray document in *Teaching in America: The Slow Revolution*, there are deep historical roots to this debate. Contrasting college professors and precollege teachers, Grant and Murray find both joined by the essential acts of teaching they share, yet radically divided as professionals. They assert that "professors and precollege teachers are not seen as members of the same profession" (Grant & Murray, 1999, p. 1). Why should this be?

That professors are mostly men and schoolteachers mostly women is, they believe, a critical part of the answer. In an early 20th century revolution, professors took charge of their teaching and research and "stripped college presidents of their powers to determine the curriculum and fire the faculty at will." But schoolteachers remained locked in a "hierarchical system in which they were treated as hirelings whose work was mandated by a male administrative elite. As schools were urbanized and centralized in the course of the 20th century, teachers . . . were treated as functionaries, not as professionals capable of independent judgment" (Grant & Murray, 1999, pp. 1–2).

Other historians attest to the utter disdain with which female teachers and their abilities and knowledge have been held (Eisenmann, 1991; Warren, 1987). Sally Schwager (1997) finds evidence that the history of women in education is linked everywhere to issues of power and privilege—including the history of education. Linda Eisenmann (1991) reports how the low regard for the practical knowledge gained and held by female classroom teachers shifted teacher education away from elementary teachers toward priviliging men who were preparing to teach high school. Other evidence points to the split between practitioners and educational researchers. Cochran-Smith and Lytle (1990) document that no research generated by teachers is cited in the 1986 *Handbook of Research on Teaching*. In fact, it was not until the 1996 *Handbook* that a chapter addressed the issue. In that chapter, Zeichner and Noffke (1998, cited in Anderson & Herr, 1999) argue that such research done by teachers should not be seen as merely an extension of the current knowledge base but rather as a challenge to existing forms of knowledge.

Grant and Murray do see a gradual accretion now taking place of efforts by schoolteachers to take charge of their practice and their profession. They call it the "slow revolution." Teacher researchers affirm it as well. Cochran-Smith and Lytle (1993), who argue that teacher research is a way of knowing, have called for a project to create a theory of a knowledge of teaching by practitioners themselves. Teachers are claiming the right to investigate and name the knowledge of practice (Duckworth, 1987; Lampert, 2000; Lytle & Cochran-Smith, 1992). Schön (1995) calls it an epistemological battle, but "a battle of snails," proceeding so slowly that you have to look very carefully in order to see it going on. But Anderson and Herr argue that we are poised on the threshold of an outpouring of practitioner inquiry that will force important redefinitions of what "counts" as research (Anderson & Herr, 1999, p. 14; see also Denzen & Lincoln, 1994).

But, even as research in teacher knowledge grew in the 1990s, as in the past, questions persist—about the justification of this knowledge (Anderson & Herr, 1999), about the nature of it, and the place of narrative in it. For example, What role does narrative play in the construction of teachers' knowledge? What is the meaning and usefulness of narrative to teachers learning to teach, as well as to experienced teachers? What is the nature of narrative knowledge? How can or should this knowledge be validated and judged?

Contemporary research on learning throws light on these questions articulating a view of knowledge as a social construction and of situated knowledge (Brown et al., 1993; Bruner, 1996; Greeno et al., 1998; Putnam & Borko, 2000). This perspective is significant because it takes into account both the importance of meaning and the knowledge of situations, contexts, and particulars—of this class of students, this school, this historical moment, and so on, rather than general rules about teaching. It calls attention to the social nature of cognition, to how teachers themselves learn, and to ways of teaching for teacher and student learning:

> Learning process goes beyond . . . individual construction of knowledge [cite omitted]. Rather, interactions with the people in one's environment are major determinants of both what is learned and how learning takes place. These discourse communities provide the cognitive tools—ideas, theories, and concepts—that individuals appropriate as their own . . . to make sense of experience. (Putnam & Borko, 2000)

Even though our sciences have tended to privilege abstract, universal theory and theorizing, Donald Schön, Eliot Mishler, and teacher researchers argue that the grounds for validity and reliability of practical knowledge—such as the knowledge of teaching—may not follow the path of positivistic science and need another kind of proof for justification and another approach to validity. Mishler suggests one alternative: the idea of exemplars and a process he calls validation.

SHIFTING THE GROUNDS OF VALIDITY TO TRUSTWORTHINESS

> Acceptance or rejection of a practice or theory comes about because a community is persuaded. Even research specialists do not judge a conclusion as it stands alone; they judge its compatibility with a network of prevailing beliefs. (Cronbach, 1988, p. 6)

Mishler first espoused his argument about validity for inquiry-based research. That research similarly, although not exclusively, makes use of narrative. Mishler describes "inquiry-guided" research as including many variants of "qualitative" and interpretive research, case studies, and ethnographies as well as analyses of texts and discourses. Characterized by a reliance on a dynamic "interplay of theory, methods, and findings over the course of a study," this model uses a "continuous process through which observations and interpretations shape and reshape each other" (Mishler, 1990, p. 416). It is this feature that marks a departure from the traditional mode of hypothesis testing experimentation. Inquiry-based researchers depend on their tacit understanding of actual, situated practices of a field of inquiry. Thus, "validity claims are tested through the ongoing discourse [about these practices] . . . and in this sense, scientific knowledge is socially constructed" (Mishler, 1990, p. 416). Mishler elaborates:

> I propose to redefine [validity as] validation. . . . The essential criterion for such judgments is the degree to which we can rely on the concepts, methods, and inferences of a study, or tradition of inquiry, as the basis of our own theorizing and empirical research. If our overall assessment of a study's trustworthiness is high enough for us to act on it, we are granting the findings a sufficient degree of validity to invest our own time and energy, and to put at risk our reputations as competent investigators. (Mishler, 1990, p. 419)

Mishler's reformulation of the problem of validity as validation rests on the concept of exemplars first promoted by Thomas Kuhn (1962/1970). Kuhn discusses exemplars as "the concrete problem-solutions that students encounter from the start of their scientific education, whether in laboratories, on examinations, or at the ends of chapters in science texts . . . that also show them by example how their job is to be done"(Kuhn, 1962/1970, p. 187). For Kuhn, knowledge embedded within shared exemplars is a mode of knowing no less systematic than that of rules or laws, validated within a community of scientists as they share ways of thinking about their work and solving problems they encounter.

Validity in this approach, then, *depends on concrete examples of actual practices, fully elaborated so that members of a relevant research community can judge for themselves their "trustworthiness" and the validity of observations, interpretations, etc.* Making validation rather than validity the key term, and "focusing on trustworthiness rather than truth, displaces validation from its traditional location in a presumably objective and neutral reality, and moves it to the social world—a world constructed in and through our discourse and actions, through praxis" (Mishler, 1990, p. 420). Further, Mishler suggests, "an important task of the less well-established areas of scientific inquiry is to develop a collection of relevant exemplars, articulating and clarifying the methods of studies and showing how work is done and what problems become accessible to study" (Mishler, 1990, p. 432). It is these concepts, of exemplars and their validation as trustworthy, that we apply to a collection of narrative practices.

The idea of alternative approaches to validity joins the insistent concerns of other researchers who also see an urgent need for alternative modes of validity for research on teaching (Linn, Baker, & Dunbar, 1991). Lee Shulman, for instance, argues for attention to consequential validity, asking what difference the practice makes to students and teachers, to their learning, and to teaching practice (Shulman, 1994). Pamela Moss's (1994) answer to the question, Can there be validity without reliability? is that there can be a lesser degree of reliability. She offers the idea of an "interpretive" approach to assessment in place of independent observers of traditional models in judging the evidence of teaching, even for high-stakes assessments such as portfolios. Moss does not argue for one mode over the other, but rather for their complementarity. Others take a more radical approach.

Donald Schön, in advancing Ernest Boyer's (1990) passionate agenda for new forms of scholarship in the academy, dramatically accelerates these arguments. Schön sees a new scholarship of teaching as demanding new forms of inquiry into it, especially "practitioner action research with norms of its own" (Schön, 1995, p. 27). Schön echoes John Dewey's belief that practice has to be the beginning and the end of investigations into teaching: "the beginning because it sets the problem . . . the close, because practice alone can test, verify, modify, and develop conclusions of these investigations" (Dewey, 1929, p. 31). But, some 60 years later, Schön (1995) recognizes that Dewey's suggestion still challenges the prevailing model of the academy, what Schön terms technical rationality—that privileges the objective investigator, not an insider practitioner, and the knowledge such an investigator might uncover.

Contemporary concerns about validity are thus intricately and politically linked to actual teaching practices: to who carries out the inquiry, what knowledge they produce, what the epistemological setting is, and how it can be validated. Exemplars of Mishler's model, we believe, directly address these concerns.

We argue that the problem of validity Mishler redefines as validation applies to narrative practices. Valued teaching and research practices are subject to a continuous process of trial and interpretation, giving way to shared understandings.

NARRATIVE PRACTICES AS EXEMPLARS OF INQUIRY

While we recognize that narrative can be a part of any number of approaches to teaching, we also acknowledge that we do *not* consider all narrative practices as exemplars (see Carter & Doyle, 1996; Gudmundsdóttir, 2001). We argue that narrative teaching and research practices, as candidate exemplars, have certain significant features and purposes: Narrative practices are intentional, reflective human actions, socially and contextually situated, in which teachers with their students, other colleagues, or researchers, interrogate their teaching practices to construct the meaning and interpretation of some compelling or puzzling aspect of teaching and learning through the production of narratives that lead to understanding, changed practices, and new hypotheses. There are several important characteristics of these practices as modes of inquiry and ways of knowing:

1. *Intentional reflective human actions.* We cast narrative inquiry as a fundamental activity of mind, constituting an intentional, reflective activity. We see the root meaning of narrative not only as an account, history, tale, or even as narrating or telling a story, but also related to "knowing" (see the *Oxford English Dictionary* for the connection of "narrative" to the Latin *gnarus*, "knowing"; see also White, 1981).
2. *Socially and contextually situated.* Narrative practices take place with a given set of people—students, teachers, in a specific context, in real historical time. Such activities are usually collaborative in which individuals in relationship interact with each other, materials, and representational systems to construct knowledge (Greeno et al., 1998; Putnam & Borko, 2000).
3. *Engaging participants in interrogating aspects of teaching and learning by "storying" the experience.* The work of narrative inquiry involves interrogating compelling, surprising, or puzzling aspects of teaching and learning that bring to consciousness knowledge that may or may not have been realized even though acted upon (Lyons, 1998). Narrative is

a way of constructing the knowledge of teaching (Gadamer, in Bernstein, 1983; Freire, 1970). This knowledge can be about new and evolving perceptions of students, teaching practices, theories and how they are refined, values, and the ethical dimensions of practice, to name some.

4. *Implicating the identities of those involved*. Because these inquiries always involve the sense of self of those engaged, personal and professional identities can be at stake in the process. We do not mean that we are not agents in our own stories. But personal and professional identities can be discovered, redirected, or affected by these inquiries and knowledge.

5. *Toward constructing meaning and knowledge*. Narrative inquiry involves the construction of meaning (Bruner, 1986; Ricoeur, 1981). This is not surprising. Teaching is fundamentally an interpretive act. Teachers in interaction with students and their learning and understanding seek to construct meaning as critical to understanding and to the advancement of practice and how it is refined, elaborated, or changed. Narrative as a way of knowing in teaching needs to be linked to existing research on epistemology, for example, that described by William Perry (1970) and Mary Belenky and her colleagues (1986). Recently Blythe Clinchy (in press) has explicitly examined the narrative elements of research on ways of knowing.

As we examine these dimensions of narrative teaching practices, they come more clearly into focus. The invitation of this work is to investigate these practices, extend these inquiries to new contexts, elaborating understandings. We do not, however, propose to accept narrative practices as exemplars simply at face value. They are not to be thought of solely as best practices, although we think of them as possible ones. We take seriously the fact that they could be problematic and need to be interrogated. To that end, we have framed a set of questions designed to illuminate and to probe narrative practices:

- What is the narrative practice? How can it best be described? What are the immediate and long-term evidences of its value?
- How are exemplars of teaching practices useful—or not—to the professional education of new or experienced teachers? To advancing the knowledge of practice?
- How might exemplars be problematic?

POTENTIAL PROBLEMS

There are at least three issues related to exemplars of which potential users need to be aware: ethical issues that may be embedded in or result from trying them out; issues surrounding reflective practice, especially a concern for what is called confessionalism; and issues of the prevailing epistemologies of institutions that may or may not support teacher inquiries suggested here and ultimately affect the emerging scholarship of teaching.

Ethical Issues of Power Relationships

Ethical issues are often encountered in interrogating practice, with regard to how work is to be conducted, entered into, arranged, written about, how people are to be identified, and how ownership of work is to be attributed. But most important is how the collaborative relationship typical of narrative inquiry is to be constructed, cared for, and realistically thought about, especially when unequal power relationships between teachers and academic researchers can be at stake. Unexpected issues may arise at each phase of the work. Researchers and practitioners need to ask together: What potential ethical issues might arise here? Who could be at risk, and how? How should this be addressed? Of particular concern are safety and privacy. If people are to share their meanings of experience, they need to be assured of the safety of the group, that it will respect their ideas and explorations; and that their work will be confidential.

Reflective Practice or Confessional Jargon?

A second issue involves reflective practice and concerns about confessionalism, that is, that reflective practices may encourage discourse of a personalistic, confessional genre. Some critics argue that what is called reflection is really self-discovery (see Bleakley, 2000). While the process of narrative inquiry can be a powerful tool for engaging in reflection, there are real issues about how it is carried out and what are the results. MacEwan and Egan (1995) argue that while narrative contributes to self-understanding, it may just as easily contribute to self-deception. It may also be that narrative in the form of creative writing, the place of the gravest charges of "confessionalism," may be more prone to self-deception. But there are important distinctions to be clear about. The self-reflection of narrative practices is a deliberate, intentional process engaging several people, frequently colleagues, directed to interrogating their professional experience to understand some aspect of teaching and learning (see Chapter 6). This is a quite different purpose. Here, however, we put a red flag on the issue, as something of which to be aware.

Institutional Epistemologies: Contexts for Developing a Scholarship of Teaching

Narrative or inquiries of any teacher research may not always be a commitment of schools or the academy. Nor are institutional contexts always conducive to it. As Schön (1995) argues, as with other organizations, educational institutions have epistemologies. They hold conceptions of what counts as legitimate knowledge and how claims to knowing are validated, even of what are to be considered legitimate topics for inquiry. Issues of complexity, uncertainty, uniqueness, and conflict—all the issues connected to teaching and learning—often fall outside the zone of what are legitimate topics for investigation within the academy. They do not fit the model of technical rationality that Schön sees still dominating the research university. Yet these are precisely the issues that would lend themselves to action research, to inquiry by practitioners, in schools or the academy. We endorse this idea and argue for reflective investigations through narrative inquiry by practitioners and researchers. And the task is urgent, especially in the light of the new scholarship of teaching that Schön defends.

The Scholarship of Teaching project proposed by Ernest Boyer generated important questions: What is a scholarship of teaching? How can it be interrogated, documented, and represented? We suggest that narrative inquiry as presented here as a way of knowing is a valued approach, one already in service of interrogating, documenting, and representing the scholarship of teaching.

At a time of intense scrutiny of higher education and teacher education and the search for new modes of assessment of students and teachers, this book extends discussion in several domains: about ways of knowing in the professions and the place of narrative inquiry in that; about the uses of reflective interrogations to examine practices, identify meanings, and knowledge; and about the epistemological issues surrounding the validity of teaching practices. Our hope is that this work will deepen a conversation about narrative, joining the work of such exquisite practitioners as Vivian Paley and Emma Rich.

REFERENCES

American Psychological Association. (1984, November) *Monitor*.

Anderson, G., & Herr, K. (1999). The new paradigm wars: Is there room for rigorous practical knowledge in schools and universities? *Educational Researcher*, *28*(5), 12–21, 40.

Belenky, M., Clinchy, B., Goldberger, N., & Tarule, J. (1986). *Women's ways of knowing*. New York: Basic Books.

Bernstein, R. (1983). *Beyond objectivism and relativism: Science, hermeneutics, and praxis*. Philadelphia: University of Pennsylvania Press.

Bleakley, A. (2000). Writing with invisible ink: Narrative, confessionalism, and reflective practice. *Reflective Practice, 1*(1), 15.

Boyer, E. (1990). *Scholarship reconsidered*. Princeton, NJ: Carnegie Foundation for the Advancement of Teaching.

Brown, et al. (1993). Distributed expertise in the classroom. In G. Salomon (Ed.), *Distributed cognitions*. Cambridge, UK: Cambridge University Press.

Bruner, J. (1986). *Actual minds, possible worlds*. Cambridge, MA: Harvard University Press.

Bruner, J. (1996). *The culture of education*. Cambridge, MA: Harvard University Press.

Carter, K. (1993). The place of story in the study of teaching and teacher education. *Educational Researcher, 2*(1), 5–18.

Carter, K., & Doyle, W. (1996). Personal narrative and life history in learning to teach. In J. Sikula, T. Buttery, & E. Guyton (Eds.), *Handbook of research on teacher education*. New York: Macmillan.

Clandinin, J. & Connelly, M. (1996). Teachers' professional knowledge landscapes: Teacher stories—stories of teachers—school stories—stories of schools. *Educational Researcher, 25*(3), 24–30.

Clinchy, B. (in press). An epistemological approach to the teaching of narrative research. *Narrative Study of Lives*.

Cochran-Smith, M., & Lytle, S. (1990). Research on teaching and teacher research: The issues that divide. *Educational Researcher, 19*(2), 2–11.

Cochran-Smith, M., & Lytle, S. (1993). *Inside/Outside: Teacher research and knowledge*. New York: Teachers College Press.

Cochran-Smith, M., & Lytle, S. (1999, October). The teacher research movement: A decade later. *Educational Researcher*, 15–25.

Coles, R. (1989). *The call of stories: Teaching and the moral imagination*. Boston: Houghton Mifflin.

Connelly, J., & Clandinin, J. (1990). Stories of experience and narrative inquiry. *Educational Researcher, 19*(5), 2–14.

Cronbach, L. J. (1988). Five perspectives on validity argument. In H. Wainer & H. I. Braun (Eds.), *Test validity*. Hillsdale, NJ: Erlbaum.

Denzen, N., & Lincoln, Y. (1994). The fifth movement. In N. Denzen & Y. Lincoln (Eds.), *Handbook of qualitative research*. London: Sage Publications.

Dewey, J. (1929). *Sources for a science of education*. New York: Horace Liveright.

Dewey, J. (1998). *How we think*. Boston: Houghton Mifflin. (Original work published 1933)

Duckworth, E. (1987). *The having of wonderful ideas*. New York: Teachers College Press.

Eisenmann, L. (1991). Teacher professionalism: A new analytical tool for a history of teachers. *Harvard Educational Review, 61*(2), 215–224.

Elbaz, F. (1983). *Teacher thinking: A study of practical knowledge*. London: Croom Helm.

Fenstermacher, G. (1994). The knower and the known: The nature of knowledge in research on teaching. In L. Darling-Hammond (Ed.), *Review of Research in Education, 20*, 3–56.

Freire, P. (1970). *The pedagogy of the oppressed*. New York: Seabury Press.

Grant, G., & Murray, C. (1999). *Teaching in America: The slow revolution*. Cambridge, MA: Harvard University Press.

Greeno, J. G., & the Middle School Mathematics through the Applications Project Group. (1998). The situativity of knowing, learning, & research. *American Psychologist, 53*(1), 5–26.

Grimmet, P., & Erickson, G. (Eds.). *Reflection in Teacher Education*. New York: Teachers College Press.

Gudmundsdóttir, S. (2001). Narrative research on school practice. In V. Richardson (Ed.), *Handbook of research on teaching* (4th ed.). Washington, DC: American Educational Research Association.

Jackson, P. (1968). *Life in classrooms*. New York: Holt, Rinehart, & Winston.

Kuhn, T. S. (1962/1970). *The structure of scientific revolutions*. Chicago: University of Chicago Press.

Lampert, M. (2000). Knowing teaching: The intersection of research on teaching and qualitative research. *Harvard Educational Review, 70*(1), 86–99.

Linn, R., Baker, E., & Dunbar (1991). Complex, performance-based assessment: Expectations and validation criteria. *Educational Researcher, 20*(8), 15–21.

Lyons, N. (1998). *With portfolio in hand: Validating the new teacher professionalism*. New York: Teachers College Press.

Lyons, N. (2000). *Portfolio project*. Unpublished manuscript, Dartmouth College.

Lytle, S., & Cochran-Smith, M. (1992). Teacher research as a way of knowing. *Harvard Educational Review, 62*(4), 447–474.

MacEwan, H., & Egan, K. (1995). *Narrative in teaching, learning, and research*. New York: Teachers College Press.

MacIntyre, A. (1984). *After virtue: A study in moral theory*. Notre Dame, IN: University of Notre Dame Press.

Mishler, E. (1990). Validation in inquiry-guided research: The role of exemplars in narrative studies. *Harvard Educational Review, 60*(4), 415–442.

Mishler, E. (1995). Models of narrative analysis: A typology. *Journal of Narrative and Life History, 5*(2), 87–123.

Mitchell, W. J. T. (1981). *On narrative*. Chicago: University of Chicago Press.

Moss, P. (1994). Can there be validity without reliability? *Educational Researcher, 23*(2), 5–12.

Nussbaum, M. (1990). *Love's knowledge: Essays in philosophy and literature*. New York: Oxford University Press.

Nussbaum, M. (1997). *Cultivating humanity*. Cambridge, MA: Harvard University Press.

Paley, V. (1981). *Walley's stories*. Chicago: University of Chicago Press.

Paley, V. (1990). *The boy who would be a helicopter*. Cambridge, MA: Harvard University Press.

Paley, V. (2001). *Mrs. Tully's room: A child care portrait*. Cambridge, MA: Harvard University Press.

Pendlebury, S. (1995). Reason and story in wise practice. In H. Mc Ewan & K. Egan (Eds.), *Narrative in teaching, learning, and research*. New York: Teachers College Press.

Perry, W. (1970). *Forms of intellectual development in the college years*. New York: Holt, Rinehart, & Winston.

Putnam, R. T., & Borko, H. (2000). What do new views of knowledge and thinking have to say about research on teacher learning? in *Educational Researcher Online*. Available: http://www.aera.net./pubs/er/aarts/29–01/putnam01.htm.

Richardson, V. (1996). The case for formal research and practical inquiry in teacher education. In F. B. Murray (Ed.), *The teacher educator's handbook*. San Francisco: Jossey-Bass.

Ricoeur, P. (1981). *Hermeneutics and the human sciences*. Cambridge, UK: Cambridge University Press.

Schön, D. (1983). *The reflective practitioner: How professionals think in action*. New York: Basic Books.

Schön, D. (1995). The new scholarship requires a new epistemology. *Change*, 27(6), 26–34.

Schwager, S. (1997). Foreword. Symposium: The history of women in education. *Harvard Educational Review*, 67(4), ix–xiii.

Shulman, L. (1986). Paradigms and research programs in the study of teaching: A contemporary perspective. *Handbook of research on teaching* (3rd ed.). New York: Macmillan.

Shulman, L. (1994). *Perspectives on the history of portfolios in teacher education*. Paper presented at the Portfolio Conference, Harvard/Radcliffe, January 1994.

Shulman, L. (1998). *The course portfolio*. Washington, DC: American Association for Higher Education.

Warren, D. (1987). *American teachers: Histories of a profession at work*. New York: Macmillan.

White, H. (1981). The value of narrativity in the representation of reality. In W. J. T. Mitchell (Ed.), *On narrative*. Chicago: University of Chicago Press.

Witherell, C., & Noddings, N. (Eds.). (1991). *Stories lives tell: Narrative and dialogue in education*. New York: Teachers College Press.

PART I

Uncovering Narrative Teaching Practices: A Sampler

> To suppose that scientific findings decide the value of educational under-
> takings is to reverse the real case. Actual activities in *educating* test the worth
> of the results . . . whether they really serve or not can be found out only in
> practice.
>   —John Dewey, *Sources of a Science of Education*

Narrative teaching practices are characterized in this volume as intentional, reflective processes in which teachers, with others (students, teachers, etc.) interrogate some puzzle or compelling question of teaching or learning through the creation of a narrative, by constructing and telling the story of its meaning. The process results in the construction of knowledge that has consequences for understanding and refining theory and changing practice. In Part I of this book, seven narrative teaching practices are described by authors who have been trying them in their own settings. All engage a collaborative process of inquiry. We see this model linked to the emerging scholarship of teaching, for it offers a way of interrogating teaching practice and a method for testing its validity—in practice. The chapters of Part I provide a sampler of such practices.

CHAPTER 2

Stories as a Way of Learning Both Practical and Reflective Orientations

VICKI KUBLER LABOSKEY

[The narrative assignment] is an important assignment and warrants the type of self-reflection that we devoted to it. Many of the words and concepts of this assignment are ones that I try to consider routinely as I deal with our "one-room schoolhouse" in the hospital.

—Hospital-based teacher

A graduate of the Mills College Credential Program, which includes a Child Life option for students who wish to teach hospitalized children, made the statement quoted above about halfway through her first year of teaching. She was responding to questions about whether or not a narrative assignment she had done in the previous year had been at all helpful in her efforts to "set the tone" in her own classroom.

THE NARRATIVE EXEMPLAR

Responses to the assignment had not always been so positive. Indeed, at one point I had become so disillusioned with the results that I came close to abandoning the idea altogether. However, because the goals of the project were so important to me, I decided to try transformation rather than elimination. In this chapter I will tell the story of the evolution of this practice and examine its short- and long-term impact on the student teachers who engaged in it. I will consider the potential of this strategy as an exemplar of narrative practice, as well as its limitations.

The Context

The Mills College Credential Program, called Teachers for Tomorrow's Schools, is a 2-year graduate program that results in a multiple subject or single-subject teaching credential and a master's degree in education. Six principles guide the goals and the design of the program around its central mission—the promotion of equity and social justice:

1. *Teaching as a moral act based on an ethic of care.* Because teaching involves human interaction, it is necessarily a moral enterprise; teachers need to base their interactions on an ethic of care and be considerate of the moral/ethical implications of their work.
2. *Teaching as an act of inquiry and reflection.* Because teaching is complex, uncertain, and dependent upon context, teachers need to engage in ongoing inquiry; they need to reflect upon their beliefs and practices in relation to the goal of equity from multiple perspectives.
3. *Learning as a constructivist/developmental process.* Because learners construct their own knowledge and do so at different rates, in different ways, and from different starting points, teachers need to get to know their learners and base their teaching on that knowledge.
4. *Teaching for the acquisition and construction of subject matter knowledge.* Because teaching is concerned with the learning of some content and because that content matters, teachers need to know both the subject matter and a variety of ways in which they might help learners understand, value, interrelate, and act upon that knowledge.
5. *Teaching as a collegial act.* Because knowledge is socially constructed, teachers need to work collaboratively with colleagues and the community, as well as include in their classrooms ways for their students to interact positively and productively with one another.
6. *Teaching as a political act.* Because education has the power to provide access to full participation in a democratic society for all students, it is by definition a political act; thus, teachers need to consider their beliefs and actions in relation to issues of equity and social justice.

The credential and half of the master's are completed during the first academic year. In that year credential candidates student teach in the mornings, beginning on the first day of school and ending on the last, and take courses at the college in the afternoons. One of those courses, which I teach, is called Curriculum and Instruction in Elementary Schools; it is yearlong and required of all 30 elementary credential candidates.

The Assignment Story

Early on in the student teachers' first semester, I give an assignment in the Curriculum and Instruction class that I call "Setting the Tone." In its original form the credential candidates had to observe two different teachers in the first few days of school. They had to spend at least one hour in each of the classrooms and then engage the teacher in a brief interview. Afterward, they wrote a short paper, a comparative case analysis on setting the tone. To do so, they needed to analyze all of their data and then compare the two classes with regard to one aspect involved in establishing classroom climate. They were to answer the question, "Are these classrooms similar or different in how the tone for the year was addressed—in what ways, and why?" Their interpretations were to be substantiated with evidence from the data and appropriately tempered. They were not to judge the value or effectiveness of either teacher or classroom. They then presented their papers to a small group of peers to get feedback and engage in further discussion of the issues. The purpose of the assignment was twofold. First, I wanted the student teachers to gather practical ideas with regard to the first days of school—things they might do next year in order to better their chances for establishing a positive classroom tone. More importantly, I wanted them to recognize the complexity of the enterprise— that there were neither simple answers nor one right way to do things; that context mattered; that it was an interpersonal activity, which should vary with the individuals involved; and that it was value laden and emotional.

I found that each time I gave the assignment I was adding more and more detail to the instructions in order to prevent the students from coming to conclusions in their papers that were judgmental of the teachers or certain of right answers. But the more I tried to control the process, the worse it seemed to get. The group discussions were also not going well; students found little to discuss since conclusions had already been drawn. Authors complained that the critiques were pointless because the papers were already written. I decided I needed to eliminate the assignment, but what would I put in its stead? What else could I do that would help me achieve my aims? This sent me back to my goals with the question, What is most important for my students to learn at this point in the year? I did want them to develop practical ideas about setting the tone in the classrooms of their future—after all, it was a methods course and they needed to acquire practical ideas somewhere. But I wanted them to learn from the get-go that the accumulation of strategies should never be just an accumulation. Even approaches to bathroom passes and seat assignments should derive from a carefully constructed "philosophy of education." They needed always to consider the specifics of their context from multiple per-spectives; to be prepared to be responsive to the situation, and to the feel-ings and actions of the humans present in the situation; and to imagine the possible long-term ethical and moral implications of their choices—that is, they needed to be reflective.

What dawned on me in this process of re-examination was that I was defining narrative knowing, in some ways the "practical knowing" that Fenstermacher (1994) describes, with the caveat provided by Clandinin and Connelly (1996), that such knowledge must always be qualified by "it de-pends." What I also realized was that to achieve these narrative goals, I had been trying to use an assignment that was constructed primarily in the paradigmatic mode. Since, according to Bruner (1985), the two modes are irreducible to one another, it was no wonder that the assignment was not working. Therefore, I decided to keep the essence of the assignment, but transform it into the narrative mode. I would still have them observe and interview in two different classrooms on the first days of school in order to insure that they would see more than one way of doing things, but in-stead of having them write a systematically analytical paper, I would have them write a story. The story could be a retelling of something that actu-ally happened in one or both of the classrooms or it could be fictional. Ei-ther way they should write it to generate an open-ended conversation with their peers about an issue that came up for them in the process of explor-ing two different teachers' efforts to establish classroom climate at the be-ginning of the year. It needed to be as nonjudgmental and unbiased as possible.

I wanted the narrative exploration to continue in the small group dis-cussions. Since I could not be present in all of them, I needed to create a facilitative structure. I put them into groups of three and gave each person one half-hour to tell her story and lead a discussion about it. After each storytelling session, the group paused and the nonauthors responded to a series of questions posted on the board:

1. Did the story elicit thinking/conversation about important issues around setting the tone?
2. Was the group able to avoid discussion that involved judgments of the teachers or situations?
3. Did the story help the group avoid having a discussion about right answers?

At the end of the class period everyone wrote a self-reflection in response to four prompts:

1. Talk about how you went about composing your story.
2. What were the strengths of your process (both the writing and discussing) and of your story?
3. What might you do differently next time?
4. Is there anything else you want me to know?

This allowed me not only to guide the discussions from afar but also to gain access to their thinking and their conversations.

What I found when I looked at the stories, the nonauthor responses, and the author self-reflections was that this process generated genuine conversations about a myriad of classroom climate issues from multiple perspectives. A closer inspection of the stories themselves revealed that they were generally free of bias and judgment, certainly more so than the analytical cases of the past. Most were quite open-ended and provocative, as in the following example:

THOUGHTS ABOUT QUIET FROM THE STUDENTS
AND FACULTY AT ADAMS SCHOOL

Quiet

Quiet
Necessary, Wonderful
Reading, Writing, Learning
A skill for the REAL WORLD
Silence

—Sherry Jones, third-grade teacher

The Best Day at School

The best day at school would be where the teacher would never blow
    a whistle.
The best day at school would be where we would get to sing.
The best day at school would have pizza for lunch.
The best day at school would be when we learned about science like
    the day we got to go outside and catch bugs in the grass and then
    look at them and then oh when Jenny screamed because she was
    afraid of the spider and then we all laughed and had a good time.
The best day at school I wouldn't have to pull a card.

—Kerry Brown, grade 4

The Worst Day at School

It is not hard to say,
What would make the worst day.
It would be one,
That is not fun,
It would make me want to run,
Far, far away.

The worst day would be where my teacher would say,
"Let's hear what Kim thinks today."
And I would squirm and shrink down real small in my seat,
My ears would burn, my face would heat.

Why can't she let me be? Doesn't she care?
I'm happy just listening to everyone else share.
I'd rather be quiet that's how I'm made.
Why do I need to talk—it's not a grade.

That would be my worst day in school, for sure

                                        —Kim Ray, grade 5

A Formula for Quiet

So you say you are confused, how much quiet should there be?
Everyone has a different answer—He, She, Me, and Zee.

"All the time! It's a skill!"
"But the spirit you might kill!"
"But the principal you might make ill if your students are too
        noisterous and boisterous and learning nothingoisterous!"

Well you are sure in luck,
Because for just a million bucks,
I will share with you my secret,
If you promise you can keep it,
For the most precise, the most exact, and so much fun
With an error margin of less than .0000000001!

So here it is, I will unveil it—
But first I need your down payment.

All right then, here it is for real—
Begin with your class size, put that number in—
Then divide by your principal's age—oh it's starting to begin!

Never mind the chortling, the bustling, and the grokemons,
Just keep inputting all those figures: your students' ages, languages,
    favorite Pokemons.
Don't forget to put in your numbers, too,
The quiet formula will not work without your issues in the stew.

There, it's almost done!
Soon, teaching will be fun!
Because you'll have the magic number—the answer—the million dol-
    lar question solved—

And so you'll know exactly when to demand quiet
Aren't you so excited? Go and try it!

—Dr. Smeuss, school psychologist

The author of this "story," Cara Taxy (now an elementary school teacher in Chicago), actually used an alternative narrative genre, poetry, to generate a debate around the issue of "quiet" in the classroom. The stories included a wide array of issues, as diverse and as apparent as they had been in the case analyses.

EVIDENCE OF VALUE

The transformation to a narrative format did seem to have positive results, but I wanted to look at the evidence more carefully.

Short Term

An examination of the author self-reflections and the nonauthor feedback revealed that virtually all (25 out of 27) of the participants felt that the stories generated rich and beneficial discussions about setting the tone. The following comment was representative: "I felt the greatest strength of the process was the insightful and interesting conversation generated in my small group. I feel like we all listened to each other's ideas and came up with some important things to think about in setting the tone on the first day."

Their responses also revealed that the struggle to avoid judgments and one right answer was both more explicit and more likely than it had been with the case analyses and discussions, especially with regard to the avoidance of one right answer. Stories seemed to invite interpretation; they triggered the telling of other related stories by the participants, which then guaranteed the inclusion of multiple perspectives. These responses to the last nonauthor question about the avoidance of one right answer were illustrative:

> We had really different opinions, which I thought was great—we weren't critical of one another's ideas but rather got some ideas from each other and new ways of thinking. Because we all have had different experiences and have seen different things work, it was really clear that there wasn't one right answer!

> We did not imply one right answer, but looked at ways in which we try to remain true to ourselves but also true to helping children learn—ensuring that they are learning something!

> We never came to the "right" answers, but rather began many of our questions with, "How can we, as teachers . . . ?" and "Where do I stand . . . ?"

The stories told of specific incidents or situations, which is where the discussions usually started. But in order to avoid judging those specific incidents or the teachers involved, they moved to an exploration of the broader questions raised by those experiences and to the implications for their future practice, which was the hope.

The avoidance of judgment was a bit harder for them, both in the discussions and in the story writing. These responses from the nonauthors speak to the former:

> We began to be judgmental regarding the teacher, but we caught ourselves digressing and refocused our discussion back to the task at hand.

> Though some judgment came into play toward the end, the flavor of our discussion group was such that we spoke about many angles of the classroom situation.

> No [we weren't able to avoid making judgments] but with every point we tried to see both the positive and negative aspects of the teacher's interactions.

The self-reflections spoke to their struggles with regard to the avoidance of judgment in the writing of their stories. What they seemed to be saying was that because stories deal with human action and intention, because they involve characterization and personalization, and because they necessarily involve perspective-taking, the avoidance of bias is even trickier than it might be in the paradigmatic mode. Thus, the story-teller is required to devote explicit attention to the question of how an absence of bias might be achieved. They seemed to respond to this challenge in one of two ways—or both. First, they tried to just tell the story of what actually occurred: "I also thought about not being judgmental so I thought I would try to portray incidents exactly how I saw them happen."

Second, they tried to tell the story from the perspective of the child. As one author said,

> Composing my story initially was somewhat difficult. I think the word "story" caused me to think in a creative tone, which led to a potentially biased voice. The story kept making me focus on the child's reaction. This was terribly positive. I think we as student teachers focus too much on our actions or our teachers when learning this craft/profession and we need to be reminded how every little thing we do impacts the children immensely.

Her comment speaks to why it was done and why it might be advantageous.

The narrative form in both the story writing and story discussion seemed to be very helpful to most of the student teachers in a number of ways, as these comments suggest:

> The strengths [of my story-writing process] I think are that I was able to just "free write" with my notes as a guide and that I was then able to revise and tighten it to emphasize the aspects I wanted to come out. The reason this is a strength is that I "choke" when faced with a project that requires writing a connected "argument" from many different sources (read: research paper!). . . . This was much more natural and I think that leads to a strength of the story: I think I captured the atmosphere.

> This process was extremely valuable especially this final portion of having two others to discuss it with. I find it so valuable to begin with this fact finding, my own observations, then a sharing and discussion! It not only validates some of my own questioning, but adds another perspective to how I might interpret my own observations.

The strength of my story lies, I think, in my subconscious decisions to take an outside point of view as an observer with no bias. That is what I believe I was trying to achieve. The next time I try this I would like to reflect for a longer time on the issues that arose from the story. I felt like the issues were there but they did not become apparent to me until I read the story to my group and discussed it awhile. Writing releases the demons and angels but sometimes it's better to know exactly what to expect before they are let loose.

As this last comment makes clear, the stories captured the emotional and interpersonal aspects of teaching, which, though not always easy to address, are an essential part of this very human enterprise and thus necessary to acknowledge and explore.

These stories and commentaries were written and discussed by preservice teachers at the outset of their credential programs. These are individuals who are at the stage in their careers when they need to call into question much of what they "know" about teaching as a result of their previous apprenticeship of observation. Thus, I believe they are particularly in need of experiences that will allow them to come to know, first and foremost, what they do not know. The telling and discussing of setting the tone stories seemed to help them do just that, as is apparent in these statements:

I composed my story both from my notes and from memory. I thought a lot about how this situation set the tone for the rest of the year. I thought about the many levels of issues that this experience raised. It made me question my own judgments. . . . All in all, this was a difficult but good experience for me. I realized through both composing the story and through some of our class discussions about setting the tone that I have a lot of preconceived ideas about what one *should* do to set the tone. Many things to think about!

I really came to an even greater understanding of how what I thought I knew about myself has been further scrutinized—and how I feel like I don't know what the best way is—since there are reasonable explanations either philosophical or theoretical for another explanation.

This process also helped me realize how riddled with judgment I am in critiquing the work of my master teacher—or of other teachers in general. I want to be sure that when I think I understand something well that I turn it over to consider it from another perspective.

This recognition then helped them to know what they needed to know:

> The group discussions were very useful. By setting up the condition that we should be nonjudgmental with one another, important questions, brainstorming, and different perspectives came to the surface. It was very interesting to see just how complex and layered situations are, even out of context.

> I am not sure what I would do differently next time because this was very helpful. I guess I had never really thought so much about "setting the tone" so in that sense this assignment has really opened my eyes. It really helped me look at the whole classroom—the teacher, the children . . . , the way it is set up—as all a part of a much bigger picture. As a teacher someday, it will be important to take note of all those details and ask myself why have I done it that way? What am I trying to promote here?

The narrative mode—the writing and discussing of stories—helped these novices to know both what they did not know and what they most needed to know, which is not only specific curricular and instructional strategies and techniques, but also the attitudes and skills of reflective practice. I believe that the narrative mode was more effective at doing this than the paradigmatic mode had been, because such knowledge is narrative knowledge and, therefore, must be acquired through narrative means.

This narrative assignment did seem to have some immediate value for most of the student teachers, but did it have any long-term benefit? The project was meant to help them generate ideas for setting the tone in their future classrooms and to develop their reflective attitudes and skills throughout their career. Thus, I decided to check in with this group one year later, when they were in the process of setting the tone in their own classrooms.

Long Term

Five graduates sent me informal messages about their ongoing efforts to set the tone in their new classrooms during the first few months of the schoolyear and seven responded to a series of written questions at a meeting in February. One of the seven had also sent informal messages; thus, I received feedback from 11 different graduates out of a total of 30. At the meeting, I gave the graduates a copy of the "setting the tone" stories they had written, as well as the responses of others in the group, and their self-reflections. After they read the material, I posed three questions:

1. Write any reactions you have to the reading of your story now. Does it have any relevance to your current situation?
2. The purpose of the assignment was to help you in two ways: (a) to generate some practical ideas, and (b) to contribute to the development of reflective attitudes and skills. Reflecting back, was it helpful with either? Did doing it in story form make any difference?
3. How would you describe the tone that currently exists in your classroom?

Informal Messages. Three of the informal messages arrived over the Internet and two were delivered to my mailbox. They came in response to an invitation to share with me anything they wanted to about their efforts to set the tone in their first classrooms. The graduates provided information about the kind of tone they wanted to set and about the approaches they were taking, both in general and in particular, to create that classroom climate. In addition, they provided clues as to whether or not they were taking an inquiry orientation to the effort.

Four of the five included comments that let me know that they were trying to set a tone consistent with our program principles, that they had some strategies for attempting to do so, and that they were taking a reflective approach to the endeavor. One said she began the year by involving her students in the process of developing a community: "The first two weeks we gathered our chairs in a circle to talk and get to know each other. We spent group time developing our five classroom rules and in playing get to know you games." She added that she "also made it very clear through my words and actions that we would have fun in this class, but we would be working very hard." She wanted to set a tone that was caring and collegial, but also serious about subject matter knowledge. She seemed to have many ideas about how to do this, though they were not always easy to carry through. She described, for instance, her many struggles with group work. Nonetheless, she ended her discussion with a validation of the process: "I will close today, feeling a little less stressed but knowing I must always find time to reflect and process if I am going to grow and feel better about my work in teaching." Another also recognized the ongoing nature of the process:

> Last year one of my biggest revelations about setting the tone is that it never stops. This year I want to be patient but persistent as I try to establish a tone that is number one safe for all students to engage in learning and number two easy-going and fun. A challenge in setting the tone that I thought a lot about was how to establish that this would also be an academically challenging class right from day one.

She acknowledged that she learned the need for a reflective stance during her credential year and that she was trying to maintain that in her current practice. She proceeded to describe in detail several activities she had used to try to begin to set the tone she wanted—a tone that, as in the previous instance, was not only caring and collegial, but also rigorous, as would be consistent with our program principles. When she ran into difficulties, she neither blamed the students nor herself and instead engaged in a process of inquiry by analyzing the problem, formulating a new subgoal, and designing and implementing new interventions.

These messages let me know that at least some of the graduates were attempting to set tones consistent with our program principles and were taking a reflective approach in order to do so. They also seemed to have learned some practical strategies. The questionnaire provided me with more specific information about graduates' perceptions of the long-term influences of the narrative assignment.

Questionnaires. The graduates who attended the midyear meeting were also attempting to create classroom environments that were collegial, caring, consistent with constructivist learning theory, equitable, and academically rigorous, and they were doing so in a reflective manner. One of them described her current tone in the following terms:

> I see my classroom as inclusive and *highly* energized. I've spent much of the first half of the schoolyear emphasizing that everyone has something to contribute and making them feel comfortable participating. Not to be immodest, but I feel totally successful on that level. I'm having a bit more difficulty meeting all the state standards but I also learned from this program to give myself a break—and do what I can do. Thanks.

The others also admitted to some real challenges but were generally positive about the process and patient with their progress, as this response indicates: "The tone in my room right now is squirrely and working towards respect. Students are good at pointing out disrespect and are actually learning to try and handle it themselves. I think I expect the students to change the tone as easily as I do, and I have to remember to go back to the basics every once in awhile."

When talking about what they learned, the graduates put greatest emphasis on reflection: "If nothing else, I gained from Mills a deep habit of reflection." Though they acknowledged that the one assignment was obviously not the whole reason for that, it did make a contribution. As one said, "I am very glad we were asked through these assignments to be more organized and critical of our observations and reactions. Any time I am able to organize my thoughts like this I find it incredibly help-ful. Writing anything in narrative form is good for me." Another spoke more specifically about how the assignment helped her: "I don't think I would have gained quite so much perspective on this assignment if it hadn't been done exactly how it was—writing in story form on my own, with license to alter it for purposes of clarity, and discussing it with a group." Someone else emphasized other helpful aspects: "I liked this assignment because it did make me think about what I considered to be important. I also liked the fact that you had us strive to be nonjudgmental because I think that being nonjudgmental promoted consideration of different perspectives more readily." She and one other were uncertain as to whether or not the story form made a difference for them. However, they and their colleagues did find the overall assignment to be very valu-able both in the moment and over a year later, and previous research (LaBoskey, 1998) has shown that the story form seemed to be a central factor in that outcome.

POTENTIALS AND LIMITATIONS

The narrative practice shared in this chapter did seem to have both short-term and long-term value for the student teachers who engaged it. Whether or not it can serve as an exemplar of narrative practice in the larger com-munity remains to be seen. The practice needs to be tested in the field by both comparing it to other narrative exemplars, and most importantly, implementing it in other contexts.

In the interest of the former, I would like to make some connections between this narrative practice and two others in the field. Significant among the possibilities is the work of Jean Clandinin and her colleagues. As she explains in one of her many writings on this topic (Clandinin, 1992), she and Michael Connelly conceive of "teacher education as nar-rative inquiry" (p. 126). Thus for them, narrative is not just a helpful addition to teacher education practice; it is the essence of the work. The primary structure they have used involves all parties in the process—student teachers and their mentors—producing stories that are shared with and discussed by the group. All then engage in a process of reflec-tive restorying wherein their collective and individual knowledge of teaching is constructed and reconstructed. They do this because they see "our teaching practices as expressions of our personal practical knowl-edge . . . the experiential knowledge that [is] embodied in us as persons and [is] enacted in our classroom practices and in our lives" (Clandinin, 1993, p. 1).

The narrative exemplar I have described also engages student teach-ers in the process of constructing their personal practical knowledge of teaching—how they will go about setting tones in their own classrooms. The assignment begins with storytelling and, though it is a story of the practice of others, it is told through the lenses of the novices and is focused on issues of concern to them. The process also includes the sharing and discussing of their stories with others and the result is a restorying: "I re-ally came to an even greater understanding of how what I thought I knew about myself has been further scrutinized—and how I feel like I don't know what the best way is—since there are reasonable explanations either philo-sophical or theoretical for another explanation." According to Clandinin, Davies, Hogan, & Kennard (1993), their participants "came to see teacher education as an ongoing process of inquiry in which there was a continu-ous dialogue between theory and practice, between themselves and chil-dren, between their pasts, their presents, and their futures" (p. 211). Ac-cording to our program graduates, they take on a similar perspective not only during the credential year, but beyond:

> Yes! Yes! Yes! with the reflective attitude. (I can't stop [smiley face]). I didn't like what I saw that first day but I didn't like what I saw my first day either. There are many things that happen in my room that I don't like or that make me stop—but I appreciate my ability to reflect on my practice—good and bad—and make changes. It helps me set the tone—I feel honest when I tell the children that we are all learning together.

The "setting the tone" exemplar, therefore, does seem well connected to the narrative practice of Clandinin and her colleagues.

Nona Lyons (1998) provides another possible exemplar of narrative practice. She describes the case of Martha, who engages in a series of dia-logues with one of her mentors during the course of her student-teaching experience. Martha brings to the interviews "artifacts as well as experiences she considered markers of her own development as a teacher—entries for a teaching portfolio" (p. 103), which are used as initiators of a conversa-tion about Martha's experience of learning to teach. The narratives are the stories told by Martha in the process of discussing her portfolio artifacts with the interviewer. Lyons concludes that the interactive storytelling pro-cess creates "texts that bring things into view—one's actions and values, what is important in teaching—and they bring into consciousness the teacher's own beliefs, ones he or she may have acted upon even subcon-sciously" (p. 117). Our student teachers and graduates expressed similar views about the "setting the tone" activity.

Lyons suggests that one of the reasons narrative practices may work well in teacher education is because stories include "interpretations of their author's meanings." Since "[t]eaching is a supremely interpretive activity taking place on many levels: in determining how children will learn a particular subject, how a subject needs to be presented, and so forth" (p. 118), helping credential candidates make appropriate interpretations through analyses of stories should be supportive of their growth as teachers. The essence of the "setting the tone" assignment is interpretation: the student teacher has to interpret the classrooms she observes in order to construct her story and she and her classmates then need to interpret and reinterpret the story in light of their own experiences, beliefs, and ambitions. Lyons's primary finding is that the portfolio interview narratives support the development of teacher reflection. The "setting the tone" stories and discussions seemed to do the same.

Though there do appear to be promising similarities between the setting the tone assignment and other narrative practices in the field, the true test of an exemplar must come in the form of subsequent implementation and debate. That process with regard to this particular exemplar has already begun. Another teacher educator, Barbara Henderson, used the setting the tone assignment in two of her classes and we analyzed the results in comparison to mine (LaBoskey & Henderson, 2000). What we found is that though the trends were similar, the outcomes were not as strong for Barbara's students. In particular, they were more resistant to the idea of withholding judgments and to not seeking the right answer. We concluded that further adaptation and scaffolding may need to occur for student teachers who are not as strong in their initial reflective orientations. In our view, this limitation did not make the practice invalid; indeed, we would expect exemplars to undergo adaptation in different contexts. In fact, Barbara has found the strategy valuable enough to continue its use in her courses. My hope is that others will engage the effort, make public the results, and debate the value of this narrative practice.

REFERENCES

Bruner, J. (1985). Narrative and paradigmatic modes of thought. In E. Eisner (Ed.), *Learning and teaching the ways of knowing* (pp. 97–117). Chicago: National Society for the Study of Education.

Clandinin, D. J. (1992). Narrative and story in teacher education. In T. Russell & H. Munby (Eds.), *Teachers and teaching: From classroom to reflection* (pp. 124–137). London: Falmer Press.

Clandinin, D. J. (1993). Teacher education as narrative inquiry. In D. J. Clandinin, A. Davies, P. Hogan, & B. Kennard (Eds.), *Learning to teach, teaching to learn:*

Stories of collaboration in teacher education (pp. 1–15). New York: Teachers College Press.

Clandinin, D. J., Davies, A., Hogan, P., & Kennard, B. (1993). Finding new ways to work together: Living in the middle ground. In D. J. Clandinin, A. Davies, P. Hogan, & B. Kennard (Eds.), *Learning to teach, teaching to learn: Stories of collaboration in teacher education* (pp. 210–217). New York: Teachers College Press.

Clandinin, D. J., & Connelly, F. M. (1996). Teachers' professional knowledge landscapes: Teacher stories—stories of teachers—school stories—stories of school. *Educational Researcher, 25*(3), 24–30.

Fenstermacher, G. D. (1994). The knower and the known: The nature of knowledge in research on teaching. *Review of Research in Education, 20,* 3–56.

LaBoskey, V. K. (1998). *"Setting the tone" stories: Opportunities for narrative knowing and not knowing.* Paper presented at the annual meeting of the American Educational Research Association, San Diego, CA.

LaBoskey, V. K., & Henderson, B. (2000). *Stories as a way to join practice and reflection.* Paper presented at the Third International Conference on Self-study of Teacher Education Practices, East Sussex, UK.

Lyons, N. (1998). Constructing narratives for understanding: Using portfolio interviews to scaffold teacher reflection. In N. Lyons (Ed.), *With portfolio in hand: Validating the new teacher professionalism* (pp. 103–119). New York: Teachers College Press.

CHAPTER 3

Narratives That Teach: Learning About Teaching from the Stories Teachers Tell

ANNA ERSHLER RICHERT

As I have reflected on the narratives I have written this year, I am struck with how uncertain I am about how much I know about my students and their English language proficiency. Initially, I believed that the equity issues that I wanted to address lay in the structure of the program. For example, there weren't enough English models in the classroom, and it was an unnecessary challenge to ask the students to work with a different teacher for English language instruction. However, after putting my narratives together and reading them as one long reflection on my own practice, I realized that a huge gulf existed between myself and my English language learners. I simply don't know what they know.

—Teacher

Serena, the teacher who wrote this reflection, is a member of the Mills College/Bay Region IV teacher research project, which houses the exemplar of the narrative methodology that will be described in this chapter. Many have argued, as I will here, that narratives of teaching practice provide special access to the world of schooling—access that is immediate, real, and importantly unique. Serena's work demonstrates all three. Her stories are immediate and "real" in that they are true accounts of current practice. This makes them unique in that they describe events that occurred at a particular place and time. Because they captured real events from her classroom in a form that she could ponder over time, Serena's narratives provided an important window onto her teaching—one without which she was unable to untangle certain complexities of her work. Interestingly, whereas we would expect Serena's narratives are important to her, we learned that they are interesting and important to other teachers as well. It appears that because narratives speak the truth of teachers' lives, they are compelling to an audience broader than the teachers who write them (Richert, 2001).

This quality of "speaking the truth" about teaching is one reason that narratives create a rich context for teacher learning; as texts that describe teaching practice, they invite teachers to reflect on their work. Serena saw in her four narratives an opportunity for "one long reflection" on her practice. She believes that the narrative process moved her toward new understandings that ultimately made her a "better teacher." How this happened is the subject of the pages to follow.

METHOD

I will begin by describing the narrative component of the professional development program that Serena participated in during the academic year 1999–2000. Using the exemplar format that frames this volume, I will then review the work of two teachers—Serena and her colleague Tanya—who engaged in this narrative work over the year's time. These descriptions of the method and the outcomes allow us to consider both its strengths and the challenges it presents.

Stage 1: Creating the Text

The teacher narrative methodology I will describe here is the first part of a 2-year professional development project directed toward equity pedagogy in urban classrooms. The narrative process unfolds over one full academic year in a sequence of three interrelated steps: (1) writing the narratives; (2) reading and reflecting on them; and (3) sharing them with colleagues. All three steps are designed to foster both individual and collective reflection on classroom events.

The narratives themselves are story texts written by the teacher participants about events in their classrooms and/or schools. Over the course of the year the teachers write several of them; in the partnership project described here, each teacher wrote four, which were two to three pages long. There is only one immutable criterion for the stories: they have to be true.

The goal in writing the narrative is to create in the reader or listener a vicarious experience of the events it describes. The narratives are less analytical in form than they are descriptive. The details of the events described are important. They convey what happened, to whom, when, how, and to what effect. The process begins with the teacher participants reading narratives from earlier years of the project and talking about the events they describe. This opening activity familiarizes the teachers with the text form and begins to demystify the process overall. Importantly, it also establishes a culture of shared inquiry.

Early in the year we also spend one session practicing narrative writing so that the teachers become familiar with the elements of narrative text writing (Zachariou, 1999). In guiding their writing, we ask that they include as many details and as much dialogue as they can remember so that the reader will have a sense of the interactions involved in the event. As they describe the circumstances, we ask that the teacher writers try to remember what they were thinking as the events unfolded and include that thinking as "internal dialogue" in the text. What they were feeling is part of the story and should be included as well.

The teacher writers bring their drafts to meetings where they share them with their colleague writers for feedback and review. The collection of narratives becomes an authentic text about teaching written by people who know it from the inside out. The stories the teachers write are not only real in the sense described above, but immediately important. They describe the unique circumstances of each classroom while at the same time revealing the ubiquitous qualities of life in school. As a collection they are full of life, love, struggle, joy, pain, disappointment, and triumph.

Over the years I have used this methodology in numerous settings, each with a different overall purpose. Different purposes suggest different foci for the writing segment of the work. For example, in the project I draw on as the example in this chapter, the focus of the work was on equity pedagogy. Our goal was to engage our teacher colleagues in professional learning that would lead toward excellent and equitable outcomes for all children. Given the persistent, predictable, and growing achievement gap between white children and their black and brown peers, our ultimate goal was for the teachers to develop their professional capabilities for better meeting the learning needs of their students of color. Consequently, in this instance the teachers were directed to write narratives of practice that revealed the equity focus of the project. Given the broad range of understandings about equity among the teacher participants, the range of stories in terms of topics and depth of understanding of equity issues was vast. This provided a rich collective text for the second step of the process: reflection on the narratives.

Stage 2: Reflecting on the Text

The process of creating the narratives is rich with opportunities for teacher reflection. Choosing what details to include, remembering the conversations that occurred, thinking back on the feelings that were part of the event, remembering who did what, who said what, and so forth, are all parts of the writing process that spurs the teacher-authors to reflect on their classroom work. Beyond this informal reflection, however, the methodology requires the teacher authors to choose one or more of their narratives to analyze more formally. In preparation for this analysis, we spend one meeting time thinking about how to analyze these texts. In this session we consider such techniques as identifying the issues revealed, raising questions about those issues or about the events themselves, looking "between the lines" of the story to see what details might be missing, and so forth.

If there is a focus for the narrative work such as the equity focus for the project described here, the analysis can be geared toward understandings in that domain. There were suggested questions to guide the analysis in the narrative project where Serena's stories were told; for example, What does your narrative suggest about the matter of equity in your classroom? What issues of curriculum and pedagogy are revealed? What do you notice in the narrative about who has access in your classroom and who does not? Whose story are you telling, and why?

Stage 3: Sharing the Narrative with Colleagues

The last step of the narrative work is to share the work with teachers who are one's colleagues. Whereas, as I am describing here, this sharing of the work appears to be the final of three steps, in truth, there is considerable sharing of the work throughout the process. By the time the teachers present their final draft narratives to one another for discussion and review, they are familiar with one another's work; the conversation between and among colleagues has long since begun. In fact, the sharing of the stories generated as part of the ongoing conversation about their work is what is at the heart of the culture of inquiry and learning offered by the narrative methodology overall.

Establishing safety and trust is essential to this process—essential, and somewhat challenging to create. It is not part of the culture of most schools for teachers to talk about the details of their practice. In particular, they seldom discuss the challenges they encounter, the puzzles they have not solved, the things they don't know. The narrative methodology challenges this "conspiracy of silence" by raising for careful examination the inherent uncertainty of teaching's work (McDonald, 1992; Wasserman, 2001). Because this sharing of one's uncertainty is uncommon in teaching, the process can make teachers feel vulnerable. Therefore, it is important to set ground rules or norms for the sharing process such as confidentiality, for example, whereby the teachers agree not to share the details of one another's classrooms with people outside the narrative group. Guidance for how to respond to one another's work needs to be part of the process as well. Even with guidance, creating a safe environment that fosters a rich and honest sharing is challenging indeed.

Once the sharing format is established, the narrative text becomes the focal point for numerous conversations about teaching and learning in schools. Depending on the purpose of any given exchange, the topics can range from those embedded in the narrative itself to conversations across narratives in a particular collection to issues noticeably absent in the narrative as a group. This process of "going public" with some aspect of one's work is critical to the learning outcomes that are possible from the process.

OUTCOMES

So what *are* the outcomes of this methodology for teachers? One way to answer that question is to consider narrative work of teachers who have engaged in doing it. Let us move, then, to doing just that: examining the work of two novice teachers who participated in the Mills College/Bay Region IV partnership narrative project on equity during the academic year 1999–2000. Both of these teachers teach at Melvina Elementary, an inner-city elementary school that serves a population of poor and working-class children. Serena is a third-year teacher whose current class is a one-two combination. Most of her students do not speak English as a first language. Serena herself is bilingual in Spanish and English; she teaches in both languages. In her narratives she considers the opportunities to learn English for Spanish-speaking children in her classroom.

Tanya is a colleague teacher of Serena's. She, too, is a novice teacher. This is Tanya's third year teaching at Melvina Elementary. All three years she has taught a third- and fourth-grade combined class. Like Serena, most of Tanya's students do not speak English as their first language. Many are from Southeast Asia; her narrative work focused on this particular population.

Over the course of our working together last year Serena and Tanya each wrote four one- to three-page narratives describing instances of practice in their classrooms. Tanya included in her narratives a brief analysis of the events she described as well as an analysis of the group of four that she wrote at the end of the process. Serena did not include an analysis with each narrative, but rather wrote an analysis at the end of all four. Both teachers also wrote two brief reflections about the narrative process. The narratives and reflections provide an interesting window onto the work: it is clear that the process was a unique learning opportunity for both teachers. Since both teach at the same school, they experienced a collective outcome as well. What can we learn from Serena and Tanya about the narrative methodology by looking at their work?

Working with Students from Backgrounds Different from One's Own

Most important of all the things Tanya and Serena learned from the narrative process is what they learned about their students. Both began their narrative work concerned about language and culture issues in their classrooms. Given that their students come from cultural backgrounds different from their own, both teachers expressed significant motivation for learning more about the children they teach. Their narratives reveal how little they feel they know about their students. At the same time, they portray the dismal reality about how little opportunity and access they have to learn more. Both teachers seized on the narrative work as an opportunity to write about experiences working with these children; all eight narratives reveal the depth of their struggles. Both Tanya and Serena pinned hopes on the narrative work as an opportunity to learn more. Serena's year-end reflection explained how her hopes began to be realized:

> When I began this year . . . I had generated a lot of anger and frustration about the ELD (English Language Development) program at Melvina. I felt frustrated for the students, frustrated for the families, and frustrated that I felt as if I wasn't doing a good job teaching my students English. Because I was so frustrated, I initially spent a great deal of time complaining about the situation. Although the complaining didn't feel particularly constructive, it was an important part of my process. My grumbling ultimately was the fire and passion that I put into my narratives.

Both Serena's and Tanya's narratives reveal how that "grumbling and passion" came together in the narrative process. Take this example from Tanya's third narrative where she describes an incident with Josie, a Vietnamese student of hers whom she is trying to support but whom she is having difficulty understanding. In this episode Tanya speaks of her confusion and frustration. Her passion is evidenced as well. The narrative begins with her pondering Josie's latest news that once again she can't go to her after-school language program. Tanya sees this after-school program as Josie's best hope for success in school—getting her into it was what Tanya considers one of her greatest accomplishments of the year. Josie's mom, however, has other plans for Josie's time. She needs Josie to pick up her younger sister Karly after school because she is unable to do it herself. Josie's inability to attend the language support program is a constant stress and disappointment for Tanya. She describes an encounter with Josie one day after school:

> I can feel the heat rising in my face as we march to the kinder- garten room to pick up Karly and I corral Josie into the office to call her mom. I speak in staccato, "Tell her your teacher said you have to come to the program." My jaw clenches. I sit in a chair next to the phone. I feel the weight of the day sink into my body.
>
> Her tiny fingers push the buttons. She turns her body to the side when someone answers and she speaks Vietnamese for only a few seconds. She hangs up. Her eyes are wet. Her lip shakes. "She say I have to go home with Karly." By the time the sentence is said she is crying. She turns away from the people who are waiting in the office. I feel a wetness in my own eyes. Josie's face wrinkles and tears splash into her hair as she pushes it behind her ears again. I wince. *Oh you sweet child. I just want you to have what you deserve. I'm sorry honey. I'm sorry. It's not your fault. I'm sorry.*
>
> "Josie honey, I'm not mad at you." I turn her so her back is toward the others in the office. My face is inches from hers. I speak in a soft, almost whispering, voice: "I'm not mad at you, it makes me very sad when you can't come because I want to help you and if you're not there, we don't get to work on things you are learning." She nods her head.

Acknowledging What They Do Not Know and the Frustration That Creates

By writing and reflecting on this narrative and others like it, Tanya's frustrations and the causes for them became clearer to her. She explains that as she wrote about her encounters with Josie and Josie's mother, she began to realize how hopelessly uninformed she was about Josie's life and family—and about the lives and families of many of the children in her classroom. "I personally know very little about the families of my Southeast Asian students," she explains at the end of one narrative. "I believe that as a staff, we collectively don't express a solid understanding of their experiences." In her concluding analysis, she writes, "My inability to identify Josie's learning issues with confidence points to many causes as well as a myriad of effects." Importantly, the effects of "not-knowing," of which Tanya writes in her analysis, are ones that have troubling consequences—

something Tanya comes to understand more deeply by writing the narratives and sharing them with her colleagues. She explains the impact further in the final analysis: The fact that I know virtually nothing about her home life and culture has an enormous impact. I do not know what she already knows. I don't know her family's understanding of the U.S. educational system. Without knowing these things, I cannot plan culturally congruent experiences for her. I also feel incredibly frustrated by Josie's inability to regularly attend the after-school program. Because I can never get a handle on the specifics of her situation, I tend to blame her family for not making school a priority.

Without the opportunity to look systematically at their practice, teachers often find themselves feeling feelings they cannot attach to accurate or appropriate causes. Understandably, their frustrations mount. Unexamined, these frustrations lead to misunderstandings. Even more damaging is when the frustrations lead to the kind of "blaming" that Tanya bravely reveals in the analysis she shares with us here.

The same uncertainty or sense of not-knowing that Tanya describes in her narrative mirrors the frustration Serena describes as she reflects her starting point for the beginning of the project. As Serena examines her narratives, she, too, realizes how she had misidentified the appropriate antecedent for her frustration. She writes:

> Over and over again in my narratives I express frustration that my students are not speaking English or that I am only hearing Spanish being spoken. I also have tremendous concern about particular students who seem to be "stuck" [as measured by their reading score]. My assumption is that they are not learning English and that there is something within the structure of the program that is preventing them from being successful.

It was only after reading her narratives and then thinking about them that Serena began to understand things differently—a process similar to Tanya's whereby Tanya began to see the antecedents to her frustrations more clearly by writing about her practice, and standing away from it to analyze the stories she had written. Serena continues,

> However, as I was rereading my narratives it dawned on me: how do I know that they aren't learning any English? I know that they are not speaking very much English, but I have no idea what their listening, reading, or writing skills are like in English. My entire measure of success and failure has been based on their oral English capabilities.

WHAT IN THE NARRATIVE PROCESS BRINGS
ABOUT THESE RESULTS?

Serena claims here that "rereading (her) narratives" gave her access to information about her teaching that she did not have before. In looking at Serena's work more closely, however, it is clear that the learning process began before she read her narratives—and it continued beyond. The work of both Serena and Tanya reveal how each step of the process contributes differently to the overall impact: (1) telling or writing the narratives; (2) reading the narratives; and (3) talking about the narratives with colleagues. Let us consider each step in turn.

Telling—or Writing—the Story

Telling their stories of practice provides teachers with an opportunity to focus on particular instances of teaching and to examine those instances more deeply than they are able to during the busyness of their classroom work. In this project, the teachers *wrote* their stories, which provided a focus and attention that simply telling them does not. Interestingly, both Tanya and Serena suggest that this ability to focus may extend beyond the particular narratives that they produce in written form. For example, Tanya describes how the narrative work has begun to take hold as a "habit of mind" that began with the writing step of the process, but then continued beyond. She explains:

> As the year went on it was harder to keep up with the narrative assignments. I thought about future narratives often and I wrote many narratives in my mind that never made it to paper. I think that's a good sign. I was breaking down elements of my day and putting them into this narrative format (if only mentally).

Tanya's move to thinking about "future narratives" suggests that she began to think of her work as clusters of activity worthy of documentation and analysis. Serena described a similar feeling; she explained that the narrative process helped her view the details of her day-to-day experiences in school as meaningful in new ways. "My interactions with students, teachers, administrators, and parents suddenly became valuable in a new way," she explained. "It was anecdotal data that could inform and improve my practice."

Writing the stories of practice provided both teachers a chance to "go public" with the details of their work. It drew on their creative and emotional selves and provided a powerful opportunity for the expression of those aspects of themselves that are highly engaged in the work of teaching, but seldom expressed publicly (or possibly even privately). "The narrative process was incredibly empowering for me," Tanya wrote. "I got to use my creative side while being forced/allowed to critically examine elements of my practice." Part of "using their creative side" involved exploring their feelings, according to Tanya and Serena—exploring their feelings and letting others know about those feelings at the same time.

This opportunity to explore their feelings is particularly significant when considering the impact of the narrative methodology for teacher learning. Teaching is a highly emotional enterprise, but teachers have little opportunity to make note of their emotions much less tell others about them. Since feelings are so much a part of teaching, however, they are centrally important to the narrative work. Serena explains, "Personally, (writing my narratives) gave me an avenue with which to express my frustrations, observations, and feelings about my own teaching and my experiences working in a school."

Ironically, the emotional side of teaching that is ubiquitous in the work is seldom identified or discussed by people who talk about teaching. In the narrative methodology described here, however, the emotional side of teaching is seen as not only legitimate, but essential. Since the emotional state of teachers provides the barometer that heralds the puzzles of practice (Dewey, 1933), the narrative methodology requires attention to the emotional in new ways that are welcomed and valued deeply by teachers. Teacher narratives provide extraordinary witness to the emotional demands of teaching—witness that is seldom revealed when teachers talk about their work to others who are not teachers. It strikes me in reading the narratives from this project and others how valuable these texts are for understanding the emotional content of teaching by understanding the toll it takes on the professionals who do it. Interestingly, the narrative process, by its invitation to name feelings, also makes these emotional demands clearer to the teachers themselves.

The narratives examined in this chapter provide ample examples. Consider, for a moment, the *stillness* Tanya presents when she describes her meeting with the resource teacher who called for a "referral" after a notably brief conversation about Josie. She begins by describing how the meeting began:

> I remove the rubber band that attached the SST form to the file. "I wanted to talk to you about a referral I'm making. . . . It's Josie T. She's reading a high five [high first grade level] and I had to drop her from the after-school intervention program because of lack of progress and poor attendance." I make myself take a breath and slow down. We have only 20 minutes. We have two other children to

discuss after Josie. I feel like I could talk forever about this child whom I've known for 7 months now. In my mind I can see myself on my knees in the hallway one morning two weeks ago in an attempt to be on eye level with Josie. I remember searching for the kindest words to tell her she couldn't come to the after-school program anymore. . . . "Well," the resource teacher states, . . . "it sounds like a solid referral. Who else do we need to talk about?" I sit *still* [emphasis added] for a moment. I can hear the happy screams of children outside the window. Children playing four-square and jump rope.

Serena's narratives are similarly replete with emotional content. The feeling in the pit of her stomach that she describes in an early narrative is part of the "evidence" Serena found when she studied her collection of four narratives and discovered what she did not know about her English-language learners. In this instance she describes Maria who, having memorized its contents, is reading her book upside down:

Maria reads *cow* for *dog* and self-corrects after checking her illustration. All the students are busy finishing or reading their books. I have a pit in my stomach and my mouth feels dry. *Where else do you speak English? How can I get you to speak more English? What is going to happen to you? What can I do to help you learn this language?* Janet is speaking in Spanish to Valeria. Julie sits quietly next to Zenaida. George is speaking Spanish to Marisol. *Is anyone speaking English? They must be tired of listening to me talk.*

Her feelings are equally clear in another bit from the same narrative:

She is small—smaller than almost all of the other children. Her hair is all over the place. Her arms hang limp at her sides. Her shoulders fall forward slightly. Her lip is still in her mouth. I reach for her hand. "Maria, let's go outside. This really isn't OK. I know that you can talk and that you have wonderful things to say. I want to hear your beautiful voice."

Reading and Reflecting

Writing the narratives is one step in the learning process; reading and reflecting on them is the next. Serena's reflections at the end of the year provide particular insight about how this works. She explains how she began to understand her teaching in new ways when her analysis revealed that certain details appeared "over and over" again:

> Over and over again in my narratives I express frustration that my students are not speaking English or that I am hearing Spanish being spoken. I also have tremendous concern about particular students who seem to be "stuck" (as measured by their IPT score). My assumption is that they are not learning English and that there is something within the structure of the program that is preventing them from being successful.

Having the narrative text to examine offered Serena the opportunity to see her frustration while not being in the middle of it. She could see in the stories themselves, the repeated expression of her concern about certain students. She was also able to identify what she later realized was possibly an erroneous assumption concerning her lack of success. With this window opened up, Serena was able to turn her thinking in a new direction. She explains:

> However, as I was rereading my narratives it dawned on me: How do I know that they aren't learning any English? I know that they are not speaking very much English, but I have no idea what their listening, reading, or writing skills are like in English. . . . I began to think about other areas of my practice where I feel in touch with my students and what they know and don't know. I thought about my primary language reading program and how much the students and parents are an active part in their learning to read. . . . I realized that the biggest difference between my English program and my reading program is the use of standardized routine assessment. I am able to make changes to my reading program on a regular basis because I know what my students know and don't know.

The narrative methodology gave Serena an opportunity to see in her work that which she was not able to see without it. By reflecting on her work we are able to understand what she means when she describes the narrative process in her reflection at the end of the year: "Suddenly our incidents of practice became texts (from) which incredible discussions and questions emerged." The "incredible discussions and questions" that Serena alludes to in this quote moves us to the final step of the narrative process, the sharing of these narratives with colleagues.

Discussing the Narratives with Colleagues

Both Serena and Tanya identify their collegial conversations about the narratives as important to their learning as well. From them they claim new insights, new questions, and a new sense of shared work and professional responsibility. None of this was gained easily, however. Teachers are not used to sharing their work with one another, especially those parts of their work where they feel uncertain. There seemed to emerge from the process a two-way cause-and-effect process whereby the sharing of the narratives built trust among the teachers and the building of trust allowed the teachers to be more open in sharing their stories. "First, writing and sharing the narratives with one another facilitated the three of us getting to know one another better and trusting each other with our fears and inadequacies (perceived?)," Serena writes. She explains later, "We all felt very vulnerable sharing our narratives but with time we grew to trust one another with our most private teaching moments."

Both teachers explained that ultimately, sharing those private moments—and the realities of their day to day work—offered them the chance to "go deeper" in their understanding, and therefore to develop new and richer understandings of their work. Tanya explains, "I feel that my team members and I have a deeper understanding of how we must structure our conversations about language development with our colleagues to encourage looking specifically at each population and also for allowing diversity of experience within that (cultural) group." Serena shared that sentiment:

> Writing and sharing the narrative helped to ground us in our day-to-day experiences with our students and our English curriculum. We were able to move through our hunches and frustrations towards the asking of deeper more meaningful questions of our practice and the ELD program as a whole.

This notion of "wholeness" that Serena raises captures some of what the collective aspect of the narrative work contributed to the overall impact. When the teachers shared their work, new questions were raised, as Serena mentions above. The new questions pushed the teachers to think more deeply. They were moved from their typically isolated existence into a collaborative consideration of the complexities of their teaching practice. This sense of connection and its potential contribution to what teachers can come to know is not to be underestimated. Tanya says, "I believe I have a more holistic understanding of the root causes of the inequities in our ELD program." Similarly, Serena explains how the new directions of understanding are both toward the more whole and the more specific at the same time:

> We began our discussions with [a consideration of] broad-sweeping inequities that felt impossible to address . . . but through our analysis of our narratives, we were able to be more specific about the equity issues (i.e., What we have in place for certain groups of students at Melvina that is not evident for other groups).

FINAL THOUGHTS

For ages, people have been using stories as texts from which learning can occur. Drawing on that tradition, the narrative methodology described here provides teachers an opportunity to tell their stories of practice and then build from that telling, various opportunities for reflection and learning. The process values what teachers do because what they do is the subject of the narratives they write. Through the process, "What [they] do all day long was made to feel important and powerful," Serena claims, "and this was very encouraging."

As encouraging as it is, however, keeping the momentum going for the narrative work is challenging, given the many demands teachers have on them every moment of every day. Perhaps at the root of this difficulty is our profession's low value for practice-based teacher learning in the first place. Since schools are notorious in their disregard for teacher's professional growth (Sarason, 1990), establishing a context where the narrative work will take enough priority for the teachers to engage consistently in the various steps of the process is a constant challenge. It is both difficult— and yet critical for the method's success—to keep the momentum going by providing incentives and supports for accomplishing the work, at each stage of the process.

One incentive that the teachers claim is particularly powerful for their engaging in this work is the opportunity it provides for being acknowledged as competent knowers in the professional world. It feels good to be seen as competent. The narrative process is clear in its valuing what teachers know because it requires that teachers write about their practice. What they write typically reflects what they know. The narratives produced in our project are filled with brilliant insights about children and learning, about subject matter and teaching, about the workings of school. It would be impossible to read them and not have an enriched image of how complex the work of teaching is and how vast the knowledge base must be to do the work well.

Interestingly, while on the one hand the narrative methodology reveals what teachers know, it also allows teachers to explore what they don't know, which may be the greatest gift of all. Without an opportunity of naming what they don't know about those aspects of practice that are at the center of their concern, teachers are never invited into the critical process of asking their own questions and pursuing the exciting journey of coming to know new things. To not have that opportunity can leave teachers and their students in a frightening abyss of ignorance leading to unfulfilled hopes and expectations. Alternatively, to have that opportunity presents teachers with an invitation to become better at what they do and thus to rekindle the spirit that brought them to the work of teaching in the first place. This, in turn, restores their hope that they can serve their students well. The work of Tanya and Serena demonstrate how this might be so. It is on the basis of their experience and the potential for learning we witness there, that this exemplar is offered as part of the collection included in this book.

REFERENCES

Capitelli, S. (2000). *Narratives and reflections.* Unpublished manuscripts from the Teacher Research Project on Equity Pedagogy in Schools. Oakland, CA: Mills College/Bay Region IV Consortium for Professional Development.

Dewey, J. (1933). *How we think* (Rev. ed.). Lexington, MA: Heath Publishing.

Loomis, T. (2000). *Narratives and reflections.* Unpublished manuscripts from the Teacher Research Project on Equity Pedagogy in Schools. Oakland, CA: Mills College/Bay Region IV Consortium for Professional Development.

McDonald, J. (1992). *Teaching: Making sense of an uncertain craft.* New York: Teachers College Press.

Richert, A. E. (2001). Narratives as experience texts: Writing themselves back in. In Lieberman, A., & Miller, L., (Eds.), *Teachers caught in the action: The work of professional development.* New York: Teachers College Press.

Sarason, S. B. (1990). *The predictable failure of educational reform.* San Francisco: Jossey-Bass.

Wasserman, S. (2001). Quantum theory, the uncertainty principle, and alchemy of standardized teaching. *Phi Delta Kappan, 83*(1), 28–40.

Zachariou, P. (1999). *Exploring your creative writing potential.* Unpublished guidelines for teaching writing.

CHAPTER 4

Out of Despair: Reconceptualizing Teaching Through Narrative Practice

REBECCA AKIN

When I recently heard stories described as being much like maps (Winterson, 2000) I was suddenly able to understand in a fuller way the nature of the narratives that have become part of my teaching practice. Maps allow one to see the layout of the terrain from above so that mountains can be seen as bounded rather than as insurmountable obstacles, valleys can be seen as finite rather than inescapable chasms, and oceans can be understood to be navigable rather than experienced as a vastness within which to be engulfed. I imagine that Winterson was not thinking literally of geography when she made her analogy, but it certainly has been the terrain of all the many and varied landscapes of teaching that have come into much clearer view for me through the writing of stories of my teaching.

The writing of narratives began almost incidentally for me, first as assignments in graduate school, then as material to present at conferences, and finally as a part of research I have been doing in my classroom. It was what amounted to a series of very synchronistic opportunities that provided the structure for me to write consistently, until I came to a place where I realized that I needed to purposefully make this writing a part of my practice.

I didn't come to narrative practice consciously, thinking that I would begin to write and in doing so make some sense of teaching. On the contrary, the incorporation of this practice into my teaching has been a slow process of discovery, one that is not so much about the technique of writing narratives as it is the development of my understanding about my teaching through the purposeful articulation of the dilemmas, experiences, and situations in which I have found myself over my novice teaching years. It is that process I will describe here as an exemplar of narrative practice.

CONTEXT

Describing both narrative and how it has become an actual practice requires a story, one that illustrates why the need for writing narratively exists for me in my professional environment and where that writing has enabled me to go. Like all of the narratives I have written, the story that follows entails context, interactions with students and colleagues, dilemmas, reflection, sharing, and the articulation of new understanding. And like all of my narrative work, this one is fluid in that it moves in and out of these varied perspectives in an attempt to represent as authentically as possible the richness and complexity of teaching.

The View from Inside

On Monday mornings I take great care to avoid the familiar chatter of my school office, where teachers busily gather around the copy machine to ready themselves for the new week. When I do find myself there and am politely asked about my weekend, I am uncomfortable because I feel that a particular type of response is anticipated, one that either acknowledges my joy at being away or my displeasure at having to come back. Such is the culture of my school site, where the atmosphere is one of compulsion rather than engagement. Bordering on lying, I simply say it was too short. The implication taken, of course, is that I wanted more time away, time for my "real life" and the relief that returning to it brings. I don't know how to talk about the fact that I spent those two precious days trying to better connect to the work of the week and make some sense out of what I'm doing in my classroom. The fact is, I have only one life, not two. I have never been able to be someone different at specific times, at one moment being Ms. Akin the first-grade teacher, and the next Rebecca the swimmer, spouse, reader of books, housekeeper, thinker of adult thoughts. I certainly don't begrudge that Monday morning group the distinction between real life and work life. In fact, part of my struggle as a teacher comes from my confusion about having to make that distinction. When it was finally brought to my attention that as a teacher the work I do is almost entirely defined by others (Richert, 2000), I realized that as an act of survival we often choose to see our lives as real only outside of our schools.

I imagine that there are many of us who are lesser teachers for having to make this distinction between the person we are and the teacher we have been named. And I witness the results of this unnatural schism all too often as apathy, feelings of mediocrity and failure, cynicism, and sadly, flight. Trying to hold on to a single identity has been without a doubt one of the most difficult and draining challenges I have faced in the 5 years I have been teaching in an urban public school.

Defining Teaching: A View from the Outside

A few weeks into this new year, on a day in which the sunshine finally broke through the cloudy gloom, my students and I were out on the blacktop tracing each other's shadows. Somehow the winter sun broke through at a time in which the shadows cast by our bodies were fairly proportional to our real selves, neither unusually elongated nor comically short. The children who drew labored with delight in trying to move the porous chalk over the rough surface of the asphalt. Their partners worked with intense concentration to hold still enough to keep their wavering shadow within the already completed sections.

During the discussion that ensued upon our return to the classroom, Nina, a particularly brilliant 6-year-old, reflected on the fact that although these shadows were our own, all of the details of our physical appearances were lost. Instead of seeing a pink blouse with buttons, blue pants, eyes, and individual strands of hair, she saw only the outline, as if everything were one indiscriminate form. Although the actual articulation of these thoughts came with great struggle through broken, halting English, it was clear that Nina was stunned by this incomplete view of herself, by the fact that a sort of anonymous form of herself could exist. I remember being struck by the metaphorical nature of her discovery. In the world of public schooling the most essential players, the students and teachers, are often mere shadows for others to define as they will, choosing particular descriptors, ignoring others, all the while making what amounts to very definitive interpretations about the nature of that which casts the shadow, often without actually having seen the student or teacher to whom the shadow belongs.

It has been my experience that as teachers we are not positioned to define our work or our roles in a meaningful way, a fact of my life that I have found to be supported by many structural components of my school site and district. The issue of an almost complete lack of time for collegial discussion hinders significantly any type of reflective analysis that would render a shared conceptualization of our work. What brief time is allowed for talk is always either taken up by faculty meetings, where the agenda is dominated by the administrator, or staff development, which as the name implies is typically a training involving "experts" from outside coming in to teach specific, predetermined strategies. Time to do the necessary work of thinking, reflecting, evaluating, and modifying our own work is simply not provided.

It has been through purposeful and emphatic movement against this suppressive environment, by actively examining the space I occupy as a teacher, that I have been able to sustain myself thus far. This idea of examining the space I occupy as a teacher entails both reflection and a process of making sense. Importantly, this examination is not looking at what is wrong with the intent of trying to fix it, but rather focusing on some aspect of my teaching experience in the service of learning from that experience. It is this learning itself that lies at the center of teaching for me.

LEARNING AND THE STORYING OF EXPERIENCE

As a teacher I've given a considerable amount of thought to the nature of learning and knowledge. I've come to hold a fairly standard constructivist view of learning, where I believe numerous and varied learning opportunities are essential to the individual's ability to develop knowledge. Implicit in my understanding of learning is the conceptualization of knowledge as fluid—the idea that knowing is a way of being and interacting with the world, rather than the possession of information imposed from a particular source. Above and beyond achievement of district standards, what I most hope to provide for my students is the opportunity to become powerfully in control of their learning, to use critical thinking skills, intuition, inquiry, and communication with others to continually reevaluate and expand their understanding of the world around them and their place within it. Such learning, I believe, is at the core of living an engaged and responsible life.

Yet not only have I found the structure for such learning opportunities for teachers to be entirely lacking in the context of schools, but in fact there exists a very purposeful disregard for our need to learn. It took my own purposeful articulation of my experiences through writing to situate myself in a position where I could begin to reconceive of myself as a learner.

For 3 years now I have been writing about the experiences in my own classroom because it is the primary way in which I make sense of my teaching. I began this writing my 3rd year as a teacher, at which time I completed my master's degree at Mills College. An integral part of this program was a class taught by Anna Richert that focused on understanding theory through teaching practice. A central component of this class entailed writing narratives of practice, stories that in some way illustrated dilemmas we faced in our classrooms and/or school sites. Guidelines for the writing of these brief three- to five-page narratives were open-ended and simple: they had to address some aspect of our teaching, and they had to be true. These narratives were then used as a text around which discussion was focused.

That the writing of these narratives uses the classroom and school site as the stage for the events depicted was immediately significant. Anyone who has spent time in a classroom understands that it is a complex environment. Individual personalities and moods, varied curricular requirements, externally imposed time constraints, management issues, administrative demands, and the regularity of unexpected occurrences are all issues with which teachers must contend, often simultaneously and in perpetually changing configurations. It is the complexity of the environment that makes the lived situation of the classroom somehow greater than its parts, which is partially what renders teaching so difficult for those of us who are novices. Being new, we tend to see the chaos of the many parts rather than the continuity of the whole. Part of the power of narratives is in stopping the action long enough to theorize about it. Even more importantly, however, because of this contextual grounding narrative allows one to reflect on particular issues in the context in which they occur, which is essential if connections are to be made among experiences.

What I want to focus on, because I think it gets to the core of what keeps me in the profession, is not simply the learning that results from the writing of narratives, but that this writing has also allowed me to reconceptualize myself as a learner.

In *The Narrative as an Experience Text: Writing Themselves Back In* Richert (2000, p. 17) points to the use of narrative as a way for teachers to write ourselves back into the text of teaching. She explains that through the creation of this text "teachers write themselves into the situation they describe, either literally or as the observer/author who defines what matters most. Writing themselves into the text is critically important to the learning opportunity the narrative methodology affords novice teachers. Too often, novices' experience is written out of the teaching text by the plethora of programs and policies that neither ask what they think, nor care how they feel."

WRITING

This idea of writing myself back into the text of teaching has helped me to realize that the narrative work I have been doing over these novice years has been more than reflective. It has allowed me to insert myself more fully into a vision of teaching that I have taken part in constructing. In writing these narratives, stories of teaching as I perceive my experiences, I make conscious choices about how to conceptualize myself and my role. It is only through that act of articulation that I have been able to contest, resist, and revise, to use Ritchie and Wilson's (2000) terms, who I have been named as a teacher and to actively reconceptualize myself. What I have found I have been doing narratively is to "write myself back in" as a learner.

Richert's theory on the value of teacher narratives is one of those transformative ideas. I now realize that my use of narrative has impacted me in three fundamental ways. Through writing narratives I place myself in a position where I can learn from my work, I participate in the definition my own practice, and finally, I assume responsibility for who I am as a teacher.

Acknowledging Perspective: Simply Beginning

I began this whole process of writing narratives, it now seems, simply trying to make my classroom and my teaching experiences concrete. I was completely terrified about my first assignment to write authentically about my teaching. I knew I couldn't simply present the vision of my classroom as I thought it should look: ordered, rational, populated by students eagerly learning, and a teacher in full control of every shift and movement. Although I believed this was what I should have been able to represent, I could not write this because it was not even remotely true. The story that I did end up telling was one of my bitter failure as a teacher. I had addressed issues here that I worked daily to hide, issues that dealt with my inability to support even the most basic emotional needs of my students because of our language barrier. I was failing, I felt, in an area so fundamental that it preceded subject matter. As a new teacher the perception of the classroom that I experienced daily was so far from the conception I had of what it should look like that I could not reconcile the two, and consequently assumed that the problem was the result of my own inadequacy. As I wrote:

> Although a great majority of my students were born in this city, all but three had come to kindergarten a year earlier not speaking English. Our frequent inability to communicate often seemed a humiliation to them. An eager hand would go up in response to a question or idea, a mouth would quickly open, and yet nothing would come out. I could see the wheels turning. The excitement in the child's face would quickly fade, however, when the words would not materialize. Silence. Head hanging, face red, the student would manage a whispered "I forgot." Hmm . . . "Did you forget, or you don't know how to say it?" I would ask. I asked this all the time, thinking I was clarifying the problem. I felt I was helping the student by pointing out that he or she really did have an idea, but

just couldn't find the words. I meant for this to be a good thing. But maybe I was actually drawing boundaries that they didn't feel able to cross. They never were able to articulate this lack of vocabulary. It remained always, "I forgot." We just didn't have the language to talk about deep academic matters or the fundamental social issues so important to first grade. You have to be able to talk about all of these things or they get away from you. I felt that was the way it was with my whole class that year—everything important just got away from us. I couldn't understand what they were really saying. I couldn't help them communicate with each other. I couldn't help them treat each other with respect. We couldn't talk about things that really mattered. And I felt that somehow my inability to talk with them always ended up as their humiliation. (Akin, 1997, p. 3)

I finished writing that first story at 6:30 in the morning the day it needed to be done. Still unhappy with the product, I was embarrassed that it had taken me so long and that I had spent the whole night reworking it. I battled with myself on the drive to school that morning over issues of grammar. I had never written anything more than a standard college paper. I was terrified at the prospect of actually having my Mills colleagues read what I had written; a fear all mixed up in exposing myself as a teacher who didn't know what she was doing and as a graduate student who, it would be clear, didn't know how to write. The whole endeavor played on every insecurity I had, and my lack of sleep served to heighten my already strained emotional state. But even as vulnerable as I thought I had made myself, I felt a kind of resigned relief. At least at that moment of sharing, I could come out of hiding. Although I couldn't articulate why, it was in this simple act that I first felt myself being pulled out of the blindness of despair into which I had fallen as a novice teacher.

The Need for Focus

Part of my fear in feeling safe enough to articulate what I was experiencing in my classroom was that I came to the profession with a conceptualization of teaching as methodological, purposeful, and goal oriented. I was completely caught up in what Clandinin and Connelly (2000) describe as the "grand narrative" of teaching, where behavior is conceptualized as objectively identifiable, predictable, rational, linear, and consistent. And yet, what I experienced in my classroom as a new teacher seemed like a series of individual moments and various isolated episodes, which in their fragmentation appeared anything but methodological or goal directed. It was the gulf between what I thought should be possible for me and the seemingly minuscule circumstances that actually consumed me that threw me into disequilibrium. It was what I conceived of as the peripheral aspects of classroom life, not the lessons and learning but the interactions that occurred in process, that so absorbed my attention:

> "Teacher! Teacher! Teacher! Teacher! Teacher!" It's never long after the eight o'clock bell before John makes his presence known. The usual urgency in his voice increases with each pleading call. I purposely ignore him. "Teacher! Teacher! Teacher! Teacher!" He does not even look to see where I am. Nor does he wait for a response. The words roll off his tongue in quick succession. "Teacher! Teacher! Teacher! Teacher!" Finally it's too much. I make eye contact across the room and motion silently for him to come to me. Innocently, he responds as though I am the one who wanted something. "Yes, teacher?" I ask him if it's okay to yell across the room like that. "No teacher. Teacher, cccc . . . cccan I play animal families?" At times like this when he's excited, one continual initial letter sound struggles in his throat until, at length, his first word finally appears. This articulation delay does not stem from a lack of vocabulary. John's English is as fluent as his Vietnamese. I've come to think that the power of his thoughts are so great that he's trying to keep the words from exploding out of his mouth. But try as he might to control himself, the longer it takes him to get that first word out, the more force and speed with which the following words burst forth. I ask him if this activity is one of his choices this morning. "No, bbbb . . . bbbbut teacher, can I play animal families?" I remind him, as I remind him every morning, that he can only work at the centers listed under his name. I remind him also that animal families is not a choice for him this morning, and that if he wants to, he can choose it later during free choice time. We look together at the possibilities and he quickly decides where to go. Within five minutes, however, he's back. "Teacher! Teacher! Teacher! Teacher!" This time, too impatient to wait for me to respond, he's quickly at my side interrupting a discussion with another child. "Teacher, cccc . . . ccccan I play animal families now?" Without explanation, I quickly sit him in a chair and sternly tell him he can stay there until he decides to remember the rules for morning work time. I am immediately embarrassed by the severity of my decision. It's a purely emotional response on my part. John's really not doing anything wrong. He doesn't work where he's not supposed to. He only asks if I'll make an exception. Yet his relentlessness drives me crazy and I usually let him get the best of me. (Akin, 1998, pp. 1–2)

I express throughout that narrative my frustration at my complete inability to get John to work. I shamefully interpreted my experiences as failures rather than analyze why these experiences seemed to me to be problematic. However, I came to realize, as Maxine Greene writes, that "without articulation, without expression, the perceived world is in some way nullified . . ." (1978, p. 223). It was only through this process of writing that I began to realize that this articulation, this giving voice to these perceptions, wasn't a betrayal of my incompetencies, but rather a way of making my perceptions tangible and finally recognizing the validity of their reality.

Making Connections

It was through making myself describe what I was experiencing and naming what I was seeing that I then began to make connections among those experiences, my thoughts about my practice, and my role as a teacher. Rather than just a statement of my confusion, I began to see this writing developing to include the recognition of the dilemmas I felt I faced:

> "Ivy did a beautiful job on her work. She has a story, a picture and it's colored. But there are always ways to make work better. Who has a suggestion for how she could make her work even better? Two suggestions please." My poor kids. They hear this same speech four times a day. I wonder that they don't get sick of my voice. Yet hands shoot up immediately. Ivy examines the potential participants, staring back at the pleading eyes for what seems like an eternity. She finally selects Nancy. We wait again as Nancy gathers her thoughts. Is she trying to think of a suggestion only now or is she searching for the words in English? My frustration mounts as more empty time passes. I bite my lip and remind myself over and over how important discussion is. Somehow, we all sit silently for her. "Why you don't . . . , um, . . . , why you don't . . . , um . . . , why you don't color the window?" Nancy finally asks. Ivy stares silently at her work. My heart grows a little heavier. A few of my kids can make suggestions, but most, like Nancy, don't seem to understand. I muster as much enthusiasm as I possibly can, "Oh! So you think it would be better if she colored the window. Is that your suggestion?" Nancy happily agrees. As we proceed I am sidetracked by the thought that I am asking too much of my kids and wasting their time. If they're not developmentally ready for this, all the practice in the world won't help.
> My principal walked in once as this type of journal sharing was about to begin. In a panic, I fabricated some pretext for having to postpone this until after the next activity. I was terrified that she would see so much empty wait time go by unused. I imagine that other kindergarten classrooms are churning out voluminous product, racing through the curriculum, always occu-

pied producing tangible evidence of growth and development. I always think I am the only one who struggles with getting my kids to move along in their development. I believe strongly in what I do and could argue intelligently for why I make particular curricular choices, but still I am insecure. Though never challenged, I feel completely unsupported. I am alone in the choices I make, and my panic and insecurity seem clear evidence of my professional isolation. (Akin, 1999a, pp. 3–4)

By making my perceptions tangible I find myself finally able to take responsibility for them—I begin to reconceptualize those experiences, make sense of them, and resituate myself.

Reconceptualizing Myself as a Learner

My struggles around what my classroom and teaching should actually look like were themes that I began to see running throughout my narrative work. The more I wrote, the better able I became to purposely focus on these issues, and in focusing on them, begin to make sense of where they were coming from and then reframe them. It was in the actual process of the writing of the narrative from which the following excerpt comes that I found myself purposefully challenging the role I had been placed in as a learner:

> We sat in a semi-circle in the auditorium, some thirty elementary school teachers, clad in shorts and tee shirts, hiding yawns and sipping tea in attempt to fight off the effects of the late August heat. Most of us were wary of this in-service, hearing from colleagues at other schools that this district sponsored "Efficacy" training was another monumental waste of time. I had no argument with the facilitator's central premise, which was that it made sense to think of learning happening if people are pushed to level of complexity just beyond what they already possess, which is the Vygotskian concept of proximal development (although the facilitator refused to attribute the idea to Vygotsky). What offended me so deeply was the implied assertion that followed; that the reason our students were doing so poorly was because teachers weren't working hard enough to help them succeed.
>
> There was that familiar beast raising its ugly head again: "If only you would work harder. . . ." I know I must always try harder. And yet I don't know that simply working harder, putting my nose closer to the grindstone, will move us anywhere except into greater frustration. It was with these conflicting feelings battling inside of

me that I raised my hand and tried to express some sense of my concern.

I addressed my concern that by talking about student learning and teacher responsibility in such an objective, linear fashion and restricting our conversation to particular variables, that the job of teaching and the phenomenon of learning were both represented as simplistic. And it is this simplicity that grossly distorts the nature of learning and what we as teachers are being charged with.

As I spoke I looked around and realized I was talking to a blank audience. Although many of my colleagues had earlier expressed similar concerns to me, no one now offered one word of support, nod of agreement, or glance of acknowledgement. I tried giving an example from my classroom, one that drew directly from my own research the previous year, addressing essentially how I wasn't thinking clearly about a phenomenon going on in my class because I was stuck in one particular conceptualization and was not seeing the possibility of other interpretations. A teacher finally responded with a very sincere but specific suggestion about the example I had just given and how I might have handled my student better. I remember being dismayed at her response. She completely missed my point, which wasn't about particular inter-ventions, but about what that event symbolized for me as a teacher—about the learning that had taken place as a result of thinking differently about that situation. I tried again to clarify what I was talking about, but these words too were met with silence. (Akin, 1999b, pp. 1–2)

This was traumatic. But both this event and the writing about it were pivotal moments in my conceptualization of myself and my role as a learner. It was through putting this event down on paper and locating it among other faculty meeting situations in the whole of that narrative that I began finally to step outside of the "grand narrative" in which I saw myself as passive recipient of information, to a place where my resistance and challenges were indicative of a different conceptualization of my situation. It was in this new place outside the margins of the story constructed for me, that I began to understand the need to purposefully reconceive of myself as a learner.

"Writing Myself In"

It is the process I have described here of articulating thoughts and situa-tions through the telling of stories of my experiences, of positioning myself purposefully amid those experiences (Richert, 2000), of the revision of understanding that develops through this writing and sharing of this work (Ritchie & Wilson, 2000) that I offer as an exemplar of narrative practice.

Through the writing I've done over these novice years I've arrived at a place where I understand that to write narratively as part of my practice, to make tangible the contradictions and complexity of my daily experiences, is to pull myself up out of the numbing confusion imposed by these very immediate challenges. Most importantly, through this writing I put myself back into the text of teaching in a meaningful role, as one of learner and engaged participant. I gain an important sense of ownership over my work, an increased ability to focus, and a stronger, more confident sense of myself as being in control of my teaching and learning. I've come now to a place where I understand that reimagining myself as capable in light of the uncertainty I experience daily, seeing my struggles framed as part of the work of an inherently complex profession, valuing my perspective in a professional culture whose very structure discourages deep thought and reflection, and liberating myself from the isolation that is fed by a fear of being exposed are all essential for engaging in the difficult work of sustaining myself intellectually and emotionally as a teacher.

It is important to acknowledge, however, that I feel this narrative work holds huge risk for me. I feel vulnerable doing the writing that I am and have never shared it with my school site colleagues or administrators. This vulnerability stems from the very real fear of being deemed inadequate, of breaking the institutionalized silence around the acknowledgment of uncertainty, and the exposure to close scrutiny in what has proven to be a hostile environment. These risks can be insurmountable obstacles. I don't imagine that this labor of making sense, of gaining clarity, of defining teaching, and of sustaining myself will ever be easy. Yet it is the power inherent in writing myself into the text of teaching that compels me to stay.

REFERENCES

Akin, R. (1997). *I forgot.* Unpublished narrative, Mills College.
Akin, R. (1998). *Teaching toward disengagement.* Unpublished narrative, Mills College.
Akin, R. (1999a). On my knees again. *Teacher Education Quarterly, 28*(3), 7–10.
Akin, R. (1999b). *Talking in circles.* Unpublished narrative.
Clandinin, J., & Connelly, M. (2000). *Narrative inquiry: experience and story in qualitative research.* San Francisco: Jossey-Bass.
Greene, M. (1978). *Landscapes of learning.* New York: Teachers College Press.

Richert, A. E. (2000). *The narrative as an experience text: Writing themselves back in.* Paper presented at the meeting of American Educational Research Association, New Orleans.

Ritchie, J., & Wilson, D. (2000). *Teacher narrative as critical inquiry.* New York: Teachers College Press.

Winterson, J. (2000, November 10). Lecture. Booksmith. San Francisco.

CHAPTER 5

Teaching Through Relationships and Stories

NANCY M. CARDWELL

For my 10th birthday, my mother gave me a story she received on her 10th birthday from her grandmother, my great-grandmother. The story told of how my great-grandmother spent a spring, summer, and early fall with her father's tribe in upstate New York when she was 10 years old. Listening to my mother's voice as she retold this decades-old tale breathed life into my Native American heritage. I remember asking my mother to tell me the story again. Each time, it changed slightly depending on her mood and my questions. In this way, this narrative became a coconstructed lesson in my heritage, culture, and a cross-generation connection with my mother, grandmother, great-grandmother, and great-great grandfather. It helped me find a place in which to locate myself.

Each of us has the need to organize our experiences around the important moments in our lives. Stories help locate us in the broader sociocultural landscape by naming our connections with culture and power (Bakhtin, 1981). Children construct the meaning of the people, places, and objects in their lives through interaction (Piaget, 1967).

Piaget found that the emotions drive the intellect. In teaching, it is important for teachers to establish emotional equilibrium in order to create intellectual disequilibrium with increasingly difficult academic challenges (Piaget, 1967). Lev Vygotsky looked more closely at the role of social interaction in facilitating learning (1978). To Vygotsky, children of varying skill levels do better when working together than the sum of their abilities might indicate. The more advanced partner can rediscover mastered knowledge, ask new questions, and explore new avenues of inquiry, which creates the ability to discern deeper and more nuanced meanings from the material being revisited (Vygotsky, 1978).

Through story, the meaning individuals make of their experience is entwined with an individual's conception of themselves. For women and girls in particular, the site of this negotiation and renegotiation of connection to facilitate cognitive and emotional development takes place within relationships, which provide the psychic space where closeness and vulnerability commingle, creating the safety to narrate one's experiences freely (Gilligan, Lyons, & Hanmer, 1990).

Teachers who share their personal narrative in the classroom offer students a window into their life experiences and the meaning they have made of it. Weaving together personal narratives and academic work helps create a broader context of the children's and teachers' collective experiences into which the academic lessons can fit.

Such storytelling is an intentional act. It is the purposeful choosing of personal narrative to make concrete connections between teachers and students in service of academic achievement. In this chapter I describe such narratives and offer them as examples of narrative exemplars, illustrating different ways teachers in varied urban settings seek to make these connections with their students. The first and second examples focus on the stories teachers tell their students. The third focuses on the stories teachers tell students and the stories they tell themselves about their students, ones not shared with children. Each of the school settings profiled in these examples shares the task of teaching economically disadvantaged black and Latino students in academically rigorous environments. In each school, the vast majority of the students perform at or above grade level expectations that are measured by standardized test results in reading and mathematics.

MS. ANDERSON

The Hopedale Elementary School is a predominantly black public elementary school serving children from low-income families who live in a nearby housing project in New York City. Hopedale Elementary enjoys a reputation for academic excellence ranking in the top 20% of schools in this large urban city. Ms. Anderson, an experienced fifth-grade teacher, participated in a larger research study that looked at black women teachers' reflections on their classroom practices with black girls. As part of this study, I observed Ms. Anderson's teaching practice and asked her to reflect with me about her practice during follow-up interviews.

Ms. Anderson said she had a repertoire of stories she told the girls during her informal all-girls' lunches. These stories allowed the girls to hear how Ms. Anderson's intentions shaped the choices she made. Ms. Anderson said she told stories to provide the girls with the guidance she felt she didn't get from her own teachers. During an interview, Ms. Anderson told the following story from her college days to illustrate the connections she made between her personal choices and her academic goals:

> I went to a small school of 2,000 black students in the south. It was a Christian school and we had the church right on campus. All the freshmen had to be in the dorms on the weekends by 11:00 and during the week by 10:00. There was this concert and everybody wanted to be there! Of course, nothing really got started until 11 pm. So we decided we were going to go to the concert and then sneak back in the dorm, because we knew one of our nerdy friends wasn't going so she would be the lookout. We went to the concert and tried to sneak back in the dorm at 3:00 in the morning, we threw rocks up to the window to wake up the lookout. But some- body accidentally threw a rock too hard and broke the window, which set off the alarm. That brought the security guards from all over the campus. We went berserk! I was the one saying "oh my parents" because I was the first one in my family to go away to college. Now I was going to disgrace my family because they were going to kick me out if we got caught. We ran all over campus to get away from the security guards. We finally did by slipping over this wall that separated the girls' dorms from the boys' dorms. Thank God we didn't get caught!

Ms. Anderson realized that her expulsion would be a shared disgrace, diminishing her family's years of collective hard work and sacrifice along with constraining her own prospects:

> In the beginning I was going to college because my parents sent me. Then, I wanted to make my parents proud. I didn't want to disap- point them [by getting expelled for breaking curfew for an Earth, Wind, and Fire concert]. And I wanted to prove something to myself. I wanted to graduate. I wanted to march with my class. I wanted my parents to be there. I wanted my family to see me in a black robe with a black hat and the cum laude around my neck. This was something I wanted to do for myself. I constantly tell them, you're not in school for me. You're not in school for your parents. You are in school for you.

Here, Ms. Anderson described her shift from being in school for her fam- ily to being in school for herself while remaining connected to and repre- sentative of her family. Embedded in this is the message that it is okay to be in school for themselves because these girls are inherently valuable and deserving of an education for no other reason than being themselves.

This experience prompted Ms. Anderson to reflect on her relationship with authority:

> From this, we learned that you've got to think about the consequences of things. Later, I thought that maybe if we had gone to the dorm counselor and said, "Well we want to go. We have the tickets. Can we have permission to go?" Maybe she would have said yes. But we didn't know you could do that, and so we didn't think to ask."

Hearing this, I wondered about the relationship between Ms. Anderson's early experiences with not being allowed to ask questions and not feeling entitled to approach her dormitory counselor. She discovered that there are adults children can approach for permission to break the rules. She further discovered the entitlement of negotiating rules rather than merely accepting and following them. Given this and her desire to offer black girls the guidance she didn't get, I suspect that she tells these stories to let her young listeners know that she is the kind of adult they could approach to renegotiate the rules to live in ways Ms. Anderson never had as a child.

This was also a story of self-discovery as Ms. Anderson narrated the shift she made from being in college for her parents to being there for herself as the embodiment of her family's hopes and dreams:

> I share these stories with them to let them know that I did things and I wasn't always the teacher with the glasses on her nose, saying don't do this and don't do that. I don't hide anything from them. I tell them, yeah, I did things but I learned from the things I did and it made me the person that I am today.

In this analysis, Ms. Anderson provides her students with a glimpse of her own mistakes by letting them know how she became the woman they know as their teacher. With this approach, Ms. Anderson offers herself as a role model for her girls to follow. She is not a role model in the conventional sense of arriving in the classroom "preassembled" (Britzman, 1993). Instead, she offers the girls her mistakes, struggles, and lessons to provide a more fluid and authentic "rolling model" (Britzman, 1993).

In spite of Ms. Anderson's purpose in telling this story, the lessons learned are up to the listener to interpret and ultimately discern. The lessons her students take away from the stories they hear are connected to the questions and dilemmas they bring. Ms. Anderson wanted her students to learn about her reasons for being in school so perhaps they could think about their own reasons for being in school. She also remained open to the unanticipated lessons her students took away from her story. Ms. Anderson found that the girls tended to respond to her story with surprise:

> At first, they laughed, saying, "Not Miss Anderson, it doesn't seem like she was bad." The reaction from some of them is, "You mean, Ms. Anderson, you had fun in college?" It's almost like they don't believe you can be a student and still have fun.

From this, the girls learned that there was joy and fun being a student. Perhaps, their surprise revealed the lack of joy these girls may have felt in their own school experience. What the listener learns is connected to the questions the listener brings.

MS. KELLY

Considering the questions the learner brings is the approach Ms. Kelly uses in her seventh-grade classroom. Ms. Kelly was a student in my child development course. She created an environment in her classroom in an all-girls Catholic school in the South Bronx that provided an invaluable opportunity for the students in my child development class to explore the possibility of establishing connections across the boundaries of race and class using personal narratives. Bank Street College is a small, progressive college of teacher education. We prepare teachers to create democratic classroom communities using the developmental interaction approach to education. As children's worlds of home, school, and neighborhood intersect, each teacher's task is to surface and identify issues that contribute to and obstruct academic achievement and democratic life. Identifying these issues is a critical step in constructing a learning environment in which questioning, communication, experience, and active participation are essential to learning. When I teach child development, the theories become tools teachers can use to understand children's social interactions and academic performance (Nager & Shapiro, 2000).

Ms. Kelly's seventh-grade students came from low-income black and Latino families. Ms. Kelly said she grew up in an upper-middle-class, midwestern suburb in an upper-middle-class family. Early on, Ms. Kelly felt her students didn't seem comfortable with her. She believed this discomfort contributed to the girls' reluctance to take the intellectual risks of asking questions, making mistakes and explaining their thinking that are necessary for academic success. Ms. Kelly said she suspected the emotional distance stemmed from her students feeling she couldn't know them because they saw her as "a rich white girl." Ms. Kelly knew that the girls were right about her not knowing their reality of being a person of color from a low-income family. At the same time, there was more to Ms. Kelly's life story than the girls knew.

Ms. Kelly knew that, developmentally, 13-year-old girls were beginning to define and redefine themselves, integrating external perceptions of their maturing bodies and with their increasingly complex psyches, which is characteristic of early adolescence (Erikson, 1963; Gilligan, 1982; Piaget, 1967). Given the girls' focus on constructing and integrating their internal and external identities, Ms. Kelly made the decision to tell the girls her own story about her ongoing efforts to construct and reconstruct her own identity as an adopted child. She wanted to connect with her students' developmental struggles across their race and class differences.

Ms. Kelly believed it was her job to put her students emotionally at ease in the classroom so they could face the intellectual demands she placed on them (Piaget, 1967). To this end, Ms. Kelly described a strategy she used in her seventh-grade classroom:

> I tell them that even though I'm white with blond hair and blue eyes from the suburbs, I know what it feels like to struggle to find out who I am and where I fit in my family and in my community because I was adopted. I know that my being adopted doesn't mean that I know what it feels like to be black and Latino. But I am saying that I do know a little about what it feels like to be different and not feel like I really belong.

She shared this part of her life experience in this way early in the schoolyear to establish a nascent comfort level with her students. Ms. Kelly wanted them to know that even though she didn't share their life experiences she could relate to some of their feelings, which left room for the girls' experiences and interpretations to create a new classroom "we" that connected across race and class differences. By naming her connection and the limits of that connection, Ms. Kelly could then create an emotionally safe space in which her students could teach Ms. Kelly about their lives. She, like Ms. Anderson, offered a "rolling model" where the teacher has some of the answers but not all of them.

Ms. Kelly took her students' questions about the connections between their lives and academic work seriously by making explicit connections between what she learned of the girls' lives, in ways that made the girls feel seen but not spoken for during the academic lessons she taught. This strategy required emotional courage on Ms. Kelly's part to see herself "in the unflattering light of another's angry gaze" in order to understand an unfamiliar perspective (Delpit, 1988).

With her story, Ms. Kelly gave her students a window into her own struggle to reconcile external perceptions with her own internal sense of reality, which was a struggle that resonated with her students. She didn't elicit the girls' sympathy by burdening the girls with her own emotional pain. The deeper lesson they learned together was the ability to discern the shared dilemmas of development through the differences of race and class. After Ms. Kelly shared her story she said that she found that the girls in her class felt more comfortable with her, more connected to her, and were willing to laugh with her and trust her when she asked them to risk making a mistake in order to learn something new.

Once Ms. Kelly shared this experience, I noticed that the students in my course referred to it throughout the semester trying to think about ways to make similar connections in their classrooms. Over time, I've also noticed that there is a connection between the ways my students began to interpret children's behavior using developmental theory and their own life experiences in term papers.

As we discussed their interpretations in class after they handed their papers in, I noticed a number of students saying that thinking of attention deficit/hyperactivity disorder (ADHD) or molestation wouldn't have occurred to them because it wasn't a part of their personal experiences despite the assigned readings. However, hearing their classmates' stories made them more aware of it and willing to consider it as a possibility in their own classrooms. For Ms. Kelly and my other students, stories can hopefully create connections to personalize a standard curricula, making it easier for students to take the intellectual risks necessary to achieve academically.

MR. RIVERA

Smoothing the emotional landscape of intellectual risk-taking in the classroom is the task Mr. Rivera takes up in his classroom. Unlike the previous examples, Mr. Rivera keeps his personal struggles to himself, choosing to use them as sources of insight into children's behavior. As part of a professional development project in a predominantly Latino public school, serving nearly 2,000 newly arrived immigrant families, two colleagues and I worked with a voluntary group of teachers to strengthen their relational pedagogy by strengthening their knowledge of child development and teaching strategies designed to improve students' academic achievement. The principal has set the standard in this school by knowing every child's name, family story, and academic standing. Much of our work centered on the role of narrative in sustaining academic success.

We began our work together reading and discussing Virginia Axline's *Dibs: In Search of Self* (1964). Because we had a cross-section of participation from teachers, staff developers, and administrators we were able to engage in discussions of practice across role and responsibility looking closely at the meaning of their collective efforts to create emotional stability and foster academic success. During our meetings teachers began to share their personal stories with each other as they described the behaviors they saw among their students (Brunner, 1994).

After hearing about these conversations and readings, Mr. Rivera joined our group. Mr. Rivera believed his work as a teacher centered on making explicit connections between his third graders' life experiences and their current school experiences. His 8-year-old students are leaving the early childhood stage of developing skills to enter middle childhood where they will begin to use those skills to learn new content information. This transition from learning to read to reading to learn can help to deepen their basic understandings of the world in which they live. Helping his students successfully navigate this transition requires attention to both the emotional and academic dimensions of development.

With his diverse group of Spanish-speaking students from the Caribbean, Central America, and South America, it has been a challenge for Mr. Rivera to bridge the subtle yet significant cultural gaps that a shared language alone doesn't close. To invite his students' stories, Mr. Rivera told brief anecdotal stories about his school experiences as a native Spanish speaker in an English-dominant school. Through these stories, Mr. Rivera's students got a sense of him and learned about the culture of the school they were attending. He further said the purpose of this approach was to let his students know that they have a place in the English-dominant society they now share in the United States.

Mr. Rivera had firsthand experiences with love, nurturance, betrayal, and trauma as a child. He recalled with colleagues the ways in which his behavior, emotions, and achievement changed in the wake of his trauma. However, Mr. Rivera kept his personal stories brief in the classroom to avoid unwittingly revealing his own childhood traumas that he appropriately keeps from his students. At the same time, these untold stories have helped him decode his students' behavior and achievement patterns.

For example, Mr. Rivera noticed children who seemed to be overly quiet or frightened by unexpected noise or movement. He also paid close attention to his students' behavior, making sure they seemed safe and unharmed without intruding on them with a lot of questions. Because of his attention, children who had experiences that troubled them often came to him on their own for help. The help he offered was emotional safety and stability in the classroom and the outside support they needed with the principal's help. He was able to notice early warning signs of trauma among his students but also took care not to cross the line between teaching and therapy.

Maintaining his students' sense of physical safety and emotional stability is a paramount concern as he challenges them academically (Piaget, 1967). Mr. Rivera believes that the classroom is not a place for him to unburden himself. Instead, the classroom is a place for him to help his students succeed academically. To this end, Mr. Rivera uses his story in two ways. First, he tells selected stories to help create a shared classroom culture among diverse students, easing the children's transition to a new country, culture, and language. Second, he uses his untold experiences to help him interpret his students' behavior patterns in ways that help him foster their academic success and emotional well-being.

PROBLEMS AND POSSIBILITIES

These three examples provide a view of narrative teaching practice in a variety of settings used by a diverse group of teachers. In their individual ways, all the teachers were clear about why they told or didn't tell certain stories. Because of this clarity, the teachers shared enough to engage but not so much as to burden, overexpose their students. These teachers used narrative as a vehicle through which the possibility for a new "we" of shared experience and language can become a classroom reality across individual differences (Dyson & Genishi, 1993).

But this work is not without its potential problems. When teachers share their own personal narratives with their students, in service to their students' academic achievement and emotional development, they offer children a model of how to simultaneously manage closeness and vulnerability in an academic setting. It also elicits teachers' need to maintain enough emotional distance so that the stories that teachers tell respond to children's needs. A key aspect of remaining clear is for each teacher to maintain the boundary between his or her private stories and those stories that are available, as resources, to their students. Navigating these boundaries to maintain this balance may not be easily achieved at a time when test scores come before relationships and personalized curricula in urban schools. To do this, teachers need to develop a repertoire of strategies so that the classroom is emotionally safe enough for children to take the intellectual risks necessary to learn new academic material.

Yet passion and perseverance are still significant components of in-novation (Britzman, 1993). The unscripted, spontaneous stories teachers tell invite children to make connections, creating shared meaning and cul-ture within the classroom. Ultimately, the lessons learned are shaped by the questions and interests the learner brings. Every time I heard my mother tell the story of my great-grandmother's journey, I found new details that raised new questions. As the teachers in these three examples illustrate, there are multiple ways to create connections with children in urban schools across the boundaries of race, gender, and class.

These connections allow everyone the gift of stretching academically and emotionally to understand the lives of others beyond their own indi-vidual experiences. As educators, we need to have the capacity to value all children by valuing the connections they make with the stories teach-ers tell, which can enable children to succeed academically, emotionally and in life. Teachers set the example by sharing the lessons they learned from their own experiences in ways that make children think more deeply about themselves, their classmates, their families, and the world in which they live.

REFERENCES

Axline, V. (1964). *Dibs: In search of self.* New York: Vintage Press.

Bakhtin, M. M. (1981). *The dialogic imagination.* Austin: University of Texas Pres.

Britzman, D. (1993). *Practice makes practice: A critical study of learning to teach.* Al-bany, NY: State University of New York Press.

Bruner, J. (1996). *The culture of education.* Cambridge, MA: Harvard University Press.

Brunner, D. D. (1994). *Inquiry and reflection: Framing narrative practice in education.* Albany, NY: State University of New York Press.

Delpit, L. (1988). The silenced dialogue: Power and pedagogy in educating other people's children. *Harvard Educational Review, 56*(4), 280–298.

Dewey, J. (1963). *Education and experience.* New York: Collier Books. Original work published 1938.

Dyson, A., & Genishi, C. (1993). *The need for story: Cultural diversity in classroom and community.* Urbana, IL: National Council of Teachers of English.

Erikson, E. H. (1963). *Childhood and society.* (2nd ed.). New York: W. W. Norton.

Gilligan, C. (1982). *In a different voice.* Cambridge, MA: Harvard University Press.

Gilligan, C., Lyons, N. P., & Hanmer, T. J. (Eds.). (1990). *Making connections: The relational worlds of adolescent girls at Emma Willard School.* Cambridge, MA: Harvard University Press.

Hopkins, R. L. (1994) *Narrative schooling: Experiential learning and the transforma-tion of American education.* New York: Teachers College Press.

Jalongo, M. R., & Isenberg, J. P. (1995). *Teachers' stories: From personal narrative to professional insight*. San Francisco: Jossey-Bass.

Josselson, R., & Lieblich, A. (1995). *Interpreting experience: The narrative study of lives*. Thousand Oaks, CA: Sage Publications.

McEwan, H., & Egan, K. (Eds.). (1995). *Narrative in teaching, learning, and research*. New York: Teachers College Press.

Nager, N., & Shapiro, E. K. (Eds.). (2000). *Revisiting a progressive pedagogy*. Albany, NY: State University of New York Press.

Piaget, J. (1967). *Six psychological studies*. New York: Vintage Books.

Vygotsky, L. S. (1978). *Mind in society*. Cambridge, MA: Harvard University Press.

CHAPTER 6

The Personal Self in a Public Story: The Portfolio Presentation Narrative

NONA LYONS

In this chapter I introduce the portfolio presentation narrative to open it to scrutiny. This narrative, created for a public presentation of a teaching portfolio, is usually drawn from the contents of the portfolio but different from it, a creation in its own right. It is essentially the story of professional learning a portfolio maker tells, accompanied by samples of evidence of that learning. To illustrate, I turn to one example from an apprentice teacher of physics, capturing some of the words and flavor of his presentation narrative in order to ask, What is the role of narrative in this presentation? Does it warrant consideration as an exemplar of narrative inquiry?

THE PORTFOLIO PRESENTATION NARRATIVE

Addressing his undergraduate classmates and college faculty at the end of his student teaching, the teacher, John, begins his narrative by suggesting his dissatisfaction with an earlier attempt at a teaching portfolio. He enumerates his complaints: the portfolio couldn't easily be changed or added to; there was only one copy; it couldn't be sent overseas where he was looking for a job; and it certainly could not be left with a prospective employer without the fear of losing it. "Thus," John announces, "this is my new portfolio." With a flip of a computer switch he powers onto a website and there appears on a large screen "Experiments in Education: A Teaching Portfolio" (Lyons, 2000).

Explaining his title, John says: "I would like to take a moment to comment on the title and theme of this portfolio. When I was looking for an idea to act as the center of this creation, I wanted something that would embody both the spirit of a portfolio and the essence of myself. The idea of an experiment came to mind. . . . As a physicist, I am an experimentalist. As a teacher I am a practitioner. Theory is like a game to me. I enjoy listening to an idea develop, but I want to see it in action. Finally, I was only at the start of my training as a teacher, everything was an experiment to me. Thus, Experiments in Education." Continuing, John shares other portfolio entries—a teaching philosophy and, importantly, an entry he calls the "teaching experiment." The experiment, the centerpiece of his portfolio, is his effort to translate a Japanese style of teaching math into his high school physics class. Adapted from reading a comparison of Japanese and American methods of teaching math, John was eager to try this experiment with his students:

> It was the idea of student-developed lessons. Students are not passive in this approach. They are given puzzle pieces and asked to put them together themselves. Students are able to play with the materials. . . . Students tend to limit their respect for things they are not really interested in. . . . [With the Japanese project] they worked harder, were willing to work harder. . . . I was very proud of that.

When queried by another intern about problems that emerged with this project, John replies:

> Most kids were looking for me to show them. When I didn't show them, they worked with each other and looked at previous problems with very little help. But, still, there were kids who . . . let it slide by. They got left behind. I had told them that we were going to do things differently. The top of the class was really turned on. . . . But there was a group of kids who didn't. They complained: "Why won't you show us?" We were switching from "I show you how to do this and you show me you know how to do this" to "You have figured out how to use these tools, now you figure out a new problem."
>
> I also felt the project would have been more successful if I had followed the Japanese model more specifically.

John then introduces other entries from his portfolio: some interviews he did with a student and a special unit on engineering, a teaching project he did as a service to the school. He turns next to the entry, "Teaching and

Physics." A physics major just completing a senior research thesis, John explains:

> I love physics. I feel like physics is something that is very important to me. The development of physics is something I want to be part of. I was coming to realize that I don't think I am ever going to make an earth-shattering impact myself. And it was a reality that was very hard to take at the time. But it was something I realized I could change. If I moved to a level where kids were just starting into science, starting physics, I could bring those minds to physics and get them working. That was something that really turned me on. That is really powerful. And that is something I am doing, trying to give a mind a focus.

Later, in an interview, John offers his own reflections on this portfolio process:

> The first term, it was portfolio by searching for stuff to put into it. This term, it was actually doing what the portfolio was asking you to do, take something and really play around with it. That's what I have in my portfolio, more things I've played around with . . . that's where the Japanese lesson came from. I wanted some continuous experiment to weave through, to weave in as an actual experiment . . . it really tied the portfolio together and helped me a lot. . . . I wanted to find out more about independent learning and independent work I expected from my kids. It was more like a radical shift in the way I was teaching. I enjoyed putting it together. It was lots of fun to see things plummet like a rock, and "Why does this happen, this made so much sense on paper? What on earth happened." So you pick it apart and say, "Well, maybe if I tweak this a little," and "The problem with that is . . ." But it is such a long and slow process, because what I got out of this lesson, I am not going to be able to apply until next fall [when I start teaching]. But it is a chance to sit down to reconfigure your classroom to handle that kind of thing.

Here, the portfolio maker through a series of narratives, stories of his experiences, describes his own inquiries into teaching and learning and articulates new understandings: about his teaching, the learning of his students, and how he understands his own teaching and learning. But where has this understanding come from? What part did the portfolio and its presentation play in his discoveries? This chapter takes up these questions to ask: Is the portfolio narrative an exemplar, something others ought to know about and try in their own practice? This chapter asserts and seeks to demonstrate that the portfolio narrative can be a significant exemplar, a way of making a metainquiry in the service of integrating learning, of scaffolding reflecting on reflection.

THE PRESENTATION NARRATIVE WITHIN
A PORTFOLIO PROCESS

I consider that the use of narrative in teaching is almost a natural kind, what might be called a natural fit. Narrative finds its earliest manifestation in the delight the youngest children take when they hear, "Once upon a time . . . ," which is the usual response of most adults to the anticipation engendered by these words. Toni Morrison calls them the "opening phrase of what must be the oldest sentence in the world and the earliest one we remember from childhood" (Morrison, 1998). Narrative, Morrison believes, is one of the principal ways we absorb knowledge. That may be why narrative is so compelling a teaching mode. But there are other reasons why narrative remains necessary to learning across the life cycle. Psychologist Jerome Bruner points to another, significant reason. Stories, even the simplest, can carry all the ambiguity, the mystery of the ways in which human intentions and actions can go wrong. As such, story deals fundamentally with meaning, peoples' interpretations and constructions of meaning. Narrative, Bruner argues, is itself a way of knowing (Bruner, 1986)—one particularly suited to capture the complexities and mysteries of teaching.

Most portfolio presentations are the culminating event of the portfolio development process. At that point, the portfolio maker, in a public forum, in the presence of colleagues and mentors, presents his or her portfolio, and seeks feedback from peers and faculty. The portfolio presentation narrative is defined here as the intentional, personal story of meaning a portfolio maker constructs through reflection and orally presents in public. The portfolio is usually composed of a series of entries, evidence of significant experiences in learning about teaching. While a portfolio narrative can be used to organize portfolio evidence and structure its presentation, how it is involved in personal learning through a presentation has not been much discussed in the research literature. Most audiences consistently note the varied, personal, and compelling narratives of learning that characterize these presentations (Lyons, 1998). Yet little has been written about them. Indeed, some teacher-education programs do not require or even include presentations as part of their portfolio process. Here

I want to ask, What purpose is the narrative serving in this process? Should educators pay special attention to it? What do beginning teachers find in it?

To address these questions, I draw selectively on my research data from a sample of 10 portfolio narratives derived from a longitudinal study of 20 teacher interns who developed and presented a teaching portfolio as part of their credentialing requirements. These undergraduate students participate in a teacher education program at a college located in the eastern United States. Data are from two sources: audiotapes of portfolio narratives presented by the students and data from interviews with interns who took part in a retrospective review of the portfolio process or wrote about it and its meaning to them. Data were taped, transcribed, and analyzed. Although three contrasting models of portfolio narratives were defined in this research, I focus on describing the Intentional Reflective Narrative, the most frequently found narrative in this sample, in contrast to the Simple Narrative (little or no reflection) or the Extended Reflective Narrative, which were minimally represented.

Ultimately, I argue that constructing a portfolio narrative and presenting it can constitute a special performance activity that

- supports and scaffolds a process of intentional reflection that brings to conscious awareness and understanding critical learnings an apprentice teacher achieves over a course of learning to teach; that is, the knowledge of practice;
- affirms, disconfirms, or redirects the teacher intern in the process of identity formation, the identities of both a personal self and the emerging professional person; and
- provides a portfolio maker with an explicit performance experience as a self-directed, reflective learner, interrogating one's practice, and ultimately authoring one's own learning—a potential model for lifelong professional development.

I see the portfolio presentation narrative as an important exemplar of a teaching practice. I recognize, too, that there are potential threats to its validity as a narrative exemplar.

To address these issues, I first briefly describe how the portfolio narratives presented here are embedded within a larger portfolio assessment and support system. I then present several examples of portfolio narratives that teacher interns have constructed, returning to the work of John and his colleagues. In conclusion, I problematize the portfolio narrative as exemplar, indicating some challenges that might be encountered by those who wish to try it in their own teaching or research.

THE PORTFOLIO NARRATIVE REVEALS
INTENTIONAL PROCESSES

Lee Shulman, who introduced the portfolio idea into teacher assessment (1998), argues that serious portfolio making is far from frivolous: it is, he claims, a theoretical act: "It is important to keep in mind . . . your theory of teaching will determine a reasonable portfolio entry. What is declared worth documenting, worth reflecting on, what is deemed to be portfolio worthy is a theoretical act" (Shulman, 1998, p. 4).

Serious portfolio makers know this. They eschew the portfolio as a scrapbook activity or one-shot event. They experience portfolio making as a series of significant processes and elements that emerge in the act of creating such a history of learning to teach. These processes, usually embedded within the student teacher's teacher education program, include five elements:

- The process of being mentored in portfolio development, a collaborative activity taking place through critical conversations with mentors and peers over the course of a teacher-education program (portfolio making is not a one-time, end-of-program experience)
- Some set of goals or standards about what teachers entering today's complex classrooms should know and demonstrate, including knowledge of one's subject matter, of child or adolescent development, of authentic assessments, and so on, adopted by the teacher education program as its standards
- A body of entries, evidence collected by the portfolio maker to demonstrate understanding of the program standards and his or her learning about teaching and student learning, including videos of classes, student portfolios or other work, curriculum units, lessons that failed, and so forth
- A set of reflections, or critical interrogations about what exactly was learned about teaching and learning that accompanies each portfolio entry
- A public presentation of the portfolio to a community of colleagues, cooperating teachers, and teacher educators, after which the portfolio maker can claim the authority as a teacher to take responsibility for a class, and a teacher educator can confirm or deny this judgment and decide the student's readiness for certification

A critical context of portfolio making is, then, a set of collaborative activities taking place over the course of a teacher education program. But what is the actual experience and sense of a portfolio maker in creating a portfolio narrative?

In the teacher education program under discussion here, each portfolio maker engages early in the program in the portfolio process, usually meeting with her or his peers who serve as collaborators in gathering the evidence that will fashion a teaching portfolio. Students begin by developing a statement of their teaching philosophy or identifying a piece of evidence they think significant to their development as a professional. In their final portfolio, these students will assemble a set of entries as evidence of their growth as teachers and their competency in meeting the set of standards adopted by the program. The intern is reminded that they will be making a formal, public presentation of their portfolio, narrating the story of their learning and development. But how is this narrative constructed?

A prospective history teacher, Ron, provides another example of a portfolio narrative, revealing especially the workings of narrative within the portfolio construction process. Like other portfolio creators, Ron introduces his portfolio, opening a large notebook inscribed with his theme, "Creating a Classroom Community: A Portfolio." He states: "The idea of community is the unifying idea of my teaching philosophy. It is an idea not easily defined, and thus not easily achieved. . . . when it is achieved there is no doubt about it. The most important first step in establishing a viable classroom community is to create an environment of respect. It is a respect where all ideas and individuals are honored. This respect is absolutely necessary for the free exchange of ideas that is an education. I believe learning is essentially relational, and relationships do not exist in a vacuum. They come to be in the context of the classroom, where outside barriers can be broken down and we all show our vulnerability. For this dissolution to occur, every member of the classroom community must work together to create a caring, safe, respectful environment that encourages risk-taking and reflection. In this portfolio, each entry in some way makes a contribution to the rise of this classroom community. Some of the entries bring us closer to a true community, while some pull us away from that goal. . . . I shall begin my tour of my portfolio with a brief look at my philosophy of education."

A sampling of the entries from his teaching philosophy, what he calls his "Creed," include the following:

ON TEACHING

I believe that a great teacher is vulnerable. He must disclose his passion through teaching and this disclosure involves risk-taking. He must join his students in the conference of souls that is the classroom.

I believe that the teacher must join in a partnership of inquiry with his students, recognizing that he himself is a learner. It is through this partnership that true learning occurs and the ideals of community come alive in the democratic classroom.

ON HISTORY

I believe that history provides a lens through which we can view ourselves. History is the study of humanity, and is a reflection of our collective strengths and faults. I believe that facing and understanding our history is a means of reconciling past injustices. Healing historical wounds comes about through acknowledgement and discussion of them, especially as these wounds teach a new generation.

I believe that the ability to put oneself in historical context is an instrumental step in learning how to empathize with other human beings.

Later, in an interview, Ron responds to a question about what stood out for him in the portfolio-making process:

Having to spell out a teaching philosophy. It was the first thing that I did as a real entry—and trying to put down words that you felt your philosophy could be pinned to. At first it was a little bit intimidating, but I grew to really love it and I learned a lot about why I was doing what I was doing that I hadn't really thought about that was important to me. So just the act of binding yourself to those ideas was a very educational experience. I also pulled out two narrative essays I had written on the vulnerability of teaching that I couldn't quite capture in a couple of brief statements. . . . One was about one of my own high school teachers.

During a lot of the portfolio process I found myself going back to his class and reflecting on what he had done to influence me. From 10th grade I always felt he was head and shoulders over other teachers. But I could never figure out why. And there were other students who did not think he was a great teacher and I was trying to figure out why his style did not work for all. So I found myself going back to his class for Experiential Learning. He and I would plan these trips at our school—we had a special semester for making trips. On one trip we went to the Mississippi delta to study the "Blues as an Art Form" using literature, the music, the entire art form. We just rode bicycles around with 40 students. Another year we did "Road Scholars." [Rethinking] all that, I kind of got behind his teaching philosophy. It was a lot of reflecting on those experiences that I knew I learned from in high school. When we went on the road we were always a community—that was the ultimate student-centered classroom. So I went back to that idea and that is where the whole theme of my portfolio came from—the classroom community. During my internship in the spring when I was teaching the Holocaust it further spelled out the idea of community was the essence of the democratic school. The most effective form is when students are involved and are empowered, having an arena where they are in control.

In his reflection, Ron presents the story of the evolution of his thinking about community, going back to his own high school experience to uncover a theme of his own. His portfolio narrative—like the physics teacher's—is linked by a set of stories. Each entry is constructed as an intentional search for meaning, and then cast as a narrative.

The portfolio excerpts in this chapter reveal that the portfolio narrative and its presentation involve an intentional act of retrospective reflection constructed as a set of narratives that

- looks back over a semester of teaching experiences;
- is organized and integrated into a teaching philosophy and/or a theme; and
- has for the portfolio maker an immediacy, pointing to a seen future, of being in a classroom and having to act on what one knows, aware that one's actions do and will have consequences, hoped for or not.

The portfolio narrative, then, serves to provide the scaffold for engaging in intentional reflection. Narrative here is both a mode of inquiry for the student and a means of organizing a description of the larger meaning of their reflective learning. But do portfolio makers themselves see this? Of what significance is this reflection to them?

Bringing One's Learning and Knowledge to Conscious Awareness

When asked to respond in writing to the question, What would you say the process of creating and presenting a teaching portfolio meant to you?,

Eva, a prospective Latin teacher, offers one explanation. At first, she tells us, she found the process and idea of a portfolio new and intimidating:

> [The] idea of creating such a large piece of writing that expressed my work as a student teacher, including as well as my teaching philosophy scared me. I was unaccustomed to reflecting on what I had learned; reflection has not been a standard practice in the classes I have taken. However, as I learned more about the process of creating a portfolio, I grew to like the concept.
>
> The experience of creating my own teaching portfolio has impressed on me the value of reflection. I was forced to think about what I had learned from different experiences, and while it was difficult at first, I eventually saw that these reflections had great value. Reflecting made me think about and *consciously* realize what had happened in a particular situation, which allowed me to learn more from my mistakes and my successes. It would have been very easy to remember what had happened with a particular lesson, for example, while forgetting about learning *why* it happened.

Another portfolio maker emphasizes the act of putting ideas together and anticipating sharing them with others:

> What I take the most pleasure in doing is writing, putting in words things you have been mulling over, things I know I am learning. I have never been a teacher before. When you begin to put it into a language that you can share with other people, you say, "I really did learn that." We learn things every day but we might not really know it.

A critical aspect of the portfolio narrative is identified: that the reflective process brings to consciousness knowledge one may have acted on but not fully realized or elaborated, making possible future, purposeful action.

Directing the Formation of Identities:
The Personal Self in a Public Story

Intern assessments of the portfolio process point to a second element of significance—that is, that the process as well as the experience can affirm, deny, or redirect one's emerging professional and personal identities. In the portfolio narrative presented above, John, the physics teacher, commented on the importance to him of coming to understand himself not as a researcher of physics but rather as a teacher of physics. He indicated a critical reevaluation of his emerging professional identity as he redirected a potential career path into teaching. Commenting in an interview after the portfolio presentation about how he now saw himself as a teacher, John indicates how a professional identity is linked to his personal sense of self and some of the ambiguity he still finds in that. "I feel like the term of teaching helped me to become more comfortable with myself, . . . where I was confident of myself as an adult, as a person. . . . Most of last term I didn't know where I stood. I was partly a student to my cooperating teacher and partly a teacher to the kids. . . . I was in limbo between an authority figure and friend. . . . I feel like if I were to go back there now, I'd know where I stand."

Another teacher offers a more dramatic view of the link between presenting a story of a teaching portfolio and professional identity formation. The student intern, Emma, had faced a serious crisis in her student teaching when, early in the fall semester, she found herself unable to speak or direct her class, with no idea of what her role should be in the classroom. Recovering sufficiently and successfully completing her student teaching, Emma reflects back on the role portfolio development played in her sense of self as a teacher. She describes her own transformation as she contemplated creating a portfolio and its narrative:

> What I chose to put in, I thought, really highlighted me changing, me taking a risk, me taking a risk in the curriculum, or even me taking a risk in explaining how I felt as a teacher. It felt like this portfolio in the end wasn't just a documentation of the curriculum I had done, or the work students did for me, but really of how I changed myself and how I changed my perceptions of the classroom and how I changed the classroom—I had to change it!

As Emma suggests, "It is hard to reflect on something that isn't perfect. But in the end that helped me. . . . We talked about metacognition in class, but rarely do you get a chance to look at your work and say: What is this to me? Is this an accurate explanation of what I wanted to do in this class? The portfolio just doesn't give you a chance to present, but it gives you a chance to respond to it—to respond to what was hard to deal with." In the end, Emma believes she could say, "This isn't a failure. This isn't me being a bad person—or a bad teacher or a bad student. This is my trying to understand something. This is me going through a whole process. And it is validating in the end."

Forging an Explicit Performance of Self-Directed, Reflective Learning

Portfolio makers in discussing the role of the reflective process in their development highlight a third element: their creation of an experience of self-directed learning:

> As a teacher, my job is to be reflective in ways that students can see. . . . It's a questioning, not taking anything for granted, connecting things to other things . . . internalizing. Engaging with materials is what reflection is about. I think reflection is the most valuable part of education and having a portfolio process is one way that makes you realize that.
>
> Reflection is the way you take observations and see your evolution—your teaching style, your planning and assessment, how you move from one place to the other. If you do not, you have to rely on someone else's interpretation.

A graduate of the program talks of one implication of learning to be reflective: "I had my students do reflections similar to what we did. Reflecting helps them know what they know: by that I understand what I have done myself and ought to do differently."

PROBLEMATIZING THE PRESENTATION NARRATIVE AS AN EXEMPLAR

The portfolio narrative process as presented reveals it to be a potentially critical experience in a beginning teacher's development. A process of narrative inquiry engages an intern in the task—itself intentional—of telling the story of one's learning. Then, through a process of reflective interrogation of experience, critical stories of a student's learning emerge. Three important outcomes characterize the process: the scaffolding of reflection that brings to consciousness important knowledge; the affirming, disaffirming, or redirecting of personal and professional identities; and the forging of an experience of professional learning. While this research is clearly limited in numbers and its sample, the evidence presented here warrants the identification of the portfolio narrative as a significant teaching practice, an exemplar for inquiry. But what might threaten its validity? There are at least two issues of concern: how reflection is defined, and whether reflection can be cast as a serious professional activity.

Self-Reflection, Self-Confession, or Other Interpretations?

Alan Bleakley (2000), writing on reflective practice through journal writing in the first issue of *Reflective Practice*, issues a sharp warning about the dangers of what can be construed not as professional reflection but as "confessional writing." He argues for a need to be cautious about

> repeating the Enlightenment mistake of treating language both as a transparent medium for explanation and closure. . . . As Barthes [cite omitted] suggests: "[I]t is language which speaks, not the author." (p. 5)

Bleakley asks just what is being created through language and how we should interpret it. While Bleakley refers solely to journal writing, could a portfolio narrative be prone to similar dangers? How, then, should we consider it? I suggest that we look carefully at all the evidence a teacher intern presents in a portfolio and at those who do intern assessments. A portfolio is not a single-item document but a set of entries, a collection of significant evidence. It ought to have other confirming or disconfirming elements within it. Others, such as mentor teachers, also give testimony and weigh evidence regarding an intern. But Bleakley's warning is important.

Reflective Development: What Is It?

A second issue of concern is how to consider reflective development. Reflective ability is considered a core competency of accomplished professionals. Yet little consensus exists on the terms used to define reflection. Copeland et al. (1993) ask, What is reflection? What does it actually look like or mean to teachers?

The work reported in this chapter defines reflection as an intentional act of mind engaging a person alone, but especially in collaboration with others—students, other colleagues, researchers—in interrogating a compelling or puzzling situation of teaching or learning to construct an understanding of some aspect of it. Such an act looks both backwards and to the future. It is in the service of understanding that will shape action. It likely takes place over long stretches of time, involves narrative for it is the story of meaning, and often raises ethical issues for people involved. But no clear, ongoing body of research exists to examine these observations. The process Mishler (1990) suggests, of testing the trustworthiness of an exemplar by research of other scholars, could both verify the exemplar and contribute needed research to document and more fully describe reflection.

REFERENCES

Bleakley, A. (2000). Writing with invisible ink. *Reflective practice, 1,* 11–24.

Bruner, J. (1986). *Actual minds, possible worlds.* Cambridge, MA: Harvard University Press.

Copeland, W. D., Birmingham, C., De La Cruz, E., & Lewin, B. (1993). The reflective practitioner in teaching: Toward a research agenda. *Teaching and Teacher Education, 9*(4), 347–359.

Lyons, N. (1998). *With portfolio in hand: Validating the new teacher professionalism.* New York: Teachers College Press.

Lyons, N. (2000). *Research project: Reflective development and the portfolio process.* Unpublished manuscript, Dartmouth College.

Mishler, E. (1990). Validation in inquiry-guided research: The role of exemplars in narrative studies. *Harvard Educational Review, 60*(4), 415–442.

Morrison, T. (1998). Lecture and speech of acceptance of Noble Prize for Literature.

Shulman, L. (1998). Teaching portfolios: A theoretical activity. In N. Lyons (Ed.), *With portfolio in hand: Validating the new teacher professionalism.* New York: Teachers College Press.

CHAPTER 7

Using Narrative Teaching Portfolios
for Self-Study

VICKY ANDERSON-PATTON AND ELISABETH BASS

We want to be good teachers and we want our students to be good teachers. Previous experiences convinced us that merely reading research on
teaching is not effective in transforming practice. We started doing self-
studies in 1997 and discovered how powerful this methodology is. We
developed narrative teaching portfolios to further our ongoing self-study,
and used this narrative process to guide our students' self-studies. Here
we offer narrative teaching portfolios as a candidate exemplar.

In fall 1999, Lis conducted a practicum for new writing teachers and
Vicky was teaching creativity in elementary school; both are marginalized
courses. Our outsider status enabled us to experiment more freely, so we
engaged our students in self-studies. Self-study is a methodology for examining one's own teaching, carried out collaboratively, with the goal of
transforming one's practice. Studying one's own classroom may seem, at
first, methodologically unsound. Yet for teachers who have experienced
force-fed best practices, working with what is real is a great palliative.
However, self-studies can become cumbersome; when anything related to
our classrooms becomes data, most of us are overwhelmed. To manage this,
we used narrative teaching portfolios to scaffold a focused self-study.

We introduced our students to self-study (Hamilton, 1998; Loughran
& Northfield, 1998) and teaching portfolios (Lyons, 1998), then to research
where portfolios were used to scaffold self-studies (Cuban, cited in Lyons,
1998; Gipe, cited in Hamilton, 1998). We assigned students a narrative teaching portfolio as their cumulative assignment. Concurrently, we worked on
our own self-study narratives. This project pushed our self-study work and
engaged more educators, our students, in this valuable process.

In self-study and teaching portfolios, narrative is both research process and product. We reflect on what we do, tell our stories, and then create portfolios to share our stories with others. Narrative methods allow us to explore the complexities of teaching, incorporate self and context, and more fully understand the lives of others. Narrative enables imaginative identification (Achebe, 1990) and personal voice, two ingredients we believe are necessary for transformative learning. In the context of the stories we tell, we can see the small moves of transformed practice that might otherwise disappear. The narratives make these changes real and allow more complex reflection because they help us get outside ourselves and connect with others.

The portfolio assignment was a seemingly open-ended process, yet we carefully guided its structure. First, we asked students to write a personal narrative (their creative self for Vicky and a literacy biography for Lis). We structured reflection on their teaching values and practice through journal starters and group activities. Students discussed their teaching artifacts—such as their students' work, lesson plans, and student interviews—and captioned them. Students also experienced other classrooms. We provided a guiding question and asked students to develop subquestions to focus their portfolios (Grant & Huebner, cited in Lyons, 1998). Finally, we invited students to experiment with alter-native representations in their portfolios and presentations. To reinforce the reflective nature of the portfolio process, we required an introduction and a concluding reflection. For our self-studies, we conducted follow-up interviews with these students 3 months after the semester (Lyons, 1998).

Our self-studies included a third teacher, Jerry Allender, as part of our collaborative. We met, e-mailed, examined student work, and kept journals. We explored our living contradictions: do we teach according to our values? (Whitehead, 1993).

OUR NARRATIVE TEACHING PORTFOLIOS

Over the past 2 years, our teaching portfolios have grown to include five parts:

Part I. A reflective paper presented at a conference and published as part of the conference proceedings
Part II. A dialogue representing the process students went through while creating their teaching portfolios
Part III. Student artifacts—selections from their teaching portfolios and our version of their stories

Part IV. Alternative representations of our process
Part V. Feedback from presenting at the conference

We include segments of each part below to provide a sense of our overall portfolio process and product.

PART I: REFLECTIONS

The following two segments are from a group of 14 reflections previously presented at the Self-Study Conference in Herstmonceux, England in 2000, and published as a paper in the conference proceedings. These reflections articulate our teaching values and allow us to explore how we enact them.

Vicky asked, How do I structure freedom in the classroom to foster creative expression and development?

REFLECTION 1

Owning creativity. I tried to give students space to talk about their creativity and engage in the process. The final portfolios evidenced students experiencing themselves as creative. Furthermore, the students valued their creativity and saw the importance of role modeling it.

Lis reflected on the role of personal involvement and self-study:

REFLECTION 6

I am intellectually committed to doing personally meaningful work. I don't buy the mind-body split. I can't teach writing without making room for voice. I can't help teachers become teachers without helping them to connect deeply with themselves. It's harder this way; I become more vulnerable when I am not the expert glibly providing predigested theoretical texts. Self-study forces me to do personal work and allows students to do the personal work that they are ready for.

PART II: DIALOGUE

This narrative dialogue tells the students' story of developing their portfolios. We created it from our teaching journals, their comments, and pieces of their writing.

THEME 1: PROCESS ANXIETY

A: What does she want?

B: What's a teaching portfolio?

A: She said we could do anything we want.

B: But we need artifacts, and it has to be about our teaching.

A: What's an artifact? This is too loose for me. I need more structure. Tell me how many words, and I'll do a research paper.
   I'm good at that.

B: I just want to learn some new tricks to be more creative in my
   classroom.

A: Self study—what's that?

B: She's not clear. She said it is a process and will emerge.

A: I guess it has to be about self. That's so different than research.

B: I just don't get it.

THEME 2: COLLABORATION

A: Where are you teaching?

B: I'm teaching in West Chester; I have 22 kindergarten kids.

A: I teach adults.

B: That's interesting work, but kids are so cute. Today, they made
   pictures books with new endings to their favorite stories.

A: I'd love to see them. Could you bring them as an artifact?

THEME 3: CREATIVITY AND ALTERNATIVE REPRESENTATION

A: I'm teaching college writing and it's not creative.

B: Well, I'm not really creative, either.

A: I like creative writing.

B: Maybe you could do that for your portfolio. What can I do?

A: Didn't you tell me you redid all the bulletin boards in your
   classroom because they were so boring? That's creative.

B: What am I supposed to do, bring in 6-foot bulletin boards?

A: Why not take photographs?

THEME 4: RISK TAKING

B: It's okay for the kids, but you know . . .

A: What do I know? I'd like to see what you do.

B: Are you willing to bring in some of your writing? What have
   you been writing in your teaching journal?

A: I write about different students—they are so amazing. Once I wrote about how I was really scared to go to school and felt like an imposter.

B: That sounds like what our teacher said about self-study. You are writing about yourself and your teaching. Are you too embarrassed to share that?

A: A little.

B: Hey, I feel that way, too. But we're both new teachers.

THEME 5: REFLECTION

A: How much have you done on your portfolio?

B: I was really worried that I wouldn't have enough artifacts, but now I have so much stuff, I don't know where to begin.

A: What was your portfolio focus?

B: How can I teach for creativity when I don't feel creative.

A: But when you look at all the stuff you do, you are creative.

B: It's funny, but when I started captioning the artifacts, I realized I was being creative.

A: Because I decided to write a short story for my portfolio, I have to create student characters. I decided to interview students. I'm learning more about teaching from talking to them than I thought I would.

THEME 6: CONNECTION WITH REAL LIFE/AUTHENTICITY

B: I picked up the guitar last weekend for the first time in 3 years. I really like making music. All this talk about creativity is reminding me how important it is to nurture it.

A: Writing the short story for my portfolio has been fun, because I love to write. And I am exploring questions about my teaching through writing a teacher character.

THEME 7: PERSONAL DISCOVERIES

B: Thanks for helping me with this—collaboration really works.

A: For me, too. I really enjoyed talking about my classroom. I was willing to try what we discussed because I knew that even if the activity didn't work, I had your support.

B: I risked trying some creative things too and now I really see how creativity belongs everywhere. I discovered that I hadn't given the kids enough open-ended projects.

A: Remember how anxious this open-ended project made us?

B: But now we're done, I really like this more than a paper.

A: I feel more connected with writing, too. I decided to become a writing teacher because I wanted to do something closer to writing than delivering pizzas. Then I had to wrestle with whether academia would destroy my creativity. In the portfolio I was able to combine my interests.

B: I wasn't sure that I was going to be a good teacher, but I really did touch some kids. I'm glad I have some of their work to remind me. This portfolio is definitely a work in progress.

A: Talking to you and dealing with the whole self-study process makes me less scared of making mistakes. She made it seem important to look at discomfort and learn from it.

B: And, looking at the variety of portfolios, it's obvious there is more than one right answer.

A: The portfolio made us reflect on being teachers, what's important to us, and that is different for all of us.

PART III: STUDENT ARTIFACTS

We include a few brief excerpts from some student-teaching portfolios. These portfolios intrigued us because (1) they showed the insight and transformation of the student's ideas, (2) they resonated with our teaching (both struggles and values), and (3) they included something creative that moved us. We conclude each excerpt with a reflection.

Vicky's Student Artifacts

Jackie's Portfolio. Jackie created an imaginative storybook filled with her art, photographs, and writing. She concluded:

> I learned so much about my creativity. I will teach for creativity by encouraging imagination, non-conventional thinking, and constant exploration of the world. I will practice my creativity by being awake to the world around me, thus finding inspiration everywhere. It's too easy in life and in teaching to just keep our feet on the ground and steadily move forward, the way we always have. It's much more rewarding to fly; to shoot for the stars, to spread our wings, and see what is possible to create by leaping into the unknown, by attempting what we aren't yet sure we can achieve.

VICKY'S REFLECTION

I found the rich artistry, insight, diversity of ideas, and media experimentation in Jackie's portfolio compelling. These elements are central in teaching for creativity. Teachers must encourage students to fly, take risks, and be flexible.

Jan's Portfolio. Jan included *Thank You, Mr. Falker*, a book by Patricia Polacco as an artifact because it led her to articulate the teaching qualities she values and to grapple with transforming her practice. She concluded:

> It is important to be accepting of whatever the student is creating. This has been an important lesson for me, as I tend to be a perfectionist and a little too controlling with regards to the end result. I have seen so much inventiveness occur without specific direction or control. True creativity cannot always be planned. Students need to enjoy what they are doing to be creative. When you provide them with a stimulus that will motivate them intrinsically, creativity will follow quite naturally.

VICKY'S REFLECTION

Balancing control and structure for each student so he or she feels comfortable expressing creativity is a struggle for me, too. Developing a close relationship with each student and discovering their strengths and weaknesses, like Mr. Falker, guides me in this process.

John's Portfolio. John described gaining teaching insights from paying attention to two problem students' stories. He included their photographs as artifacts, and wrote:

> Sam was my greatest struggle this year, but he has made me a better teacher. My patience has dramatically improved, and I had been forced to find his strengths. With Ivan I learned how everything we do affects our students.

VICKY'S REFLECTION

I admire how John remained open to his problem students and learned with them. Trying to meet diverse student's needs requires being nonjudgmental and creative. Too often we focus on negative behaviors and forget to appreciate the positive.

Mike's Portfolio. Mike noted in his final video portfolio:

> I love hanging out with kids, getting to know them, and seeing what they are up to. I love recess, playing with the kids. I realized through this class that I probably will not teach as the school structure doesn't fit with my impulses and ideas when I'm working with children.

VICKY'S REFLECTION

> I was moved by the sheer joy Mike captured in the children's faces on his video. Clearly Mike has remarkable rapport with these children to reveal them expressing creativity and play so naturally. I am sad students will miss the opportunity to work with Mike who really wants to understand them. Balancing relationship, creativity, and play is integral to learning.

Brenda's Portfolio. Brenda loves music and used song excerpts to augment her artifact messages. She wrote:

> When I think of creativity, I think of music. Musicians imagine the world in many forms and approach it in many ways. With each style comes a novel approach. We should take the time to enjoy the novelty in our lives, to relish it, to teach about it and be mindful of it.

VICKY'S REFLECTION

> I found the music and notion of novelty in Brenda's portfolio powerful. They are both components that I value in my teaching and use to encourage creative thinking and expression.

Susan's Portfolio. Susan's portfolio was an artistically decorated box containing many intriguing artifacts. She wrote:

> Creating this portfolio taught me a great deal, and it is a valuable tool for self-reflection. Creativity is necessary in a successful classroom and establishing strong relationships with students is impor-

tant. I realized through this process the profound influence a teacher has. If I value creativity my students will value it, too. Self-reflective exercises like this enable teachers to check they haven't fallen away from their original teaching philosophies. This portfolio is a work in progress.

VICKY'S REFLECTION

I value self-reflection and authentic student-teacher relationships. Teaching portfolios and creativity allow us to carefully examine these aspects of our teaching.

Lis's Student Artifacts

Pam's Portfolio. In Pam's poem about her fear of teaching, she noted that her success as a teacher "depended on courage and the ability to make conscious contact with that fear." Her process became "one of remembering to incorporate into my teaching the practices that I have found helpful in my life: taking risks to push past my comfort zone, reflecting on my life experiences, and asking for help."

LIS'S REFLECTION

Unlike a victory narrative, Pam's poem maintains the tensions that she feels. She sees herself as living the contradictions, involved in the dynamic process of learning to teach.

Don's Portfolio. Don wrote, "I used the medium of short fiction to channel some of my hostility and regret." His protagonist's expectations that teaching would provide accolades and money were undermined. In Don's class evaluation, he blamed Lis for not mentoring well, the practicum for not teaching him how to teach, and the institution for not preparing new educators. Also, he wrote, "[All] the students who failed because I was not able to reach them suffered directly as a result of my inexperience." Don decided not to pursue teaching.

LIS'S REFLECTION

Direct communication with Don was difficult, but we could talk about the characters he created. I felt more comfortable raising issues from his text, and I think he could hear literary criticism.

Dena's Portfolio. Dena's creative essay incorporated the stages of the writing process as they applied to her life, teaching, and writing. She experimented with giving up traditional control (teacher in front of the room) and turned her classroom into a workshop. She found comfort and success in one-on-one conferencing, coinciding with how she learned to write. She concluded, "I learned more than I thought I would in musing about the processes of life and writing. Applying what I've learned will be a constant struggle; it is so much easier to keep the control."

LIS'S REFLECTION

I liked Dena's "aha moment" when she realized she could use the method by which she learned to write as a teaching strategy. I truly enjoyed her essay and suggested she publish it.

Joan's Portfolio. Joan's literacy biography focused on educational feedback. She concluded:

I always look for feedback to invigorate my professional growth, and yet I never examined my students' perspective. Students crave the same thing I do: reassurance and constructive criticism. I realize students' trust and look to the teacher as expert. Individual attention can be achieved in a large class through specific comments and one-on-one conferences. Being available before and after class offers students an opportunity to speak informally. This time is ideal for personal attention and shows students you are willing to listen. Students also welcome comments from their peers. Verbal and written feedback is useful; teachers need to realize, however, the power of their words.

LIS'S REFLECTION

I appreciated that she was thorough in her research. She identified a problem, figured out a way to research it, and acted on it—an action research project that clarified for her the types, uses, and problems with feedback.

Katy's Portfolio. Katy wrote:

Writing and walls are—and always have been, from my view—inseparable. I created a visual depicting the walls, which surround and confine the imaginative in writing, but also serve as a vehicle giving structure. This is even more true teaching writing in the inner city where walls take on a new significance. Basic Skills is loaded with people who are marginalized for their color and economic status, and because in a society that prizes itself on literacy, not writing well is a sentence of silence. But, educating them into the mainstream inevitably destroys part of them. I tried to gauge just how much loss occurred as students learned and I depicted those responses (from their journals and interviews) on the black paper in the form of walls, which are tumbling but are nonetheless still there.

LIS'S REFLECTION

Katy used a visual image that worked. When she described walls, she connected the structures of academia with a critical theoretical context.

Carol's Portfolio. Carol examined the multitudinous ways she built student confidence, and concluded, "I gained confidence by giving confidence."

LIS'S REFLECTION

Carol's work was pure victory narrative. The class and I questioned her about problems or tensions and she felt that there hadn't been any. At the 3-month follow-up, she had begun to question her teaching in a more complex fashion. I felt she needed some success before being able to question her teaching.

PART IV: ALTERNATIVE REPRESENTATIONS OF THE PROCESS

To facilitate transformative learning we felt it necessary to integrate the arts with research. Historically, the humanities and the arts were considered better suited to communicate the richness of lived experience. Also, a guiding principle of self-study—walking the talk—required us to incorporate alternative representations into our portfolios because we asked the students to do so.

Our first discovery was that the process is more important than the product. We struggled with how to articulate our learning in artistic forms and how to work with our vulnerability:

I was caught between my belief that the self is intrinsic to transformation and my aversion to narcissism. My three-part graphic—

Who am I? What and how do I teach? And what did I learn?—
forced me to articulate my living contradictions. I felt exposed
through this process; however, the work reminded me how central
personal voice, risk taking, and diversity, (of ideas, media, and
expression), are in my teaching. Wrestling with how to articulate
my teaching helped me stay more authentic with students. (Vicky)

The process of searching for an image reminded me that each
person's life spirals through issues, returns to them regularly, but
differently. While creating the piece, I questioned its value. Then I
got in touch with how any piece of educational research is in the
hands of a larger community. I also believe that teachers should
explain, bridge the gulf from creation to audience. That is our
profession. So, around the graphic I placed a circular sentence,
". . . frame because we cannot apprehend it all—to do that one
would need to be a mystic but we are fallen and science and
skepticism frame . . ." This phrases the dilemma of alternative
representation, understanding forms without language requires
being a mystic. We need frames to understand. (Lis)

Do alternative representations stand by themselves as art? We don't
believe so. But the process: trying something different, being vulnerable,
exposing one's self, articulating one's teaching, and interacting with a wider
world were engaging and valuable experiences.

PART V: FEEDBACK FROM PUBLIC PRESENTATION

We presented our narrative teaching portfolios at the Self-Study Conference (July 2000) in Herstmonceux, England. This process was akin to our
students' final portfolio presentations. We were anxious, as our colleagues
became our audience. After we presented, we invited the audience to become part of our living portfolio. Our primary questions framing this discussion were: Is self-study worthwhile to a larger research community?
And how do our alternative representations fit into this work? One answer
was that we would not have completed our work without the conference
deadline. Preparing for a research community energized and focused our
work. Second, the narrative articulation of our work and the audience's
response made us more conscious of our practices. Our alternative representations, however, were not as potent for the audience as our students'
were for us. On reflection, we feel our images were simplistic, and we

lacked the intimacy with this audience that we had established with our students. There was general agreement that the portfolio structure needs to be flexible so researchers can select media that will support individual expression. Additional questions addressed what institutions would allow, how to move forward with this work, and the value of alternative representation to the research community.

CONCLUSIONS

We continue to use narrative teaching portfolios because they did scaffold self-study. The process of responding to them, however, was time-consuming and stressful. Because the self-studies required individuals to examine their teacher-selves, many issues emerged. We spent hours crafting responses that were attentive to the work, respectful in relational terms, and real to us. Each student received a lengthy feedback letter. We both had students who decided not to pursue teaching, and we both agreed that it was their decision and it was appropriate. On the positive side, the relationships produced were real. Students thanked us for the feedback letters. One of the base groups continues to meet, and many keep in touch.

Another dilemma we wrestled with was how to respond to the diversity in vulnerability and insight revealed in the portfolios. We had to be aware of each student's level of proximal development and psychological comfort (Goldstein, 1999) so that we could responsibly challenge but not overwhelm them. We believed that students did their best, though the results varied. Some students' lack of confidence led them to create portfolios bordering on showmanship (Shulman, cited in Lyons, 1998). However, from students' self-reports, we believe they needed that boost of self-confidence. The process allowed what was, at the time, critical for the student to emerge. We felt it was more important to embrace what the students brought rather than compare his or her product.

Bringing the self-study process into the classroom means modeling it. We discovered that we needed to provide space and time, support the development of personal voice and group collaboration, give up traditional authority, and openly share our vulnerabilities balanced with our confidence in the process. Additionally, our experience suggests that using artistic forms in narrative teaching portfolios (e.g., music, poetry, photographs, drawing, art and crafts, videography, short story) as alternative representations support personally meaningful learning.

Developing a narrative teaching portfolio with the goal of engaging in self-study brings the self into the process at the deepest level through sharing stories. But it is vital to balance the danger of narcissism with the potential learning. We advocate harnessing the collaborative to focus on the work and check the egoism that is implicit in creating first-person narrative. For us, the integration of self and others supports change. The great benefit of self-study narrative teaching portfolios, a worthwhile exemplar, lies in the potential for teacher transformation through creative expression.

REFERENCES

Achebe, C. (1990). Hopes and impediments. New York: Doubleday.

Anderson-Patton, V., & Bass, E. (2000). How well did we structure and model a self-study stance? In J. Loughran & T. Russell (Eds.), *Exploring myths and legends of teacher education: Proceedings of the 3rd international conference on self-study of teacher education practices* (pp. 10–14). London: Falmer Press.

Goldstein, L. (1999). The relational zone: The role of caring relationships in the co-construction of mind. *American Educational Research Journal, 36*(3), 647–673.

Hamilton, M. L. (Ed.). (1998). *Reconceptualizing teaching practice: Self-study in teacher education*. London: Falmer Press.

Loughran, J., & Northfield, J. (1998). A framework for the development of self-study practice. In M. L. Hamilton (Ed.), *Reconceptualizing teaching practice: Self-study in teacher education* (pp. 7–18). London: Falmer Press.

Lyons, N. (Ed.). (1998). *With portfolio in hand: Validating the new teacher professionalism*. New York: Teachers College Press.

Whitehead, J. (1993). *The growth of educational knowledge: Creating your own living educational theories*. Bournemouth, UK: Hyde Publications.

CHAPTER 8

The Development of Teachers' Narrative Authority in Knowledge Communities: A Narrative Approach to Teacher Learning

CHERYL J. CRAIG AND MARGARET R. OLSON

In this chapter we illustrate narrative practices that place teachers' knowledge at the fore of teacher learning. We build the case that teachers filter all experience (including their experiences of coursework at both the preservice and in-service levels) through their personal practical knowledge, and express their knowledge of teaching in practice through their narrative authority (Olson, 1995). Furthermore, teachers authentically share their stories of practice in safe places that they or others may have created or found. In these, knowledge communities (Craig, 1995), their personal practical knowledge is made explicit to themselves and to others. Without productive knowledge communities where practice is consciously reflected upon, in-service and preservice teachers will not develop to the fullest extent possible the socially funded knowledge necessary to make sense of the complexities of teaching. Our examples feature undergraduate and graduate students constructing and reconstructing their personal practical knowledge (Clandinin, 1986) through the expression of their narrative authority in particular knowledge communities. In this way, their narrative knowledge becomes publicly visible, leading to transformative changes in their practices.

UNDERLYING CONCEPTUALIZATIONS

Two conceptualizations underpin the narrative exemplars we present: narrative authority and knowledge communities. In this section, we explain these narrative terms.

Narrative Authority

Narrative authority emerges from the implicit narrative knowledge individuals develop through experience and shapes the way we choose to author our lives in relation to others. As we explain to our students, it involves both living and telling stories in response to the social contexts in which we find ourselves. Because the narrative version of knowledge construction is transactional, authority comes from experience and is integral as each person both shapes his or her own knowledge and is shaped by the knowledge of others. Thus, narrative authority becomes the expression, enactment, and development of a person's narrative knowledge as individuals learn to authorize meaning in community with others. Because teachers' lives are not lived in isolation, each person becomes simultaneously both an author of her or his own stories as well as an actor in stories authored by others. Thus, the narrative authority of each educator is both enhanced and constrained by the narrative authority of others and the unchallenged assumptions they hold. Conventional attempts to cultivate individuals in the positivist paradigm has led to the valuing of the authority of position (Munby & Russell, 1994) and epistemic authority at the expense of individuals' narrative authority. When officially authorized versions of professional knowledge are presented as givens, narrative authority can be thwarted or silenced. Ironically, however, the choices teachers and preservice teachers make and the actions they take necessarily continue to come from their individual narrative authority, however unexamined it may be. Unless there are spaces for stories to be brought out into the open and shared with others, they become the unreflective bases for professional practice and decision-making.

Knowledge Communities

Knowledge communities are safe, storytelling places where educators narrate the rawness of their experiences, negotiate meaning, and authorize their own and others' interpretations of situations. They take shape around commonplaces of experiences (Lane, 1988) as opposed to around bureaucratic and hierarchical relations that declare who knows, what should be known, and what constitutes "good teaching" and "good schools" (Clandinin & Connelly, 1996). Such knowledge communities can be both found and created.

In knowledge communities, teachers validate and consolidate their experiences as individuals and as members of a professional community. Tensions are revealed and insights are offered that enable situations to be revisited, reassessed, and restoried (Olson & Craig, 2001). Such reflective turns (Schön, 1991) lead to more informed practical actions. Teachers explore the upsides and downsides of experiences, making their practices transparent and their knowledge public in the presence of others. In these personal public exchanges, profound meaning in teachers' everyday experiences can be found. Participation in communities of knowing allows teachers to transcend the challenges of particular situations and to recognize and name latent opportunities for growth that situations might hold. Teachers' knowledge communities support shifts in personal and collective perspectives that would be impossible to achieve through individual reflection alone. In knowledge communities, the scholarship of reflective teaching is nurtured.

INTRODUCING OUR NARRATIVE PRACTICES

Olson begins by describing written responses and what are known as base groups as interrelated examples of one narrative practice that promotes the development of narrative authority and the cultivation of knowledge communities with preservice teachers. She shares examples of narrative awakenings from several students in a required first-year bachelor of education course. Craig then describes the use of journal writing in developing narrative authority in knowledge communities. She focuses on examples of narrative shifts over time with one teacher in a group of teachers whose school reform plan included in-school graduate coursework for faculty members at her school.

READING RESPONSE AND BASE GROUPS
IN PRESERVICE TEACHER EDUCATION

These interrelated narrative inquiry practices are used in a first year, first term sociology of education course. There are four sections of this course that two other instructors and I have worked closely together in designing and redesigning. We have approximately 30 students in each section. The narrative practices we have developed are buttressed by several other interrelated narrative practices in the course and are also embedded in our program goals of teaching for diversity, equity, and social justice, and the valuing of experience.

Most of our students come from Nova Scotia, a small maritime Canadian province of picturesque fishing and farming communities. While the capital city, Halifax, has an obviously diverse population, in smaller communities ethnic groups have not tended to mix. Yet within a 4-hour drive are communities of Acadians, Mi'kmaq, Scots, Dutch, Gaelic, and black

Nova Scotians. Most of our students are of European ancestry. A few Mi'kmaq students comprise the most obvious ethnic minority. Most enter our program hegemonized into beliefs such as, there is little or no diversity within their community, they are representatives of a homogeneous group, or they are different from everyone else and therefore are not "normal." Here I describe my use of reading responses and base groups to enable students to surface and examine unchallenged assumptions embedded in their narrative knowledge about equity and diversity.

A main focus of the sociology course is to become aware of the implicit social structuring of inequality in our schools by "examining our own 'taken for granted' assumptions about the purpose of schooling in order to transform ourselves and our schools in more democratic ways" (course syllabus). One major understanding we want students to develop is that "teachers need to examine the attitudes, values, beliefs, and knowledge that they bring into the classroom" (course syllabus).

Reading Responses as a Narrative Practice

Students prepare one-page written responses to assigned articles, videos, and in-class activities. The course outline describes the assignment as follows:

> The purpose of the reading responses is to help you begin to make explicit and explore your own underlying assumptions about the contents, goals, practices, and/or effects of schooling within their social contexts and from a variety of perspectives. These assignments have two sections: First, summarize two or three points in the article. Identify whether these are things you resonate with, things you resist, and/or things that make you stop and wonder. The next step is articulating WHY you feel the way you do. It is important to connect your beliefs to your own past, present, and future experience as a student and as a teacher. The criteria for assessment are:
>
> *Summary*
>
> * Ability to focus on key issues
> * Articulation of why you have chosen these particular issues
>
> *Insights/Reactions*
>
> * The degree to which your response connects to your own past, present, and future experience as a student and teacher

- Evidence of further understanding of existing beliefs and/or insights that lead you to interpret your experience in new ways
- Evidence that you have taken into account different perspectives

Course readings deal with issues of equity in areas related to class, race, and gender as well as other social issues such as body image, the power of the media, critical media literacy, the use of standard English, and so on. Those readings that work best to enable individuals to connect with and examine their own narrative knowing of equity issues, such as Peggy MacIntosh's (1990) "White Privilege: Unpacking the Invisible Knapsack," are used again. Others are replaced. The following student response to *Failing at Fairness: How American Schools Cheat Girls* by Myra and David Sadker (1994) is typical of how students began to become aware of and examine their narrative knowing:

> As I began to read this article I was telling myself that I haven't really been exposed to a situation this severe. I don't recall being pushed aside so that my teachers could focus on the boys. Looking back I realize that there was a sexual bias, probably in every class, but often it was subtle, repeated enough to the point of acceptance. All through high school I focused on science courses. By the time I graduated I decided to major in English in university. I did equally well in both subjects, yet I don't recall being encouraged (by my male science teacher) to pursue a degree in Science. I do not regret my decision. Yet I wonder how many males in my graduating class who were torn between Arts and Science, were persuaded to take Science.
>
> As a future teacher I will constantly be aware that I must not create a gender bias in my classroom. Every student deserves my full attention and the right to feel that they are active members of the class. (Betty)

These responses, examples of preservice teachers' expressions of their narrative authority, comprise the major portion of students' "class notes" and are used as the basis of discussions in their base groups and their final paper in which they "synthesize their thinking over the term given input from the instructor, peers, readings, and texts" (course syllabus).

Giving meaningful response to 30 students writing twice a week is a daunting task. I used to worry about this more when I believed they would need response from me as their teacher in order to expand their thinking. I now respond to 15 on Tuesdays and 15 on Thursdays. I have learned to trust that the response they receive from their peers is equally valuable to mine. I now describe the role the base groups play in enabling students to articulate, value, and examine their own narrative authority while simultaneously gaining an understanding and appreciation for the diversity of experiences and views within this supposedly "homogeneous" group.

Base Groups as Potential Knowledge Communities

I put students in base groups of three created around as much diversity of gender, ethnicity, religion, school experience, and so on as I can identify from introductory activities during the first two classes in which we discuss the importance of each individual's experience in shaping their education and the uniqueness of each individual's experience. These base groups form the primary structure used for discussion of the reading responses and other class activities. They provide the opportunity for individuals to develop sustained conversations and move past surface-level discussions by providing group continuity during our short term. While students stay in the same base groups for the remaining 8 weeks of the course, there are several other cooperative group activities. Students also sit at tables for six comprising a "double base group." The double base groups and other cooperative activities provide a wider variety of perspectives that complement base group discussions.

The following comments from students show how the base groups as knowledge communities enable students to examine and revise their own assumptions embedded in their narrative authority and expand and/or revise their narrative authority through perspectives gained from hearing others' narrative authority:

> By discussing with others, you can change your opinion on a specific idea, just as I did with my idea on poor people. I realized that I was looking at only one part of the poor people (the lazy one) and not giving attention to the rest of them. (George)

> I can change my views to be different than those of society and of those which have been passed on to me through parents, friends, grandparents. I have started to change my views, but it is difficult. (Jan)

> I wasn't aware of how much my experiences affect how I look at situations. Some things that I thought I knew a lot about were very different from what others knew about the same topic. I learned a lot on the issue of poverty by listening to others' views and experiences. (Linda)

As I saw in our groups about stereotypes, I did not see myself as someone who practices this. However, in discussing with the group I realized that we all have stereotypes that may be hidden. This is frightening when I consider how stereotypes, racism, and prejudices become hidden as people become oblivious to them. (Pat)

In the final paper, students are asked to focus on four questions. Here, I present excerpts from their final papers to show evidence of the value of using these narrative practices in examining issues of equity and diversity and transforming individuals' narrative authority.

1. *What have I uncovered about inequity in society and in schools?*

For me, as a student, equity was never an issue. I was "taught to"— based on my white race, and my middle-class family. I never had difficulty relating to subject material, or even to my teachers. The majority of them spoke and acted like I did. My cultural capital allowed me to succeed in school, whereas it forced others to fail.

Another realization I made in this course is that teachers *should* have certain expectations for students of all races and classes. It does not help a student for a teacher to "go easy on them" because they are underprivileged. Race and class are not handicaps, and teachers should not treat them as such. In the past, I was guilty of making these types of assumptions. If a student from a poor area did not do well in school, I assumed it was because he or she was from a poor family who did not care about his or her education. I now understand how damaging this way of thinking is, especially for a teacher to have. (Karen)

2. *What taken for granted assumptions have I reexamined?*

I did not even realize, before this course, that I had *so many* taken-for-granted assumptions. This course has been a truly enlightening learning experience. Certainly, the first thing that needed to be looked at was my "white privilege." I always knew, at some level, that this existed, but I did not realize the extent to which racial minority groups are treated as compared to white people. I am still not sure that I will ever *completely* understand this since I have never lived another racial experience. However, it has become very clear to me that the idea of having a special black history month says a lot about how the black experience is perceived for the other 11 months of the year. The same thing could be said for my Christian privileges and my heterosexual privilege. There are many things that I took for granted in the past by telling myself that it is "just the way it is" but I realize now that these privileges I have been living with are unearned and that people of other races, religions, and sexual orientations deserve the same treating as I do. (Sandra)

3. *What will I do individually and collectively as a teacher in my classroom to promote equity? What tools do I have?*

To approach inequity in the classroom and to challenge it, it will be necessary to look at every event, activity, or text from the point of view of the least advantaged. Our current curriculum contains the hidden curriculum. This hidden curriculum is that of our society. Through our schools children learn about social relationships and values. If we do not challenge *everything*, these children will internalize the values of society that fragment groups such as women and minorities and they will be perpetuated. Children will accept white privilege, racism, sexism, classism. In order to create a classroom that is equitable, I need to bring my reexaminations to the forefront. (Pat)

4. *What more do I still need to know?*

Although I now have a base of knowledge about issues of equity, tools to use in teaching, and a greater awareness of the issues, I still can learn a great deal more. I feel I have merely scratched the surface in knowing about these issues and I intend to examine them further. I want to read more about various perspectives, issues, and views. I still need to work on changing my own preconceived views and judgments of others . . . I will need to always think about and work on *not* falling into the trap of teaching only to the "white middle class" students. I need to think about and continually be aware of injustices to assure that I am not reinforcing them . . . For my own benefit, I will need to work on my own critical thinking skills. This is the first time I have been taught how to do this, and I know it will not happen overnight. I'm sure I will have to work on critical thinking for the rest of my life in order to continue doing it. (Leslie)

The developments and transformations that occur in this short 9-week period continue to amaze me. However, as our students begin their practicum experiences in schools, I wonder if and how they will be able to sustain the emerging awarenesses. Will they continue to value their own narrative authority and the narrative authority of their students? Will they find knowledge communities that help them continue to examine issues of equity and diversity or will the knowledge communities they encounter in schools teach them to forget what they are just beginning to know? The seeds of possibility have been sown. But how can these be nurtured within school systems?

JOURNALING IN IN-SERVICE TEACHER EDUCATION

In 1999–2000, I taught a graduate class, "Reflective Practice," at Eagle High School, a comprehensive high school in a large, urban center in the United States as part of the school's organized reform effort. Because the graduate students/teachers all worked in the same context, they were able to respond to one another and work together in ways not possible in a graduate class offered in a university setting. From the outset, the teachers were intentionally introduced to the knowledge community and narrative authority conceptualizations and the light they shed on how teachers develop knowledge in relationship with one another. In addition to a number of assignments and readings by authors like Dewey, Schön, and others, 10th-grade English teacher Abbie Puckett and 14 of her colleagues wrote reflective journals to which I responded. In this section, our journal exchange shows how Abbie and I entered into a knowledge community relationship. In this relational, knowledge-creating space, Abbie's narrative authority was legitimated and made visible to her and others.

In her initial journal entry, Abbie, who previously taught honors English classes, wrote about her introduction to

> my first regular classes [of students] in three years . . . I feel as if I have hit "the real world" with a thud. How do I best describe my kids? I guess needy would be the best way. My first-period class is small—wonderful kids—we have bonded pretty well. We wrote norms, did reflections, they responded—I am teacher of the universe. Then there is the second period full of girls who challenge me at every turn. They hate me actually. They want questions at the end of the story, worksheets, and easy grades.

Because I taught the graduate course in Puckett's school context, I was able to reply with my observations concerning the neediness and gender themes that arose early in Abbie's reflective writing. Focusing on the 68% high risk, predominantly African American and Hispanic student population, I responded:

> It is interesting that I do not see your students as being needy in their appearances. It is like the need gets covered up with designer clothing, but teachers seem to peel back the fancy packaging and uncover the real people behind the facades.

Where Abbie's relationship with "the girls" was concerned, I questioned whether the conditioning Puckett observed could be traced to cultivation, schooling, culture, other sources, or a combination of factors. I encouraged Abbie to think hard about these matters.

Abbie did so. Later in the school year, when she listened to Elliot Mishler's address at the 1999 Narrative and Portfolio Conference at Harvard University, Puckett began to connect Mishler's discussion of narratives of trauma victims with the writing of some of her students. In her journal, Abbie questioned: "Can it be that my students' lack of linear thinking or inability to sequence logically is meshed with past experiences and a combination of other factors?"

Not long after Abbie began to ponder these deep matters emerging in her classroom, she reflected on the imperatives raining down on her from out-of-classroom places (Clandinin & Connelly, 1995). Her school's standardized test scores in English had declined, and the English Department was subjected to mandatory staff development along with observers in their classrooms on a regular basis. Puckett described and reacted to the turn of events in the following way:

> We are being trained in vowel patterns; we have to teach the students patterns, decoding and fluency 30 minutes per day. They [can] only read 10–15 minutes at a time, one-half page per night. Although this may help a few kids, somehow I do not think we are meeting the needs of the majority. [A reading consultant] has observed and believes most of our students are having comprehension problems—we are totally ignoring her findings—we have been told that if we believe, our students will pass [the standardized test]. . . . What are being discounted are studies of minority children and urban kids. The hole is getting deeper—maybe we cannot climb out.

At that point, Puckett's reflective journal became filled with her exploration of the tension she felt between what she actually knew from her experiences in her classroom, and what she was being told to know and practice. Abbie's initial reaction to the outside intervention was one of anger and discouragement. Then, in her sustained writing, a ray of light shone through:

> Finally! All this English staff development is coming together. All this nitpicking is actually making me really reflect—for the first time in a long time—on my own teaching, philosophy, and practice. I needed this. I plan to carry more of my assignments into my [teacher inquiry] group. I think I can also look at others' "best practices" with a different eye. . . . This "immersion" into strategies along with my reflective readings is giving me new insights. The new book, *The Power of Their Ideas*, convinces me more than ever that the control of learning must be in the hands of the learner. How to do it is the dilemma. . . . I get so far in my thinking about it. Then I get stumped. More pondering, reflecting is needed. I think, again, the key is my [teacher inquiry] group.

At this time, I assigned a project asking the graduate students to take a fine-grained look at their beliefs in community with one another and at what was actually happening in their classrooms and school. Abbie had this to say about how the assignment related to her work:

> More and more I am beginning to see how I need this reflective research project. I have to . . . really look at what I am doing in the classroom—how do I align with my beliefs? Do I really know what is good, or needed, for an African American urban student who has not passed the standardized test? While I believe that any test cannot be the answer, the bottom line is that my kids are in a state of survival. It is like talking about the beautiful language in *Wuthering Heights* to a starving child on the street or reading Keats to someone who has no job and cannot feed her child. While I know I can free the soul that is not their need right now . . . When I spoke of real personal reflection about teaching practices today, my group began talking about what is needed to be done in administration, what the students need to do, and how the faculty needs to change. I am really excited about our research project—a little apprehensive—perhaps, we will see.

In response, I reminded Abbie that both positive and not-so-positive experiences prompt people to reflect more keenly. I also shared that I tend to do my best reflecting, writing, and learning when I am "in the throes of some less-than-pleasant situation." I wondered whether Puckett was inhabiting a similar kind of space. I added that the group reflective research project would allow Abbie to

> work simultaneously with students and with your self, and connect with other teachers and the community at large. . . . What a complex picture your work will reveal. And you will see the complexity with new eyes and a different call to action. . . . And you will temper the freeing of the soul with the need to have employment and food on the table. . . . Perhaps, most of all, you will work with the development of identities that will serve your students well in all walks of life.

Because the local office of a national reform movement financially supported the graduate course in which Abbie and her colleagues were enrolled, an external evaluator assessed the value of the "Reflective Practice" course to the teachers and to the school's "theory of action" (see Hatch, 1998) concerning how change would occur. The on-site course, Abbie's reflective journal writing, and an interview with Puckett formed a notable part of her school's unpublished report for the 1999–2000 school year. The text of the report includes the following:

> One teacher of 10th grade English told us the reflective writing she did in connection with a university course, in addition to her experiences at conferences, helped her survive a year when observers were in her classroom daily, supervising a mandated program of phonics to improve test scores. She told us that without her journaling and reflective writing, she might not have stayed teaching at the school. But in a fascinating story, she explains that the pressure she felt *in combination with* her journaling, pushed her to become a better teacher. (Coppola, 2000)

The report then directly quotes an interview with the 10th-grade teacher, in which Abbie explained:

> I am not sure how to describe it because it was really an epiphany for me about my teaching craft. And what I saw was that I could be a good teacher in the midst of this forced agenda. That good things came out of it if I was willing to be reflective. And what I have come to learn as a teacher: there are many forces that we can't control, I would say most things we cannot control, but in the midst of that I can do very well in the classroom. But the reflection, I think, is crucial. I would say for me as a teacher it is

the number one thing. . . . If you are not reflecting or taking a hard look at what you are doing in the classroom you can't make changes. . . . So how can you make changes if you don't even know what you are doing? (Coppola, 2000)

Puckett then explained to the evaluator:

[Without the journaling] I think I would have [crashed]. . . . My self-esteem as a teacher was in question. I know it had been. We were even told in the meetings that some of our facial expressions were negative . . . [and] "if we really believe[d] and if we really work[ed], these kids would [pass the standardized test]." . . . How could I care more? So I think that without the journaling, I would have allowed that to stay with me and I would not have been able to work through . . . the anger and the pain. (Coppola, 2000)

In this interview, the value of Puckett's narrative knowing not only withstands the test of time, it surfaces in a new situation, a high-stakes evaluation one. In the featured excerpts, we see how Abbie's ongoing reflective storying and restorying of her experiences gives her a resilience that enabled her to transcend a situation that others, even Puckett in another space and time, would have found unbearable. The reflective writing exchange furthermore formed a model that Abbie and her colleagues were able to sustain between and among one another after the course was completed. Abbie, for example, continued dialogue journal writing with a history teacher who taught the same students as her. Not only did the two teachers come to better understand their individual and collective experiences, they wrote a paper under review for publication in a teaching journal and a chapter that will be included in a book. The teachers made the narrative practice I modeled for them their own and were able to carve out new individual and shared spaces that honored not only their narrative knowing, but the narrative knowing of their students as well.

STRENGTHS AND PROBLEMS OF NARRATIVE PRACTICES

The featured exemplars show narrative practices assisting individual and groups of undergraduate and graduate students to explore dimensions of their personal practical knowledge, to develop their narrative authority, and to form knowledge communities that promote positive growth. Once healthy models are established and productively lived, we see that it is possible for students to seek out and extend an inquiry stance and the spirit of collaboration in their personal professional relationships with colleagues and students alike.

This major strength, however, brings with it its own set of cautions. In this work, for example, evidence of individual change—and change within small groups—prevails. Because large systems, whether they be school districts or networks of white privilege, are embedded within more positivistic and hierarchical ways of knowing, there are transitional periods where individuals may no longer fit comfortably in a conventional system but may be living a story that is yet to be or is in competition with stories of "the way things are." At the same time, we know individual educators, as opposed to schools, are where the process of change begins.

This leads to a second caution. While narrative approaches unearth complexities, help people to manage dilemmas, and elucidate more fully the human condition, they offer no quick answers. But stories can shed light on how future action may better attend to situations at hand. For narrative approaches to be most successfully lived, though, they must be consistently, as opposed to intermittently, practiced and supported in teacher-education classes, in formal groups in schools, and in other public and private spaces where educators interact. They furthermore must fruitfully merge the past, present, and future in our thinking.

This leads to a final point. We find that individual undergraduate and graduate students reflect best and develop their narrative authority most fully when they receive nonjudgmental responses to their stories that enable them to examine and revise their knowing in nonthreatening ways. Without a broad range of knowledge communities where inquiry rather than certainty is valued, there would be no place to discuss the difficult matters presented in this chapter. The failure to talk openly about perplexing topics promotes stagnation and inauthentic accounts of experience. Narrative approaches offer growth and authenticity, but the entailments that accompany them must also be taken into consideration.

NOTES

The authors have contributed equally to this article. We rotate the order of authorship in our collaborative writing. Support for Cheryl Craig's research came from the Brown Foundation, Inc. and the reform movement. The Social Sciences and Humanities Research Council of Canada funded Margaret Olson's research. Both authors deeply appreciate the contributions of the undergraduate and graduate students who participated in their research programs.

REFERENCES

Clandinin, D. J. (1986). *Classroom practice: Teacher images in action*. Philadelphia: Falmer Press.

Clandinin, D. J., & Connelly, F. M. (1995). *Teachers' professional knowledge landscapes*. New York: Teachers College Press.

Clandinin, D. J., & Connelly, F. M. (1996). Teachers' professional knowledge landscapes: Teacher stories—stories of teachers—school stories—stories of schools. *Educational Researcher, 25*(3), 24–30.

Coppola, E. (2000). *High school case study*. Unpublished report, 1999–2000.

Craig, C. (1995). Knowledge communities: A way of making sense of how beginning teachers come to know. *Curriculum Inquiry, 25*(2), 151–175.

Hatch, T. (1998). The differences that matter in the practice of school improvement. *American Educational Research Journal, 35*(1), 3–31.

Lane, B. C. (1988). *Landscapes of the sacred: Geography and narrative in American spirituality*. New York: Paulist Press.

MacIntosh, P. (1990, Winter). White privilege: Unpacking the invisible knapsack. *Independent School*, 31–36.

Munby, H., & Russell, T. (1994). The authority of experience in learning to teach: Messages from a physics methods class. *Journal of Teacher Education, 45*(2), 86–95.

Olson, M. (1995). Conceptualizing narrative authority: Implications for teacher education. *Teaching and Teacher Education, 11*(2), 119–135.

Olson, M., & Craig, C. (2001). Opportunities and challenges in the development of teachers' knowledge: The development of narrative authority through knowledge communities. *Teaching and Teacher Education, 17*(7), 667–684.

Sadker, D., & Sadker, M. (1994). *Failing at fairness: How American schools cheat girls*. New York: Charles Scribner's Sons.

Schön, D. (1991). *The reflective turn: Case studies in and on educational practice*. New York: Teachers College Press.

PART II

Embedding and Extending Inquiry
Through Narrative Research Practices

What we urgently need today is a more inclusive view of what it means to be a scholar—a recognition that knowledge is acquired through research, through synthesis, through practice, and through teaching.
—Ernest Boyer, *Scholarship Reconsidered*

The narrative research practices presented in Part II of this book expand the possibilities of the narrative inquiry process. Here under consideration are more formal situations of research: the introduction of students to doctoral dissertation study (Chapter 9), the documentation of the implementation of a new literacy program (Chapter 11), or the use of action research as a deliberate effort to align a new approach to teacher education with the implementation of a new national curriculum effort in Ireland (Chapter 10). In Chapter 12, a teacher-educator examines the effect of following and engaging with new teachers over the course of their first years of teaching in difficult urban settings, bringing together teacher interns with first- and second-year teachers all working in similar, challenging teaching situations. Through storying their experiences in the presence of each other these teachers find a reflective support, sustaining their efforts. Captured here are portraits of teacher-educator-researchers inventing new roles as inquirers, which in turn suggest the contours of a dynamic new scholarship for teacher education, advancing our knowledge of teaching.

CHAPTER 9

Three Narrative Teaching Practices—
One Narrative Teaching Exercise

D. JEAN CLANDININ, F. MICHAEL CONNELLY, AND ELAINE CHAN

In this chapter we situate our exploration of narrative teaching practices in our graduate work with novice researchers where our principal task is to teach potential researchers how to think narratively. We explain three teaching practices in the context of a single exercise. The relationship between the practices and why they appear in a single exercise will become clear as the exercise is presented. Before doing so, however, we provide an account of our learning to think narratively that led to these teaching practices.

LEARNING TO THINK NARRATIVELY

As we wrote our stories around plot lines of learning to think narratively in the introductory pages of *Narrative Inquiry* (Clandinin & Connelly, 2000), we told of how we learned to be researchers within the context of what we call the "grand narrative" of research. We began our research lives situated within times and places that Lagemann (1996, p. 5) characterized as a climate of "increasingly common faith in the value of deriving generalizations from empirical data and a widespread disdain toward knowledge based on logic or speculation." Tracing our development as members of a team rewriting Bloom's *Taxonomy* (Bloom, 1956) and drawing on other research experiences, we wrote about how narrative inquiry bumped up against what we called a reductionistic boundary associated with the grand narrative. We then explored the literature on technical rationalism and reflective practice to further develop our understanding of what we saw as this reductionistic boundary. As we turned our attention to Bernstein's (1987) work we noticed another boundary with narrative inquiry, a boundary we called formalistic.

Broadly speaking, we see these boundaries—reductionistic and formalistic—as having to do with the way researchers think and with the direction of their inquiries. For example, within the grand narrative that sets up a reductionistic boundary, inquiry tends to explorations of simpler, composite, reduced parts of the whole. Explanations are downward to the reduced part. Within a formalistic approach there is a move to overarching, comprehensive, formalistic explanations upward to abstract forms. At each of the boundaries with narrative inquiry, we described a set of tensions that we, and our students, experienced. For instance, we experienced tensions at the boundaries over the place of people in inquiry, the role of certainty, and so forth. *In Narrative Inquiry* we explored what it meant, for us as inquirers, to live at these boundaries as we tried to teach ourselves to think narratively; that is, to live our research plot lines as narrative inquirers.

As our research and teaching progressed we found ourselves supervising graduate students who wished to do narrative inquiry in their dissertations and we found ourselves teaching narrative inquiry courses. While we saw these courses partly as providing access to literature on narrative, more importantly, we saw them as an introduction to the difficulty of learning to think narratively. These courses were opportunities for students to learn to be sensitive to the tensions that would confront them as they bumped up against the boundaries.

Narrative inquiry courses are no different than other courses in that they can be taught in various ways; that is, through lecture, through discussion of readings, and so on. We determined that we needed to engage in narrative teaching and to teach about narrative inquiry narratively. We devised a list of narrative teaching practices and narrative teaching exercises. We engaged with graduate students using multiple narrative teaching practices. We singled out one exercise, the presentation of a dissertation, for this chapter because we think it is a particularly important one for novice researchers and because the exercise draws several narrative teaching practices together in one extended activity.

THE EXERCISE AS PRESENTED TO STUDENTS

The assignment of the dissertation presentation is given on the first day of class and becomes an ongoing work-in-progress for students throughout the course. The exercise reads as follows.

DISSERTATION PRESENTATION

This exercise is designed to help you accomplish three things:

1. To learn to read an inquiry text in 3 ways
2. To explore narrative forms of representation
3. To imaginatively reconstruct another researcher's inquiry journey.

Read one narrative inquiry dissertation *and* its proposal.

A. Use Connelly and Clandinin, *Teachers as Curriculum Planners*, 1988, Chapter 7. Do this reading in three ways: for recovery of meaning, for reconstruction of meaning, for reading at the boundaries.
   1. Recovery of meaning—Read from the text's inside: Read ethnographically; read as if you were the author; read uncritically; assume your opinions and biases are irrelevant or, worse, that they muddle meaning. What terms guide the construction of the text?
   2. Reconstruction of meaning—Read from your intentions: Why are you reading it? what do you want to get out of it? for what purposes? Use your biases to generate possibilities for your work, to stimulate imagination. Fidelity to the text is not the issue. What are your terms?
   3. Reading at the boundaries—Read at the interface between the text and the formalistic and reductionistic boundaries: What are the rubbing points? what questions and doubts need to be answered from either reading A.1 or reading A.2? What terms mark the interface?
B. Write a log of your three ways of reading. Discuss the narrative form that the inquirer used to represent the work. Reconstruct the inquirer's journey, paying particular attention to the tensions at the boundaries that the inquirer might have experienced. What tensions might the inquirer have experienced as she or he moved into the field? from field to field texts? from field texts to research texts in the study? Were there ethical concerns?
C. Frame a series of wonders to share with the inquirer that emerge from your readings and discussions. Engage in a conversation (in person, on the phone, by e-mail) with the researcher.
D. Engage the class in a sharing of your imaginative journey through the inquiry.
E. Contact the researcher following the presentation to discuss the presentation and any new matters that emerged.

A NARRATIVE EXAMPLE OF A STUDENT'S
EXPERIENCE OF THE EXERCISE

In order to provide a sense of how this exercise unfolds we draw on one student's course writing. We present only very few fragments of a much larger reading log.

Elaine Chan is a doctoral student in the Centre for Teacher Development at OISE/UT. She was nearing the end of her coursework and was preparing for her comprehensive examinations and writing of her dissertation proposal when she took the course. Each member of the class was required to complete the exercise. Chan chose Ming Fang He's dissertation, *Professional Knowledge Landscapes: Three Chinese Women Teachers' Enculturation and Acculturation Processes in China and Canada* (1998). Throughout the term, as she read material and wrote weekly logs following the structure of the exercise, she continued to revisit a particular topic which eventually became her dissertation topic. Furthermore, she kept coming back to He's dissertation in the context of other course readings. We present selections of her writing to illustrate the various phases of this narrative exercise.

It is important for readers to understand that Chan's writing is not presented as a formula. In the same class with Chan were students who wrote much more extensively on the recovery of meaning than did Chan. She wrote more extensively on reconstruction and reading at the boundaries. Some students had more difficulty trying to reconstruct a text. On balance, all forms of writing are accepted but are continually responded to in order to explore other possibilities.

The first excerpt is taken from Chan's reading log in week three, where one of the readings was Chapter 2 in *Narrative Inquiry* (Clandinin & Connelly, 2000). In addition, Chan was reading Polanyi's (1958) *Personal Knowledge.*

  1. *Recovery of Meaning . . . What is the author saying?*

  Polanyi's (1958) idea of frames of reference may offer some insight into the relationship between grand narrative theorists and narrative inquirers. He suggests that individuals who adhere to a stable inquiry framework often proceed without taking into consideration frames of reference that might generate approaches and interpretations different from those established.

  2. *Reconstruction of Meaning . . . What do I make of the author's text? Do I agree with what the author is saying? What difference would this text make to my research?*

I also thought that Polanyi's (1958) idea of frames of reference for personal knowledge was very powerful since it acknowledges not only our personal knowledge but also reinforces the idea that we interpret the world through our own knowledge while overlooking the views of others. Knowledge acts as a point of reference. I have been thinking about differences between the ways in which immigrant Chinese Canadians and Canadian-born Chinese Canadians view their identity. I have noted that those who come from Asia often refer to me as a Canadian Chinese while I refer to myself as a Chinese Canadian—I see myself as a certain kind of Canadian, a Chinese Canadian, while Chinese from Asia seem to see me as a certain kind of Chinese, a Canadian Chinese. Although these are merely labels and do not even begin to address the complexities of sense of affiliation, loyalty to the cultures, or how these attributes are felt, demonstrated or interpreted, they reveal interesting differences in perspective. My own preference reveals my sense of affinity to the Canadian part of my identity but in doing so, I also feel compelled to qualify the label by acknowledging my Chinese heritage. From the point of view of those who ask about my nationality, they are often asking about my cultural background. The response that I am Canadian is often sometimes not enough but if I also tell them that my family is Chinese, they nod and accept it. It is as if qualifying that I am a Chinese Canadian explains something about my identity when in fact, these are only labels. They interpret my response based on their own ideas of what a Chinese identity entails. Differences in frames of reference alter what is seen and how it is interpreted. (Chan, 2000)

3. *Reading at the Edges . . . What are the rubbing points with other works, values, methodologies in the field? What kind of critique would this work receive in a seminar/senate oral/conference?*

I agree with what the authors are saying and found this chapter especially relevant to me at this point in my work since the rubbing points that are presented in the chapter are also rubbing points in my perspective of narrative inquiry in relation to other forms of inquiry.

Learning about the extent to which the use of narrative is an appropriate means of examining my research topic has been a relief as well as a revelation. I wonder, however, about the extent of incompatibility between narrative and non-narrative methods. The emphasis on the role of experience, I think, is what sets narrative apart from other approaches. In narrative, the researcher begins with experience and then draws on what has been done to support and to explain the phenomenon being examined. Would it be possible to approach the topic through another qualitative, non-narrative approach? How would the approaches differ? Would the findings differ as well? To what extent? (Chan, 2000)

There are several things that we notice about Chan's writing as she begins to learn to think narratively. First of all, it is not clear whether Chan has started to read He's proposal and dissertation. Indeed, it is quite probable, since this is week three, that she has not yet chosen the dissertation for presentation. However, we do see from her reconstruction of meaning that she is beginning to sort out her own narrative of experience around cultural identity. She came to the course at a stage in her life, and her academic work, where the governing question, for her, was what she was going to do for her research. Our sense is that this overall concern shaped her reading of these texts and other texts assigned throughout the course. As we see in later sections, she continually refined her experience of being Chinese Canadian into a thesis inquiry.

We also see her learning to think narratively as she identifies some of the boundaries for her narrative work. At this point, she has more questions than answers, as she wonders about the relationship between the more common distinction between various qualitative approaches.

The second excerpt is from the following week's reading log (week four), where she is again reading from *Narrative Inquiry* (Clandinin & Connelly, 2000). By this point, she has chosen He's dissertation.

1. *Recovery of Meaning . . . What is the author saying?*

Memory is critical to the process of gaining understanding of this landscape since memories help to place us within the three dimensional space. As we listen to others talk about their memories, we make sense of them by referring to our own. Their stories evoke memories of our past, enhance our understanding of the existential context in which the stories of the present and the past are set, and reinforce the role of inward feelings, emotions. By referring to our memories to inform our understanding, we can't help but become a part of the inquiry. We become vulnerable to the criticism of others for thoughts, ideas and beliefs that are less than appropriate or ideal but that are our own nonetheless. In this way, narrative inquiry is a space in which individuals may reflect upon the experiences of others to inform their understanding of their own situa-

tions as well as use their own experiences to enhance the understanding of others about their situations.

2. *Reconstruction of Meaning . . . What do I make of the author's text? Do I agree with what the author is saying? What difference would this text make to my research?*

I thought of how I interpret the stories my parents and grandpar-
ents have told me about China to form an image of China as a very
primitive place to live. I doubt that my parents intended their
stories to invoke such a negative image of their home country but
when the stories, their memories, were told to me, I interpreted
them from the context of my own middle class upbringing in a
suburban Ottawa neighbourhood since I lacked the personal
experience to put the stories into the context in which my parents
had remembered them. In my neighbourhood, soup made with
bugs was not considered a delicacy, and my parents' response to
the extra work and mess of a pet dog or cat suggested to me that a
pig or cow wandering freely into and out of the house, as was done
in China, would be even messier and more work. I interpreted and
made meaning of my parents' memories by putting them into the
context of my own situation.

This story also addresses the issue of stereotypical notions of our
past selves. . . . I know that some of my ideas of China are stereotypical. Some of the stories I had heard about China presented it as a
place where I did not especially want to go. This image of China is
not something that I am proud of but it is one that was created
through stories of China that I heard from family members. The
stories were allowed to persist for lack of more accurate depictions
and from a lack of personal experience in China to refute them.
Nonetheless, it is important to present this image as I remember it
rather than changing the details to present myself in a better light
because the stories that are revealed through memories help me to
understand how the images and perceptions might have shaped my
image of China. To alter these memories to be more socially appropriate would be a form of deception, not only to others but to myself
as well.

At the same time, if memories were consciously altered to
present oneself in better light, they would be no less valid than one
based on an honest attempt to present the situation as "accurately"
as possible. Without a doubt, the stories would present the participant in [a] different light but both accounts would be equally valid.

3. *Reading at the Edges . . . What are the rubbing points with other works, values, methodologies in the field? What kind of critique would this work receive in a seminar/senate oral/conference?*

I could imagine that data based on stories and memories might be received with narrative criticism. There is an idea that research is a quest for understanding and knowledge but through narrative inquiry, I find that the more I learn, the more I realize the extent to which each situation, each event, is unique to the events and experiences that shaped it. Generalization and definitive answers are often not possible. Moreover, the extent to which each situation is only a mere speck in the context of a three-dimensional space further reinforces how much of the puzzle we are able to address. The whole thing is daunting. (Chan, 2000)

One of the first things we notice as Chan works through her reading log for week four is how she deepens her understanding of her experience. As she does this, she is becoming increasingly uncertain about how to approach her research in a credible, scholarly way. She creates stories of her parents' stories of China. They lived in China years ago, and she places these long-ago stories alongside her stories of growing up in Ottawa. Temporality has become an issue for her as she struggles to make sense out of the China her parents remember, the childhood she remembers, and her place in time now. Though she has never traveled to China it is becoming apparent why she chose He's dissertation. He grew up in China and had parents who experienced roughly the same place and time as did Chan's parents. He was now living in North America. Similarities and differences between Chan's story and He's story become important. At this point, for Chan, the focus is still very much on reconstruction of meaning as she struggles to figure out what she's going to do for her research and as she puts herself autobiographically in her research.

A third excerpt is from her reading log 5 weeks later (week nine). One of the readings for this week was Liebowitz's (1989) *Fabricating Lives: Explorations in American Autobiography.*

1. *Recovery of Meaning . . . What is the author saying?*

In the construction of a life through autobiography, many factors need to be taken into consideration. To begin with, the issue of fact versus fiction needs to be addressed. What is fact, and what is fiction? There is an assumption that since autobiography is the presentation of one's life, it must be based on "facts" and "truth." "Facts" are what we believe occurred but they cannot be "objective" since our understanding and interpretation of events is shaped by the ways in which we perceive them. The blurring of the distinction between "fact" and "fiction" becomes even more apparent when we take into consideration the role of experience and social circumstance in shaping the interpretation of the events—the ways in which we view "truth" may not be viewed as such by others. In this way, the writing of autobiographies may be considered the fabrication of lives since the ways in which we present our own life is based on our interpretation of events that may be very different from that perceived by another individual. In writing autobiographies, we are constructing or reconstructing our lives through the guidance of experience gained through events. For this reason, it might be more appropriate to view autobiography as the presentation of my life based on my understanding of the events and my history in the context of interaction with others. Moreover, the way in which the events are arranged is important.

2. *Reconstruction of Meaning . . . What do I make of the author's text? Do I agree with what the author is saying? What difference would this text make to my research?*

My own research begins with an autobiography, which includes events that I have identified as being influential in shaping my sense of identity as a Chinese Canadian. In presenting these events and stories, I am shaping the way in which I would like my readers to view me. It sounds hypocritical to say that I am committed to presenting my stories as honestly as I am able to do but to say at the same time that I acknowledge that I cannot help but select stories that present myself in a way that supports the message I would like to convey. I wondered also about whether the reader would be perceptive to the difference between making an honest attempt to present stories as I perceived them to occur, and purposely exaggerating or overlooking stories that might support or weaken my argument. How would the realization that such a deception would not be evident influence the value of autobiography as a source of information for research writing?

Moreover, in listening to and then presenting the stories of my participants, am I writing their biographies, reconstructing their autobiographies through my own experiences, or using their stories to strengthen my own autobiography?

3. *Reading at the Edges . . . What are the rubbing points with other works, values, methodologies in the field? What kind of critique would this work receive in a seminar/senate oral/conference?*

Positivists have set the standard that information gathered for the purpose of research must be "real" and based on "fact." Taking into consideration the role of past experience on shaping the way in which we perceive events in the present, I question the possibility of "fact" and "objectivity" especially when addressing issues concerning human beings and their interactions with one another. The use of autobiography as a means of accessing events of relevance to the development of ethnic identity addresses both issues of "fact" and "fiction," as well as issues of "subjectivity." (Chan, 2000)

In this log it is clear that she has made a commitment, at least a tentative one, to a narrative inquiry into her sense of identity as a Chinese Canadian. As she thinks her way through this narratively, and thinks about participants who might work with her, she raises her own questions at the boundaries. It is not as if she needs a formalistic or a reductionistic critic to make her work adequate. She raises her own questions and begins to think them through. In a sense, earlier in the course, she was imagining how different critics might criticize her work. She has now become more of a self-critic, trying to work out narrative pathways that satisfy her sense of appropriateness.

She is also worrying about the issue of narrative form as she thinks about the selection of stories that present a certain form of narrative coherence that she wishes to convey. She wonders about deception and the relation between stories and argument. In a very telling sentence, she wonders if, in her narrative form, she will be writing her participants' biographies, reconstructing their autobiographies, or using their stories to strengthen her own autobiography.

So far, in presenting Chan's work, we have shown two of the three narrative teaching practices: we have shown Chan learning to read an inquiry text in three ways, and we have shown how she is beginning to explore narrative forms of representation. In what follows, we give a fragment from her class presentation of He's inquiry journey, of which the dissertation is a part.

CHAN'S PRESENTATION OF HE'S DISSERTATION

Ming Fang He's dissertation is "a study of identity formation and cultural transformation of three Chinese women teachers as they moved back and forth between Chinese and Canadian cultures" (He, 1998; see Clandinin & Connelly, 2000, p. 50), while my study is a study of identity formation of a Chinese Canadian negotiating a Chinese identity while living in a Canadian context. Ming Fang begins with China as a reference point and moves into a North American context while I begin in a North American context and talk about ways of incorporating Chinese culture. We approach the study from different starting points but many of the issues addressed are similar. Our understanding develops in the three-dimensional space and it is humbling to acknowledge that although our own situations are unique and complicated due to the obvious and underlying influences of our personal circumstances and experiences, they are only dots in the three-dimensional inquiry space—there's so much more to know.

Ming Fang He (1998) used the idea of a composite autobiography, whereby the responses to stories told by each of her participants builds on earlier stories and elicits further stories to create a context of interconnectedness among the participants as their autobiographies unfolded. I thought this would be a fascinating way of learning about the development of an ethnic identity, while at the same time, providing a means of acknowledging the role of my own stories in shaping my sense of identity. In presenting our autobiographies in composite format, I would draw on the experiences of my participants to enhance my own understanding of the influence of the stories in shaping my sense of identity, while providing my participants with the opportunity to better understand the development of a sense of identity as well. (Chan, 2000)

This fragment is taken from a much longer printed text of the class presentation and of Chan's discussions with Ming Fang He both before and after the presentation. The presentation was a strong mixture of recovery of meaning and reconstruction of meaning. Chan presented He's work chapter by chapter using a recovery of meaning way of reading. Other members of the class, following this presentation along with its handout material, would know much about He's work. They would also know why and in what ways He's work was useful to Chan's inquiry.

This fragment was chosen to illustrate the second and third narrative teaching practices—to explore narrative forms of representation, and to imaginatively reconstruct another researcher's inquiry journey. Considerations of narrative form are seen in the second paragraph, where Chan imagines herself using He's idea of composite autobiography. Recovering the meaning of composite autobiography in He's study is the basis for Chan imagining how this form for collecting, organizing, and presenting stories could be used to give shape to her inquiry.

In the first paragraph Chan thinks through He's research journey alongside her own developing ideas. While both are Chinese Canadians, Chan develops a subtle comparative sense as she imagines each of their journeys within a three-dimensional narrative inquiry space, and realizes that they have come to be Chinese Canadians by different journeys. This understanding will make a difference to her inquiry.

SUMMARY

In this chapter we present a single narrative teaching exercise called dissertation presentation. This exercise is designed to carry three narrative teaching practices: learning to read an inquiry text in three ways, exploring narrative forms of representation, and imaginatively reconstructing another researcher's inquiry journey. We drew from Elaine Chan's reading logs from a doctoral-level course taken in the winter of 2000. The selections chosen for this chapter are designed to illustrate the exercise and its three associated teaching practices. Careful readers will notice, however, that these practices are not formulaic. Recovery creeps into reconstruction; reconstructive comments appear as she reads at the boundaries. References to He's dissertation fade in and out of prominence over the term. The exercise and its associated practices are intended as guides. Not all students were able to work with equal ease using the distinctions set up in the exercise. Furthermore, the exercise and its three narrative teaching practices are woven into a rather long list of other narrative exercises and narrative teaching practices throughout the term. For instance, to take the obvious, students are expected to share their reading logs in small groups and engage in dialogue about their different readings. This exercise and its practices are part of the life of our courses.

REFERENCES

Bernstein, R. J. (1987). The varieties of pluralism. *American Journal of Education,* *95*, 508–525.

Bloom, B. S. (Ed.). (1956). *Taxonomy of educational objectives*. New York: Longman.

Chan, E. (2000). *Reading logs for CTL4801H. Narrative and story in research and professional practice*. Ontario Institute for Studies in Education, University of Toronto.

Clandinin, D. J., & Connelly, F. M. (2000). *Narrative inquiry: Experience and story in qualitative research*. San Francisco: Jossey-Bass.

Connelly, F. M., & Clandinin, D. J. (1988). *Teachers as curriculum planners: Narratives of experience*. New York: Teachers College Press.

He, M. F. (1998). *Professional knowledge landscapes: Three Chinese women teachers' enculturation and acculturation processes in China and Canada*. Unpublished doctoral dissertation, University of Toronto.

Lagemann, E. C. (1996). *Contested terrain: A history of education research in the United States, 1890–1990*. Chicago: Spencer Foundation.

Liebowitz, H. (1989). *Fabricating lives: Explorations in American autobiography*. New York: Alfred A. Knopf.

Polanyi, M. (1958). *Personal knowledge: Towards a post-critical philosophy*. Chicago: University of Chicago Press.

CHAPTER 10

Action Research as Border Crossing: Stories from the Classroom

ANNE RATH

The last 10 years in Ireland have seen rapid and unprecedented social, demographic, political, and economic change, which has spawned an enormous societal reflection and reevaluation. Due recognition has been given to the vital link that educational investment has played in economic growth. However, alongside this recognition has been an acknowledgement of an underresourced bureaucratic educational system ill-prepared to meet the needs of a dynamic and changing society. A clear catalyst for this recognition came from the Organization for Economic Co-operation and Development Review of National Educational Policies (1991), which critiqued the dominance of a transmission model of teaching in Irish schools and the predominance of the conceptualization of teachers as "purveyors of facts and coaches for examinations." The report highlighted the necessity for educational change toward more "learner-centered, life-long" learning approaches in education, heralding a new focus on curriculum development.

Leonard & Gleeson (1999), in a review of these reform developments, identify a pervasive technical interest permeating them, and a "deep ambivalence about the practical meaning of such reform" (p. 56), especially as it relates to models of teacher education. They call attention to the gap between actual versus declared practice in Irish schools and the absence of any sustained debate around the purpose and practices of teacher education. In the same vein, Kellaghan (1999) states that there has been little change in teacher education models in the past quarter-century despite unprecedented cultural change. Teacher education has predominantly privileged theoretical knowledge over practical knowledge in many regards.

THE ACTION RESEARCH PROJECT

Against this backdrop of national curricular reform, the motivation for the Action Research (AR) was born. It coincided with the launch of the Revised Curriculum for Primary Schools, published in 1999, which heralded a new era of reform and attention on teacher professional development. It was recognized by the Irish National Teachers Union (INTO), the largest teacher union in Ireland and main sponsor of the project, that teachers' learning needs, as reflective practitioners and action researchers, deserved attention. For the previous 2 years I had consulted with the INTO on developing reflective practices in their professional development unit. The conversations around that work underscored the need to develop a partnership and learner-centered model of professional development over a sustained period as an alternative to the traditional 1-day or weeklong model already in place. An AR model was proposed, which would mirror the pedagogies and practices that the Revised Curriculum advocated teachers to embrace. The development of critical reflection was a key goal. From March 2000 through March 2001, a group of six teacher researchers came together for monthly meetings from diverse parts of Ireland to learn action research.

It is clear that the underpinning theoretical framework of the Revised Curriculum is learner-centered and constructivist. It highlights the active and situated nature of learning for children, and the central role that language and social context play in development. However, a brief look at how the Revised Curriculum has conceptualized the teacher is telling. Although the curriculum does acknowledge the pivotal role that teachers will play in its implementation, the teacher is still conceptualized unproblematically. Largely, the teacher and school are viewed as willing, passive, and committed partners in realizing the aspirations of the curriculum. The teacher is described as a "caring facilitator" and one "committed to a process of continuing professional reflection, development, and renewal" (Organization for Economic Co-operation and Development, 1991, pp. 20–21). This conceptualization of the idealized teacher and school begs a number of questions, which are central to the discussion in this chapter. Can we presume such commitment to reflection? Do teachers have the knowledge and resources to engage in continuing professional development, given what we know about the culture of schools and the problematic nature of reflection? What knowledge is uncovered when teachers engage in their own inquiry from a learner-centered perspective? In addition, questions relating specifically to this book can be posed. What were the dominant practices in the AR project? How were these narrative in nature? What function does narrative play? What evidence points to the validity of this work? And finally, can this work be considered a narrative exemplar?

MEANING IN CONTEXT:
DEVELOPING A DISCOURSE COMMUNITY

The six primary teachers who participated in the project were all female and came from diverse geographical locations in Ireland. Participants had an average of 15 years of teaching experience, ranging from the youngest member, Deirdre, who had been teaching 2 years and the oldest member, Maura, who had 28 years' experience (pseudonyms used for all participants). The participants identified six research areas to focus their inquiry:

1. Situated learning—developing social skills through the use of informational technology (IT)
2. A multicultural classroom—the integration of refugee children
3. Team teaching—moving the learning support teacher to center stage
4. Becoming a good friend—toward an understanding of social development
5. Visiting teachers for Travelers—redefining the role (Travelers are a distinct ethnic group whose traditional way of life is nomadic)
6. How preservice teachers use oral Irish in teaching

From the outset of the project, there was a conscious attention to the creation of a professional development model that acknowledged the social and active nature of learning, through the creation of a "community of inquirers" structure, where each community member became an active, responsive learning resource for the other. Partnership and active participation was key. Although the idea of a community of learners or discourse community is not new, the skill, disposition, and practice of becoming a responsive community member cannot be presumed. Acting in such a way within a professional context has to become an intentional practice and one that is given ongoing resource and attention. It is clear that the successful implementation of the Revised Curriculum presumes such a culture of thinking in schools without addressing the resource implication of fostering such a culture. Right throughout the project, participants had to be encouraged constantly to share their thinking with each other on an ongoing basis, to see this sharing as central to learning, and to pay attention to thinking as a dynamic process of engagement and change.

A lot of activities focused on getting participants into engaged, substantive conversations with each other about their projects. These included the practice of sharing preliminary drafts, research plans, research goals, problems, and contextual descriptions; responding to drafts; adopting a critical friend; staying in e-mail/phone contact; sharing reading; and so on. Initially, I consciously modeled the use of e-mailing reflections and questions, which also became an important data-generating tool, documenting the discussions and questions of our research meetings. Participants were encouraged to create a formal "critical friend" relationship with each other, a relationship that was committed to sharing and responding to ongoing thinking and writing.

There was a clear ethic of viewing research as a "work in progress," and viewing feedback as an essential part of learning. This involved an attention to the development of key thinking strategies, including learning to withhold judgment, focus on description, see thinking as interpretation and partial, and focus on asking generative questions. In order to support this practice, it was intentionally structured into meeting days, communicating its validity. Sarah, a learning support teacher, identified this practice as central to her learning. In developing a team-teaching approach to learning support in her school, she set up a collaborative discourse community with colleagues in her school:

> I would never have understood the implications of this work or stayed with it, without the support of the project. I now know the meaning of building collaborative relationships, and I see it as a process of talking together about our work. Teachers' written observations were so scant that I initially saw them as disengaged. It was only when I talked to them about what they observed that they could share what they knew. They made important links and observations, but they didn't see these as important enough to write down! What does this say about teachers and our sense of ourselves as knowers? Through the journal, I have now become my own critical friend, able to articulate my own learning needs, my questions, and my thinking. . . . But we need support and expertise on how to work collaboratively and how to use reflections. Without a caring and respectful group, I would have given up my attempts at the first obstacle.

Sarah is beginning to understand the complexity and necessity for engaged and committed conversations in building "collaboration" and a culture of inquiry in her school. This culture can generate useful data through "teacher observation" that leads to a deep knowledge and understanding about specific contextual needs.

DOMINANT PRACTICES: VOICE, NARRATIVE, AND AGENCY

The practice of engagement in one's own learning is difficult, and sus-taining that engagement over the busyness of school and family commit-ments is enormous. Participants talked of the difficulty to engage and the feelings of confusion, messiness, and uncertainty surrounding their re-search. In the beginning, the defining of practice problems well enough so that they could be studied, and identifying possible sources of data took enormous energy. The fear of "not doing it the right way" and won-dering where the project would lead was paramount. To counter this, teachers were encouraged to use "free writing" as a way of developing awareness of their thinking/interpretative process, and as a way of know-ing and viewing their knowledge landscapes. This was influenced greatly by Maxine Greene's (1978) concept of "wide-awakeness," where con-sciousness of our world pushes us toward social praxis and engagement, "a type of radical and participant knowing oriented to transforming the world" (p. 17).

From the outset, teaching was defined as a process of inquiry and uncertainty. This inquiry was modeled constantly in the structure of group meetings. The goal was always toward understanding teaching practices in a setting that acknowledged different interpretations, questions, and contexts. Actions and interventions would be generated from this inquiry and then closely documented and monitored in the various forms—obser-vations, journals, audios/videos, and collection of classroom evidence in-cluding student work and journals. Research presentations also would provide the action researcher with a context for explication, interpretation, and further reflection, thereby generating another cycle of thinking and action. Presentations became a key learning and teaching strategy, where the inquiry process could be modeled and practiced.

A core part of the project focused on developing an awareness of the teacher's own learning process, of learning how to sustain engagement with inquiry in contexts that do not support such wholehearted engagement. This involved taking a "step backward into the self" in order to move for-ward into an action intervention in their classrooms. The questions that teachers ask about their practice are indelibly linked to who they are and the contexts in which they work. Commitment and engagement to these questions is both cognitive and emotional in nature and must necessarily locate the teacher within the self as learner. The wholehearted nature of this kind of involvement and inquiry is critical for sustaining teachers in the practice of teaching as inquiry. Yet this aspect of professional develop-ment is often overlooked. Therefore, one of the key insights and questions that emerged for me toward the end of the project is: How do learners become wholehearted, responsible and open-minded in the learning process—three dispositions that Dewey (1933) identified as essential to the reflective process.

Evidence from this project suggests that narrative may be one way that teachers enter wholeheartedly into the learning process. The creation of a safe environment where both private and public stories can be told is a coconstructed community responsibility, and each story told and received opens the way for other stories, weaving connected webs of multilayered meanings. If stories are listened to with care and attention, and moved into a scrutiny of professional meanings and implications, then, they can become more expansive, uncover tacit understandings and assumptions, and move the actor into a more conscious and engaged practice.

Connelly & Clandinin (1990) define narrative inquiry as a process of telling and retelling stories of the lived experience of teaching and learning in order to live more expansive lives. However, the turn to narrative in professional education is a problematic one. For example, Bleakley (2000) calls attention to the confessional nature of narrative. There is validity in this criticism if personal exploration becomes an end in itself. But if concepts such as professional responsibility and agency are central to the learning process, by implication this moves the inquiry to the professional context of the actor. The actor is always acting in a context that carries its own accountability requirements. Explicating knowledge about this context leads to inquiry about effectiveness and professional responsibility. This demands a holding environment that provides both confirmation and contradiction (Kegan, 1982). Public scrutiny of what we know, how we know, and how these may influence action in particular contexts, become cognitive tools of a discourse community committed to development.

In the following excerpt, Maura's reflection speaks to this point. It highlights the importance of both the safety of the learning environment but also the importance of learning a new discourse. She uses the metaphors of being in a "safe house" and "offloading" to describe the support she receives at research meetings, and "embarking on a sea of adventure" to describe the learning process:

> I often came into these meetings tired and disengaged. I usually left feeling invigorated and ready to start again. It was a place to offload, but we went beyond that. . . . Being of a pragmatic nature, I would rarely have asked the question "Why?" much less have kept repeating it. . . . Many times Anne would good-humoredly say "STOP!" when the pragmatist in me would jump in with a fast solution instead of allowing my colleagues to analyze their own thoughts and practice. . . . You left feeling you had more questions

. . . you often lose direction and what you know seems invalid. But each time I came back to my classroom armed with a renewed sense of direction and hope. In class, we "sailed on a sea of adventure." Barriers became challenges. Threats became opportunities.

Here, Maura acknowledges how the practice of asking "why" becomes a new discourse tool that counters her pragmatic nature, a nature that routinely pushes her to the "fast solution," rather than staying with the uncertainty and messiness of "figuring it out." It validates the practice of the "figuring-out" process as a way of unpacking tacit embedded understandings. It also offers a contradiction to the invalidation that teachers feel about their own situated knowledge: "You often lose direction and what you know seems invalid." She identifies the need to "offload," pointing to the emotional surround of teaching and the great need for a discourse community. She links this to how teachers often "lose direction" without access to such a group. Because her "offloading" is received with care, she is free to move on to another plane of analysis and thinking. These practices are mirrored in the research project she engages with her fifth-grade students. She teaches her students how to listen with care, how to redraft thinking and ideas, and how to become a discourse community committed to inquiry and using each other as a resource.

Maura, after one of these research meetings, writes a poem entitled "Voiceless in the Classroom" to give "voice to not just my own frustration and lack of voice," but also "to those hundreds of committed teachers in the workplace, who are being stifled through the rigidity and bureaucracy used by agencies who feel threatened by questioning and enquiry." Embedded in Maura's reflection is a story about how teachers at a particular developmental stage may find schools particularly stifling and painful. The project reconnected her to important values and goals, animating her practice: "I was fired with an energy and enthusiasm, which had become only a distant memory."

The meanings of stories are not self-evident in and of themselves. Rather, these stories come to life in the conversations that are generated about them; in the retellings and illuminations of contexts that are necessary in the telling and in the listening; in the gathering of other experiences that resonate and help the participants to make sense of disparate pieces, and also in the "interrogation" of them as professional practices. Lyons (1998) defines reflection as an "intentional act of mind, engaging a person/s alone or in collaboration with others in interrogating a situation or subject of teaching or learning to construct an understanding of it . . . to shape action" (pp. 105–106). This engagement of mind in service of understanding becomes a powerful ground from which to practice teaching and to exercise professional judgment and action.

The dominant practices in the project structured an attention to voice, narrative, and agency. This grounded all reflections in the authority of the teacher as meaning maker, as interpreter, and as action researcher. The evidence from a teacher's classroom became a focal point for exploration and interpretation. Participants were challenged in these conversations to articulate tacit understandings of situated practices, to rethink their problems of practice, and "to make the familiar strange." With the validation of participants presenting their work and the adoption of a "critical friend" structure, the project validated the practice of listening with care and responding to another's "work in progress" as a necessary and required part of education. Thus, the emotional involvement of participants in both their own professional growth and other group member's professional growth was acknowledged.

ACTION RESEARCH AS REFLECTIVE PRACTICE

Action research, reflective practice, and narrative inquiry have all captured the imagination of the educational community in the last decades. However, within this literature, teacher reflection has been conceptualized variously and used to serve different purposes. Initially, I saw very little difference between the processes of becoming an action researcher and a reflective practitioner. However, from the beginning I critiqued action research models that focused too narrowly on technical aspects of "improving practice" without due acknowledgement to, and consideration of, the epistemological and value-laden nature of such a goal.

In the same vein, Leitch & Day (2000) argue that there has been insufficient attention given to both the nature of reflection in the action research process, and its relationship to purposes, processes, and outcomes. They challenge much of the rational, cognitive framing of reflection, and argue for giving more careful consideration to the reflective process itself. They also note the role that emotion plays in teacher development is underdeveloped. I believe emotional involvement plays a crucial role in the engagement process of practitioners and that this is centrally linked to narrative practices. Narrative practices give credence to the centrality of the values, histories, and beliefs that shape teachers' work. Thus, narrative practices give teachers permission to "own" their work within a value-laden frame, and to take responsibility for, and justify their actions, decisions, and judgments within a professional context.

ACTION RESEARCH AS BORDER CROSSING

The teacher as action researcher centrally casts the teacher as a border crosser, one who becomes committed and intentional about interrogating the borderland areas between the known and unknown from a situated, embodied perspective. Delgado-Gaitan (1997) argues for the necessity to create borderlands in our thinking: "Borderland suggests a space where multiple cultures, multiple consciousness, and multiple possibilities exist. . . . By remaining flexible, my psyche stretches, and I'm tolerant of ambiguity to understand my multiple identities and those of the other" (p. 37). Therefore, the teacher as border crosser must come into relationship with the self as an embodied, situated knower, a knowing that is often replete with ambiguities, uncertainties, tensions, and dilemmas. In so doing, the teacher is required constantly to step beyond the comfort of well-tested traditional boundaries and routines, and must by necessity generate a new discourse of personal meaning-making, responsibility, and agency.

In their engagement with their AR projects all participants had to inquire into their identities as teachers, mothers, trade union members, colleagues, and learners; their actions and reflections led to new ways of illuminating those identities, allowing them to view them as dynamic rather than fixed. Identities are linked inextricably to contexts and actions. This led to an inquiry about the political and ethical surround of teaching. This project fostered the creation of borderland spaces in thinking and action that invited engagement with uncertainties, ambiguities, and multiple identities. Teaching as a routinized activity rarely allows for such engagement. Indeed, the culture of teaching and schools often collude to cover up uncertainties and dilemmas. Practice tensions come to voice in the following vignette.

LEARNING TO ASK THE RIGHT QUESTIONS

Helen, a teacher of 4- to 5-year-olds for 13 years, initially focused her AR project on a "problem" student, who had not "settled in" and was creating havoc with other students. Her subsequent journaling and documentation broadens her question to the much larger frame of social development in general, and an attention to the habitual classroom routines she sees as necessary for developing a community, routines she has imposed and heretofore not questioned. Her gaze shifts to the assumptions underpinning these routines, and the meanings she brings to this work. In doing so, she has to ask about the meanings her students bring. Helen's project allows her to articulate an unexplored tension that surrounds her teaching: "I'm an organized person, I like to accomplish something tangible every day." However, "tangible" means "finishing a book," or "doing math." Although she values the social learning of her students, she realizes that she "evaluates" herself only by the "tangible accomplishments of the day," thus unconsciously devaluing the very work she deems as most valuable and necessary. Helen begins to see that she often sees this work as an interruption to the "real" work of teaching and feels pressured by the often unspoken expectations of others in the school community, including parents and colleagues, to achieve something tangible. This new consciousness fuels her decision to set aside a 30-minute daily period for social development, acknowledging the enormous learning curve that school poses for 4- to 5-year-olds, and taking responsibility for shaping this learning in a systematic intentional way:

> It is a mammoth and often unrecognized task that confronts Junior Infant teachers who have to gather 30 or so egocentric beings and gather them together to form a community aware of each other, able to cooperate and collaborate, listen, pay attention, and learn. As important as learning the concept 5 (teaching the numeral 5) students need to learn these social skills and I need to teach them, revise them constantly as the class changes, as new conflicts arise.

During this inquiry process, Helen learns to validate what she knows as essential and valuable. She engages in a number of practices that are essentially learner-centered. Rules, routines, and interventions are now viewed as dynamic rather than fixed. Rules are negotiated and revised constantly, and the diverse meanings children bring to these rules are acknowledged and explored through open discussion, drawing, drama, and art. Morning meetings become a space for children to raise their own questions and concerns. She views her own modeling of relationship building as a key teaching strategy.

Up to this point, Helen framed the "settling in" period for children as one where children were expected to adapt to her imposed routines. Now it is reframed as a two-way learning process—her adapting the environment to meet the diverse needs of children as well as their adaptation to a new environment. She documents her research in various ways, using her students as co-inquirers by introducing conflict diaries—children recording their conflicts, talking about them, and exploring different ways of resolving them. She begins to see the morning meeting as a reflection time for children: "Children too need opportunities to reflect each day."

Here Helen brings what seemed like two competing values—accomplishing tangible things and social development—into dynamic and engaged relationship, fostering an important reframing and redirection of energies. Although Helen always knew the importance of the "settling in" period on an intuitive level, she invalidated its importance by leaving it to the margins of her practice. She now has translated this to her practice in a systematic structured way. Doing so required a different capacity in terms of partnership building with students. She questions her previous mode of conflict resolution where she often adopted a "one model fits all" approach. She has learned now that skillful teaching hinges on "asking the right question" and being open to working with the diversity of students.

Embedded in her practice now is an attention to children as meaning makers and constructors of knowledge, mirroring the pedagogy of the Revised Curriculum and the AR project. The morning meeting becomes a discourse community and teaching becomes linked to knowing how students make sense of their world. Children are becoming engaged in lifelong learning capacities: learning how to evaluate themselves, to make observations, to record and review their actions, and thus becoming responsible community members. Helen connects her experience of the AR research group, where she learned to "explain, to elaborate, and to justify [her] actions," to what she now structures consciously into her classroom. In addition, Helen knows on a new level that intentionality and responsibility are necessary for learning: "One can be thinking about a concern but it doesn't become reflection until we try to make sense of it. Writing helps me know the situation at a much deeper level."

HOW VALID IS THE KNOWLEDGE THAT TEACHERS GAIN?

Deirdre, the youngest teacher in the project, recounts her new capacity for dealing with the assignment of two new visually impaired children to her classroom in the middle of the school year. Her growing understanding of the implications for such a change for her effectiveness in meeting the needs of her other students, and her ability to articulate this publicly, give her the courage to ask for a meeting structure that would facilitate the integration of these new students. Teaching in a challenging inner-city environment with a very supportive staff and dynamic principal who are already involved in many different government-funded interventions in educational disadvantage, Deirdre was already feeling under pressure in attempting to meet the needs of a multicultural classroom. Her research documents the attempts she makes to integrate refugee children into her classroom. From this work she has come to know that adding two visually impaired Travelers will have enormous implications for herself, for her other students who are just beginning to settle, and for the assigned students themselves. She is now able to articulate this complexity and able to ask for what she needs: "I would never have had the courage to speak up without this project. I have learned that what I am doing is complicated, deserves time, and support."

This crucially captures one valid source of knowledge that is gained from involvement in the AR project. Bolstered by her own growing knowledge and the conversations of critical friends in the AR group, she realizes she has a valid professional claim in asking for a meeting structure that would support her work and her students' integration. Furthermore, she knows that a meeting structure that acknowledges the complexity of integrating new students into her classroom is a practice that will change the nature of knowledge about those students, and about teaching and learning itself. She places responsibility for this work on the larger school community expanding her sphere of influence and crossing borders. In so doing she becomes an advocate for herself as a professional and for her students as learners. The importance of moving outside the confines of the classroom for teachers generally, but especially for a beginning teacher, to talk about the substantive work of teaching and learning cannot be underestimated in an Irish context.

Claire, a visiting teacher for Travelers for 18 years, had always questioned policies that foster a "culture of dependency" with Travelers. Her research heightens her awareness of her collusion with this framing insofar as she has not explicitly validated consultation with Travelers as central to her work profile. She now reframes her work to be one centrally concerned with researching what Traveler families need and building a partnership relationship with them. She locates this work within the larger political sphere and within an antiracist agenda. She brings her ongoing work with community groups to center stage where heretofore she had seen it as marginal to her work. Her research documents the consultation process she initiates by setting up a series of focus group meetings with Traveler parents, children, teachers, principals, and her colleagues. Although Claire has always valued the voices of Traveler parents and students, she says that this was more on a "theoretical" level than a clear justifiable practice.

The project gives Claire an opportunity to question where her work focus should be, and to critique an educational system that purports to serve Traveler families on the one hand, whilst on the other, not providing adequate or meaningful resources. She realizes that policy makers need to be educated about the work involved in integrating Travelers into mainstream education. With a client base of over 200 families stretching over a large geographical area, she comes to understand that the structure of the work itself is problematic. In her research with colleagues, she learns that many of them have received little or no training in antiracist work and largely work in isolation and without support and with similar problems.

Claire gains confidence in articulating the knowledge and expertise she has gained from 18 years of practice. The AR project gives her a space to articulate the assumptions and values that underpin her practice and the dilemmas and tensions she feels in working between two cultural systems. It also sustains her in her move toward translating into practice the much acclaimed and government-sponsored values of "consultation" and "partnership" between schools, parents, and Travelers. It helps her view her work from a number of perspectives and expands her sphere of influence to working with colleagues, schools, principals, and so on. She now sees her work to be primarily one of providing spaces for all partners to come into conversation with each other and to open up the "problem" of Traveler integration for all in the community to solve and linked to a larger antiracist frame.

HOW IS THIS WORK PROBLEMATIC?

The story told here has subjugated the problematics and uncertainties that surrounded this AR project to a certain extent. Multiple other stories lie embedded in this project—stories of structural obstacles; the geographical spread of participants; the amount of time, effort, and practice it takes to "animate" and engage adult learners without public structures that credential and validate that work; and the invalidation that occurs when the complexity of teaching is not acknowledged and when inquiry is not part of teaching and learning contexts. Another problematic element is the lack of professional resources that these teacher researchers faced, including access to professional reading, discourse communities, computer facilities, reflective time and space. Without access to professional resources and a discourse group, teachers may be left within their own frame of reference and an enormous amount of energy and spirit is lost.

CONCLUSION

All participants in their engagement and commitment to the project demonstrated the emergence of new thinking and pedagogies; thinking and pedagogies that attended to the complexity and situatedness of teaching. These engagement practices, as well as their practice interventions in their classrooms, had to become "intentional acts of mind." Without committed professional relationships these practices would not have been sustained. From this engagement, participants no longer expected easy answers to their questions but expected questions to generate deeper understandings and lead to more inquiry. Evidence here suggests that narrative was used by participants both as an entry point to explaining the situatedness and accompanying tensions surrounding teaching, and also as a way of sustaining interest and engagement in their work on a deeper level. Stories also were used as a way for participants to respond to each other's work, and to demonstrate their understanding of different contexts, thus forging and generating new connections and knowledge. The possibility to share and tell practice stories in a professional public sphere was experienced by all participants as a profound contradiction to the isolation and invalidation that teaching engenders. The discourse community of peers acted as a sounding board for them and fostered a necessary recommitment and reconnection to values, self-knowledge, and ideals. This became a valid professional ground, which sustained them in their inquiries and empowered them to advocate for themselves and their students in new ways.

REFERENCES

Bleakley, A. (2000). Writing with invisible ink: Narrative, confessionalism and reflective practice. *Reflective Practice*, *1*(1), 11–23.

Connelly, F. M., & Clandinin, D. J. (1990). Stories of experience and narrative inquiry. *Educational Researcher*, *19*(5), 2–14.

Delgado-Gaitan, C. (1997). Dismantling borders. In A. Neumann & P. Peterson (Eds.), *Learning from our lives*. New York: Teachers College Press.

Dewey, J. (1933). *How we think*. Chicago: University of Chicago Press.

Greene, M. (1978). *Landscapes of learning*. New York: Teachers College Press.

Kegan, R. (1982). *The evolving self*. Cambridge, MA: Harvard University Press.

Kellaghan, T. (1999). Introduction. In M. Killeavy (Ed.), *Towards 2010: Teacher education in Ireland over the next decade*. Dublin: IFUT.

Leitch, R., & Day, C. (2000). Action research and reflective practice: Towards a holistic view. *Educational Action Research*, *8*(1), 179–193.

Leonard, D., & Gleeson, J. (1999). Context and coherence in initial teacher education in Ireland: The place of reflective inquiry. In *Teacher Development*, *3*(1), 49–65.

Lyons, N. (1998). (Ed.). *With portfolio in hand*. New York: Teachers College Press.

Organization for Economic Co-operation and Development. (1991). *Review of national policies for education: Ireland*. Paris: Author.

CHAPTER 11

Narrative Research in Teacher Education: New Questions, New Practices

HELEN FREIDUS

Over the course of the past few years, Penelope Peterson has been raising a new set of questions about validity in educational research. Motivated by her son's questions about the relationship between her work on educational reform and the reality of his classroom experiences, she has taken up his challenge: "What good are you doing anyway?" (Peterson, 1998, p. 4). Why, she wonders, have the contributions of research had so limited an influence on teachers and policy makers? If research findings are only considered significant by other researchers, how meaningful can they be? What can we do to make the discourse of our work more inclusive, more relevant, more valid?

This chapter suggests that the use of narrative inquiry as a methodological tool may be one possible answer to Peterson's questions. Drawing upon data gathered during a 3-year study of a literacy implementation in an urban school district, this chapter illustrates how conversations held within the context of data-generating focus groups serve as an exemplar of narrative research practice. These conversations appear to function as both a research methodology and a professional development tool. Through the dialogue that ensues, researchers gain a more deeply layered understanding of the dynamics they are studying; teachers gain insight into their own practices and those of their colleagues.

How, one asks, can conversations—even conversations within focus groups—be considered narratives? A careful analysis of transcripts from these sessions demonstrates that through the conversations a wide range of stories were told: stories of practice, stories of context, the kinds of stories that Jean Clandinin and Michael Connelly (1996) refer to as "stories to live by" (p. 29), that is, stories of dreams and goals. These conversations began with the retelling of personal experiences. Over time, as one teacher built on the voice of another, the conversations generated collective narratives.

In these stories, the descriptors that characterize the narrative genre can be clearly identified. Individual stories are introduced by a set of details that orient researchers and participants alike to the "who, what, where, and when" that characterize the context in which the literacy implementation has been taking place. As in Barbara Kingsolver's *Poisonwood Bible* or Amy Tan's *The Joy Luck Club*, by allowing the pieces of the stories to unfold in a natural way, participants, researchers, and teachers alike also began to understand the "why."

Together, the individual stories narrated a sequence of events that brought to life what Sarason (1982) called the "prehistory" of the people involved. The composite retelling of this prehistory—experiences and relationships, attempted innovations and implementations—enabled both researchers and teachers to look at current experiences in more complex ways. Moreover, the retelling exposed tensions that had been adding drama to the change process that was being explored. And, while the telling and retelling did not lead to a state of resolution, the traditional conclusion of a completed narrative, it did bring participants to a vantage point from which tellers and listeners could look both backward and forward in more informed ways.

Thus, the narrative experience led to a construction of shared meaning about what was and what had been. For example, the change process on which this study focused was a form of literacy instruction developed in Australia. By sharing their experiences in a safe forum (one of the tutor focus groups), two professional developers helped each other and the researchers to come to a better understanding of why participants were feeling so very overwhelmed:

> This is a new program. No one has gone before us and set it up. No one can tell us, This will happen and then this will happen, and then it will work like this. . . . We've got somebody coming from another country who tells us they have used it in their country and it has been successful, but we have not been eyewitnesses to it.

> It would be different if I had used this in my classroom. But, we have never used it in our own rooms and now we are going to show somebody else how to use it. That is very difficult.

DEVELOPING A METHODOLOGY

How did these narratives come to be told? Our study was a 3-year feder-
ally funded collaboration between an urban school district, a publishing
company, and a graduate school of teacher education. It was designed as
a descriptive study, documenting the changes in teachers and students that
ensued from the implementation of First Steps, a new approach to the teaching of writing, an approach that emphasized the importance of ongoing
professional development over time. Two faculty members from Bank
Street College, the graduate school of teacher education, served as principal investigators.

The research goal was to capture the process of instructional change
by documenting changes in both instructional pedagogy and student performance and exploring the relationship between the two. Case study
methodology was chosen to enable researchers to seek out continuities,
consistencies, and patterns of meaning within a complex environment.

As researchers, we believe that teachers know a great deal about what
works and what does not work in their classrooms. We also believe that
descriptions of change processes need to take into consideration the perspectives of teachers over time. Moreover, as teacher educators as well
as researchers, we brought to the table a belief that one should take ad-
vantage of every opportunity to help teachers recognize how much they
know. We saw narrative inquiry as a tool that would provide teachers
with a way of adding their own expertise to the dominant voices in the
field. Taking the paradigmatic stance that all inquiry is value bound, all
knowledge is context bound (Lincoln & Guba, 1985; Putney, Green, Dixon,
& Kelly, 1999), we sought out research tools compatible with this double
agenda.

In developing the specifics of the research design, we hoped to ensure
the accuracy of our findings by cutting the distance between researchers
and "subjects of the study." We wanted to consider issues from the situated perspective of the teachers with whom we were working and to enable them, in turn, to consider these same issues from our perspectives and
the perspectives of other teachers and administrators within the same district. We wished to avoid the trap that Hargreaves describes: "Instead of
searching for and listening appreciatively to voices that differ, voices that
jar, voices that might even offend, we are perhaps too ready to hear only
those voices that broadly echo our own" (1996, p. 13).

Most of all, we hoped that this design might make the experience of
collaboration as fruitful for the teachers who had agreed to work with us
as we anticipated it would be for ourselves. We saw our focus groups as

forums for reflection, problem solving, and community building, forums that have been identified as essential components of adult learning and professional development (McLaughlin, 1991; Wilson, Peterson, Ball, & Cohen, 1996). We were not vested in the success or failure of the implementation we were studying, but rather in understanding *why* it was succeeding or failing and helping teachers and administrators to do the same. We believed that engagement in narrative processes—conversation and storytelling—would lead us to this understanding.

We posited that by using a combination of interviews and focus groups, we could: 1) triangulate our data; and 2) encourage participants to revisit questions in different contexts and different forms. We anticipated that some individuals would be more comfortable in a one-to-one discussion, others among a group of their peers. In either case, we speculated that the opportunity to reflect upon practice individually and collectively would create an important form of data check.

As it worked out, some teachers participated only in interviews; others participated only in focus groups. We found that, as anticipated, our richest understandings of the implementation process emerged from interactions with those teachers whom we met in multiple settings, over time. However, we found that individual conversations, be they in the context of interviews or focus groups, also served a critical function. The more perspectives we were able to access, the more we were challenged to abandon our own conscious and subconscious preconceptions and look at what was happening in new ways.

PROCEDURE

In each year of the study, we invited interested teachers at each school to join us three times for an hour of refreshments and conversation related to the implementation process. We offered a stipend commensurate with the hourly reimbursement rate specified by the teachers' union. Approximately 60 teachers, 15 to 20 at each school, agreed to participate in the series of sessions. To better ensure that each teacher would have an opportunity to actively participate in the discussion, when the numbers rose above 15 at a given school, we broke into 2 groups, each facilitated by 1 or 2 researchers.

The sessions during the first year were quite open-ended. After a brief description of our research and the purpose of the focus groups, we would begin with a question like, At this point in the year, what are you thinking about as you implement First Steps in your classroom? We chose this kind of open-ended query for several reasons:

1. We wanted to learn as much as we could about the participants—
   their perspectives on literacy, on pedagogy, on their students, on
   the implementation process.
2. We wanted to see how teachers would enter into the process of
   sharing experiences in a group setting.
3. We wanted to create a safe space, a space in which participants
   would feel comfortable telling their stories and listening and responding to the stories of others.

Recognizing that as outsiders, we could easily be perceived as "experts," evaluators, or professional developers in the traditional sense of the
term, we worked to offset this image. We sat in a circle around a table. We
used first names. We brought food. We shared our own stories about learning new things and, in a chatty way, about our experiences visiting in their
classrooms. We tried our hardest to make it clear that we were not there to
give answers or to judge but to learn from and with them.

We worked hard to engender dialogue. We welcomed all responses.
At first, teachers seemed to worry that they might be giving the wrong
answer or the wrong impression. In the first year, many were tentative or,
at the opposite extreme, strident. This suggested to us that they were not
fully comfortable with the context of collaborative critique. As in most
groups, our challenge as facilitators was to find a way to nurture the voices
of some and the listening skills of others. As researchers, our ongoing challenge was to be true to our charge: to look for patterns, to put forth hypotheses, to avoid premature conclusions, and—above all—to avoid making judgments.

We found that there tended to be a pattern in the dynamics of the
meetings. The sessions would begin with the most positive comments.
Teachers would speak out about the ways in which First Steps helped
them to understand their students' progress, gave them useful instructional strategies, and generally strengthened their writing curriculum.
Then, as the session progressed, one teacher would softly say, "But I do
feel overwhelmed."

At this point, a richer dialogue would begin—complications in the
story line, sometimes agreement, sometimes controversy. Each teacher
would tell her story, first just snippets, then, building on each other's words,
longer anecdotes, until, at the end of a session, we had heard and reheard
many, many variations on a theme. Sometimes it was a struggle to elicit
these stories; sometimes the conversation flowed.

By the end of the first year's sessions, we found that most participants were increasingly comfortable with the narrative process of the

focus groups. We became familiar with certain story lines that were repeated from school to school. One set of stories clustered around teachers' growing comfort with the teaching of writing; a second important
set clustered around the tension and discomfort of learning a new way
of teaching.

We saw dialogue growing within each group and were heartened by
it, but at the same time, we found that we were not hearing about some
topics relevant to our research questions. It seemed that we had gone as
far as we could go with this structure. Therefore, we decided to make the
next set of focus groups somewhat more guided.

When we invited teachers to join the second year's series of focus
groups, we gave them a topic to think about in preparation for the discussion. Before the first session we wrote:

> At our next meeting, we would like to learn more about the ways in
> which you are using the Developmental Continuum and the Class
> Profile [tools for recording children's literacy behaviors] to plan
> instruction. We would also like to talk about the specifics of other
> First Steps techniques that have become part of your literacy
> program.

Before the second session, we asked:

> Please reflect on those First Steps writing techniques that you have
> found most helpful and those that have been most challenging.
> What do you think has made the difference?

We discovered that posing the questions in advance enriched the conversation *provided that* the questions related to the teachers' interests and
concerns. For example, no matter how resourcefully the researchers delved
into their repertoire of facilitation strategies, the groups were unwilling or
unable to sustain dialogue around the Developmental Continuum. Some
groups were finding it useful, others not, but neither group enthusiasti-
cally joined in discussion.

In contrast, discussions in which teachers shared helpful instructional
strategies were animated and lengthy. Ways of using the Developmental Continuum may have been of primary interest to the researchers, but
the teachers' primary focus was on the instructional strategies they were
learning. The most effective focus groups were clearly those in which
the topics of discussion were directly relevant to teachers' needs and
interests.

MAKING SENSE OF THE NARRATIVES

The sense-making process (data analysis) began with the first conversations in Year 1. Steeped in the literature of literacy education, school reform, and the learning processes of both adults and children, the researchers were sensitive to categories that might emerge. However, there was no prior commitment to these categories. On the contrary, the primary goal was to follow the stories as they emerged. Researchers sought to engage in their own constructivist process as they documented the teachers' construction of knowledge.

Following each focus group, the three researchers engaged in a retelling of what happened. Experiences were summarized and emergent insights and questions were articulated. We revisited past conversations seeking to confirm or challenge what we thought we had heard. Frequently, these insights and questions were then shared in teacher focus groups. For example, we might say, "In the focus groups we had on Monday, teachers talked about how First Steps was helping them to recognize the importance of modeling instruction on an ongoing basis. How do you feel about this?" As teachers confirmed or challenged the perceptions of their colleagues and/or the researchers, they contributed a valuable member check (Lincoln & Guba, 1985) on current interpretations of the implementation process.

At the end of Year 2, themes and categories that had emerged were used to construct an initial set of conclusions. These were shared with teachers and administrators in meetings and focus groups/feedback sessions. The goal in these sessions was to be both positive and candid, to acknowledge the tremendous effort that was being made, to affirm the progress we saw, but also to put hard questions on the table. The responses from these sessions were used to inform the data collection in Year 3.

MEASURES OF PROGRESS

As we moved into Year 3, we began to search for evidence that the research was actually serving as a professional development tool. We talked about this in focus groups, looked for evidence in transcripts and, at the beginning of the 3rd year of the study, we administered a survey designed to elicit more specific evidence about teachers' perceptions of the impact of our research on their school communities. The survey was composed of five open-ended questions.

Although we anticipated that this open-ended format might discourage some teachers from responding, we nonetheless felt that such a structure was most consistent with our goal of hearing and representing the voices of participants. We felt it would be better to receive fewer responses than to risk premature structuring of participants' thoughts and feelings. As it worked out, we distributed 60 surveys to focus group participants and received 15 responses from participants.

The responses that we received suggested that, at least with this core of teachers, we were meeting our goal of providing professional development through the conduct of research. Three significant themes emerged from the responses: validation, community, and professional growth. These themes were then triangulated through data that had emerged in transcripts of teacher interviews and focus groups and in transcripts of interviews with administrators and professional development personnel. The responses quoted below were typical.

Validation

Respondents spoke of the ways in which focus groups validated their professional identity as teachers: "The group discussion helped me to feel that I was on the right track, that the things I have been doing in my classroom all these years were worthwhile." They also referred to the ways in which participation in the research process acknowledged and validated the effort they were making to change the ways they structured their classrooms: "Individual teachers (and the group as a whole) received affirmation that they were making positive changes in their practices."

Teachers emphasized that these efforts to restructure their instructional practice were difficult and anxiety provoking. They made it very clear that they needed the support provided by the ongoing group discussions: "Our meetings with the research team have helped to make us more accountable in our struggle to make writing more meaningful. They have helped us to see that our efforts in taking risks do count."

Community

The teachers who participated in the focus groups were engaged in a common goal, the implementation of First Steps. They did not, however, all share the same beliefs about teaching and learning. Survey responses suggested that the conversations in focus groups helped teachers to move beyond their own personal perspectives, to explore new ways of thinking about their own practice and that of their colleagues. As one participant put it:

The focus groups have given me an opportunity to listen to others share successes and ask questions that I might not have considered. . . . They helped keep the dialogue going between teachers who might not otherwise have had the opportunity to keep communication open.

Another response voiced similar feelings even more candidly: "The groups have helped to bring together a difficult staff and make writing a priority."

Teachers wrote that focus group conversations provided "an opportunity to learn from each other and to gain insight into our students' experiences as well as our own." The discussions reminded teachers that they and their colleagues had a collective pool of expertise that could be put to good use on an ongoing basis: "The group was always beneficial. I found that I learned more from sharing with coworkers than I did in any workshop. I believe we are the most valuable resources we have."

Professional Growth

Survey response after survey mentioned that the groups "kept us focused." Teachers were quite clear that participation in the ongoing conversations had promoted their own professional growth: "Being part of the research study kept First Steps on the front burner for me and kept it from becoming something I would use once in a while. I am now very aware of its impact on my class."

Teachers discussed the ways in which these conversations helped them to become more reflective and more assiduous in the implementation process: "The study has encouraged us to closely examine how we are implementing First Steps and to continuously find ways to improve our implementation." They made reference to the ways in which the forum provided by focus groups enabled them to acquire new skills and new ways of being in the classroom:

> I have learned a great deal from being a participant in the focus groups. I have learned how other teachers are using First Steps and come away with many new ideas. I think I am more thoughtful in the way I use First Steps due to my involvement in the focus groups.

Individual interviews and classroom observations were also cited as contributing to implementation success. As researchers, we had been fearful that we might be intrusive. We struggled with the tension between wanting to ensure that teachers felt affirmed and wanting to ask hard questions that would further reflective practice and engage voices in a discussion of hard issues. We found that it was possible to do this but that it took time, practice, and patience. As teachers began to see that we were sincere in our stance of wanting to know what they knew, they began to be more and more willing to tell us their stories and show us who they were as professionals. In doing this, they pushed themselves more and more to integrate the implementation process into their ongoing classroom practices:

> The presence of the Bank Street ladies has kept us on our toes—particularly those of us who have had visitors in the classroom. It has motivated us to try many of the activities in the First Steps resource book to see if they are useful or not. It has encouraged us to do long-term planning that integrated reading and writing so that our visitors could see the growth made by the students.

CONCLUSION

We know that schools as institutions tend to isolate teachers, compromise their decision-making abilities, and encourage them to become dependent on the opinions of outside experts and evaluators (Fullan, 1993; Hargreaves, 1996; Lortie, 1975; Sarason, 1982). These data suggest that narrative research practices that encourage and support teachers to share and reflect upon the stories of their own practice serve in some small way to counteract these conditions. As in those conversations reported by Belenky et al. (1997), hearing and sharing stories appears to have enabled participants to "get beyond their own mess," nurture new habits of mind, and engage meaningfully in the tasks at hand.

The teachers who collaborated in narrative research practices over the 3 years of the study began to develop:

- A better understanding of self and context
- A growing awareness of the needs of children and the ways in which these needs can and should drive curriculum
- A greater repertoire of instructional strategies
- A vision of themselves as a community of learners
- A stronger foundation for working collegially and collaboratively

The influence of the focus groups on the last is particularly significant. As teachers shared stories, they began to understand the thinking and caring behind the teaching of colleagues whose classroom practice frequently looked quite different from their own. With this understanding, they could begin to see these teachers as supports rather than barriers to their own efforts to help students learn.

CAVEATS

This study does not suggest that narrative inquiry is a panacea for changing the attitudes of teachers and policy makers toward research. Not all teachers chose to participate in these groups, and of those who did only 25% responded to the survey on which much of the evidence for this chapter is based. While the faithful, prompt attendance of most participants suggests that the sessions were in some way satisfying, we cannot be certain that all voices are being fully represented.

Moreover, the study does not suggest that all forms of narrative research practices will elicit the kinds of responses we are describing. Reflection on our own process suggests that there were several reasons for the success that has been documented. First and foremost, participating teachers were committed to the implementation around which the discussions revolved. Teachers wanted to learn more about First Steps; they were eager to hear the stories of their colleagues' experiences.

Secondly, we, as facilitators and researchers, brought a set of beliefs and a fund of knowledge that shaped the nature of the conversations. We began with a genuine interest in what teachers had to say. We knew that their perspectives were essential to our understanding of the reform process. We were outsiders; we could not know what had happened in years or administrations gone by. This gave us permission to ask questions that put many hidden issues on the table for reexamination.

We came to these conversations, inevitably, with our own biases and assumptions, but we worked hard to keep these from getting in our way. Over time, we found that our own conversations coupled with the focus group conversations were gradually leading us to modify our perspectives. As we reflected on our own learning, we shared our process with the teachers. This was not always easy to do; it required us to depart from the more secure stance of "expert researcher" and assume a more vulnerable collaborative stance. Making the effort to engage in this more open relationship proved to be worthwhile but anxiety provoking. In retrospect, we came to realize that this form of sharing provided a model of reflection-in-action (Schön, 1984), a model that helped both us and the teachers with whom we worked to engage in a more open exploration of the meaning of authority and professional stance.

Moreover, as stated before, our kit of research tools included individual interviews and classroom observations across the four schools. These enabled us to come to the focus groups with additional insights into the real world of these teachers, their classrooms, and their students. We were able to draw on these insights to model the storytelling process.

We could also invite teachers to share with their colleagues' relevant experiences we had observed in their classrooms. Over time, the transcripts show that our prompts became fewer; teachers became independent storytellers who invited and encouraged their colleagues to do the same.

Finally, we, as researchers, came from an institution in which a form of focus groups called conference groups serve as the core of the teacher-education curriculum (Antler, 1987; Ayers, 1991; Shapiro & Nager, 1999). Consequently, in addition to our understanding of theory and practice in the field of literacy, we brought a background of experience in adult development, teacher development, and group dynamics. This helped us, as facilitators, to keep our eye on the goal of engaging teachers in conversation when the dynamic of early groups would have made it easy to drift into a format of questions and answers. And, even with all our experience, we did not see the beginnings of the narrative flow for which we were striving until the end of the first year. Had our meetings been more frequent, monthly rather than every 2 to 3 months, the process might well have moved more quickly. Nonetheless, the data suggest that the responses we received were in many ways related to the amount of time that we were willing and able to invest in the process.

And yet, with all of these caveats, the data strongly support the supposition that the use of narrative inquiry as a methodological tool offers new possibilities for both the conduct and impact of research. When conversation in caring contexts is used as a research tool, it engenders a coconstruction of knowledge by researchers and practitioners that is more inclusive, more meaningful, and more valid. It helps teachers to know more . . . and to know that they know more.

REFERENCES

Antler, J. (1987). *Lucy Sprague Mitchell: The making of a modern woman*. New Haven, CT: Yale University Press.

Ayers, W. (1991). Spreading out its roots: Bank street advisement and the education of a teacher. *Thought and practice*, 3(1), 25–29.

Belenky, M. F., Bond, L. A., & Weinstock, J. S. (1997). *A tradition that has no name*. New York: Basic Books.

Clandinin, D. J., & Connelly, F. M. (1996). Teachers' professional knowledge landscapes: Teacher stories—stories of teachers—school stories—stories of schools. *Educational Researcher*, 25(3), 24–30.

Education Department of Western Australia. (1996). *First steps*. Melbourne, Australia: Addison Wesley Longman.

Fullan, M. (1993). *Change forces: Probing the depths of educational reform.* New York: Falmer Press.

Hargreaves, A. (Jan./Feb., 1996). Revisiting voice. *Educational Researcher, 25*(1), 12–19.

Kingsolver, B. (1998). *The poisonwood bible.* New York: HarperCollins.

Lincoln, Y. S., & Guba, E. G. (1985). *Naturalistic inquiry.* Newbury Park, CA: Sage.

Lortie, D. (1975). *School teacher.* Chicago: University of Chicago Press.

McLaughlin, M. W. (1991). Enabling professional development. In A. Lieberman and L. Miller (Eds.), *Staff development for education in the 90's: New demands, new realities* (pp. 61–82). New York: Teachers College Press.

Page, R., Samson, Y., Crockett, M. (1998, Fall). Reporting ethnography to informants. *Harvard Educational Review, 68*(3), 299–333.

Peterson, P. (1998, April). Why do educational research? Rethinking our roles and identities, our texts and contexts. *Educational Researcher, 27*(3), 4–10.

Putney, L., Green, J., Dixon, C., & Kelly, G. (1999, July/August/September). Evolution of qualitative research methodology. Looking beyond defense to possibilities. *Reading Research Quarterly, 34*(3), 368–377.

Sarason, S. (1982). *The culture of the school and the problem of change.* (2nd ed.). Boston: Allyn & Bacon.

Schön, Donald. (1983). *The reflective practitioner.* New York: Basic Books.

Shapiro, E., & Nager, N. (1999). *A progressive pedagogy: Legacies and new directions.* Albany: SUNY Press.

Tan, A. (1989). *The joy luck club.* New York: Vintage.

Wilson, S., Peterson, P., Ball, D. L., & Cohen, D. K. (1996). Learning by all. *Phi Delta Kappan, 77*, 468–476.

CHAPTER 12

Professional Conversations: New Teachers Explore Teaching Through Conversation, Story, and Narrative

FRANCES O'CONNELL RUST

Christie is a first-year teacher with a fourth-grade class in Brooklyn. It was my first visit to her class, the first time, in fact, that I had ever seen Christie teach. From reading her work when she was a student and listening to her conversation, I had a pretty good idea about what I'd see. So, we spent the day together. I watched as she and her class of 27 kids got through drug education with a "specials" teacher first thing in the morning. Then I watched as the class moved into individual silent reading and Christie conferred with four different children. She didn't listen to them read; rather, she talked with each of them about their reading and writing: what they enjoyed about the books they were reading, how their reading connected with their lives, and what they were writing about. Next came math.

Christie's class grew to 40 as kids from other classes came to her and some of hers left. The "new" class formed itself quickly into three smaller groups of 10 to 15 students and each group began to try to figure out the area of an irregular polygon using a variety of manipulative materials including cubes, rulers, string, and graph paper. They worked intensely and relatively quietly for 40 minutes. Christie told me that although most of them had seen the algorithm for area, she knew that they didn't really get it. "They need a lot of time with this sort of investigation," she said. As they finished up, she asked them to write an evaluation of their work in their math logs and respond to the question, "What do you think you'll have to do tomorrow in order to solve this problem?"

Christie and I ate lunch in another classroom so that some of her students could play and do housekeeping in their classroom. Lunch was followed by a social studies inquiry group. The class was beginning on a topic that Christie calls "Freedom Fighters." "Let's think of what we know about Martin Luther King Jr.," Christie said. Their conversation drew up on the poetry that they had written in the morning and the stories that they had collected as children growing up in New York City. Christie took notes on their conversation.

At the end of the day, there was library. Five students stayed in the room while Christie took the others to library. I stayed, too. I was intrigued by the subtle way this group had managed to stay behind. One boy was sweeping the floor; a girl was cleaning the blackboard; two boys were in the rug area singing a song softly with each other and really working to harmonize their voices. There was another boy who was roaming.

Christie returned. I checked to see that this was indeed the final period of the day. She then explained to me that she keeps kids out of "specials" (designated groups for additional instruction in reading, etc.) in this way so that she has some time with them. She said that the class is too large for her to get to know each child if she doesn't do things like this. I thought this was my cue to leave in order to give her time and space with her kids. I began putting my coat on and remarked about how I had liked the contributions of the girl who had stayed behind to the poetry discussion and her questions later about Martin Luther King Jr. "Yeah. She's pretty interesting," said Christie. "I worry a lot about her, though," she added. "She and her twin brother down the hall are being raised by their 88-year-old grandmother who has put them up for adoption since she feels she can no longer take care of them. Their mother, who is in Florida, wants nothing to do with them."

I was stunned. Thoughts and feelings came flooding over me. The child's 11 years old, I thought. Who's going to adopt her and her brother? What does this mean? Does this mean a foster home? "I'd adopt them if I could," said Christie. "They are such nice kids. Their grandmother is a very old lady and her old-fashioned ways show with these children."

I looked at this little girl who suddenly was no longer a stranger to me. Then Christie started to tell me about the others who were there horsing around with each other, being kids. Each of them had a story.

This is not an overcrowded school of desperately needy children in a high-poverty area of New York City. Christie's class is heterogeneous in every way. It reflects the diversity of New York City. There are children who do come out of difficult family settings, but there are also children who are coming from intact, single, and two-parent families.

Christie went on to talk about her class, her goals, their goals, whether she will stay with fourth grade next year or move up with her class to fifth grade. We explored that some. She feels that this is a wonderful age group to teach, but so much has already happened to these kids and some of them are so far behind that she thinks maybe she should move to second or third grade where she could, perhaps, stop what seems to her an inexorable slide toward failure on the part of some of her students. She worries about who her students will get for fifth grade. She likes the idea of taking a class through two or three grades. We left the kids, and Christie walked me downstairs to the front door. I hated to leave. I knew there was so much more to talk about, but I knew that she had to get back to her kids.

This story incorporates several lessons that I have learned over this past year in conversation with my students and graduates of the undergraduate Early Childhood, Elementary Education Program at a large New York City university about the transition from preservice to in-service teaching and about the first years of teaching. It raises for me some powerful and troubling questions about the work of teacher education and instructional supervision, about preparing young teachers for work in urban schools, and about support for professional development during the first years of teaching. Christie seems to be handling her first year well, but other recent graduates have experienced tremendous difficulty. What makes the difference? What role does teacher education play? Are those of us who are doing teacher education in urban areas preparing our students for the schools and children that need them? Are our students developing the knowledge and skills essential to their working in smart and caring ways as teachers and change agents in schools?

BACKGROUND

Christie's story emerged in a context of conversation and story, a context that had been carefully crafted by student teachers, beginning teachers, and teacher educators for the express purpose of ongoing professional growth and development. The conversation group that provides the context for this and other stories is one of 10 such groups developed by teachers and researchers who are participants in the Sustainable Teacher Learning and Research Network Project, a network of 10 distinct Professional Development and Inquiry Groups in the United States, Canada, and Israel. These are small groups that were formed voluntarily by teachers and teacher educators to examine issues of professional development associated with preservice and in-service teacher education (see Clark, 2001). The groups meet regularly to pose and pursue teaching problems and issues and to provide intellectual and moral support to one another. Their social and intellectual work is done by means of story and personal narrative shared in what Florio-Ruane and Clark (1993) describe as "authentic conversation." This is face-to-face conversation conducted in an atmosphere of safety, trust, and care between people who share a common ground and to whom it is clear that everyone in the conversation from the least to the most experienced has something to offer and something to learn. Authentic conversation is not edited and defensive. It is not distorted by fear of negative consequences regarding what is said. The common thread relating these diverse groups is that the members actively work on learning and change in their professional lives outside their groups.

Fundamental to the project is the idea that teachers, working together to frame and solve education-related problems, can create their own powerful opportunities for learning (Cochran-Smith & Lytle, 1992; Fullan, 1991; Lieberman, 1995). We take the position that adults engaged in the process of teacher education, whether they be teacher educators, preservice or in-service teachers, need supported opportunities to reflect upon their own funds of knowledge, explore their attitudes and beliefs, and extend the repertoire of skills and strategies that form the underpinnings of their work (Darling-Hammond & MacDonald, 1997; Lieberman, 1988; McDiarmid, 1990; Moll, 1990).

Our inquiry into these conversations has been informed by understandings of story and narrative that draw on the work of Bruner (1990), Florio-Ruane (1991), Schubert (1991), and Witherell and Noddings (1991). We see the stories that the new teachers in the New York City group tell as "acts of meaning" (Bruner, 1990) through which they are making sense of the work of teaching. These stories emerge in our conversations as spontaneous vignettes—generally triggered by something someone has said or a question that has been asked. They are focused on classroom-related issues that are in some way problematic: such things as concern about a particular child, an aspect of curriculum, the requirements set by an administrator, or relationships with other adults in the classroom and the school. Stories, told mostly by the new teachers in the group, account for fully half of the discourse of every meeting of the conversation group. Theirs are stories told to prepare one another for the first year.

To an experienced teacher, there is little that is new in the stories that are told by these beginning teachers in conversation night after night, but newness is not the point. They have engaged in these conversations to learn about what it means to become a teacher and to support professional development. These stories constitute teacher lore, as Schubert (1991) describes it. They contain the new teachers' theories in action. Making sense of the day-to-day in a supportive, collegial environment where reflection, careful listening, and thoughtful, informed response are constants enables them to look at their work in ways that are not available in the bustle of the schoolday.

Like Witherell and Noddings (1991), we see the stories that these teachers tell of their work to be opportunities for discovery, learning, and sense-making about themselves and their profession. As such, these stories can be seen as essential pieces in the construction of the narrative about learning to teach and teaching itself that is the focus of this chapter. And, as such, these conversations can be considered as a way of knowing, a narrative teaching practice in the service of the construction of the knowledge of practice—an exemplar.

THE CONVERSATION GROUP

We began 4 years ago, these new teachers and I. On a warm spring night, we came together for the first time and began with stories of ourselves that were embedded in stories about our schools and classrooms and about children who puzzled, intrigued, or challenged us. We knew a lot, or thought we did, about good teaching. The teachers were energetic, well-prepared, and committed to working in "difficult" schools; I was an experienced teacher and teacher educator committed to supporting them in their first years. So we started a conversation group as a way of inquiring into and marking their professional development as teachers (Clark, 1995; Florio-Ruane & Clark, 1993). Hoping for a group of 10, I initially invited 15 participants: 4 first-year teachers, 8 seniors, and 3 juniors; and I asked for a 3-year commitment so that we could really explore the transition between preservice education and the first years of teaching. My colleague, Susan Haver, joined us at our second meeting and has been with us ever since. We've grown in number and changed as members graduated and moved away and new members were invited by current ones. The fact that almost every time we meet there is at least one new face hasn't seemed to matter. The threads of our stories intertwine.

It took two and a half hours to go around the table that first evening as we made introductions. Stories sparked other stories and the conversation moved in and out of their lives, their work, and their dreams. Here is a sampler taken from my running notes made during that first evening:

James is a junior. A 30-year-old undergraduate, he's had a lot of time to think about teaching and to study it. He says that he can't remember a time when he didn't want to do this, that growing up in the suburbs of Chicago, he was keenly aware of racism and the power of teachers as leaders. He wants to teach in emancipatory ways to empower students.

Sara is a first-year teacher in a public school in Chinatown. "I am teaching sixth grade," she says. "I have 46 students. I went into teaching because I wanted to help my community. I love this work."

Lee is also a first-year teacher. She is working as an assistant teacher in a private school and has begun on her master's at Bank Street. She feels that teachers can really change things; she's not at all sure that every problem can be handled by the schools.

Rebecca, a senior, picks up on Lee's remark about schools as problem-solving institutions and tells us about "power lunches" in her public school—businesspeople come in to have lunch and read with the children in the gifted program.

Diane, a first-year teacher, steps in with her story about her year in a class of sixth graders in Harlem. She tells of losing her voice from yelling, of breaking her wrist as she intervened in a fight, of having no support from her principal or the union, of talking on the phone with Sara and e-mailing me, of learning to catch them being good, of learning how to listen and move her students toward accepting responsibility for their behavior. She's now looking for a new teaching job not because she hasn't grown to like these kids a lot but because she feels that the school is so unsupportive of good teaching.

Introductions over, we agreed to meet again after graduation. We met twice more during the summer. These were times of looking for jobs, of planning for the first year of teaching, of looking forward. The first-year teachers were mentors to the recent graduates.

During our meeting in the second week of August, Diane once again told the story of her year with the sixth graders in Harlem. This time, though, we heard Diane talk about what she did to transform the class, and how they moved from five fights a day to one a month.

Then it was September and the first week of school and the group came together to talk about their first 2 days. Our first meeting of the new schoolyear began informally an hour and a half early when Marcy, who first came to the conversation group in August when she got her job, came to my office in tears and deeply distressed by her first 2 days of teaching. Two hours later, she shared the same story with the conversation group:

> The first 2 days of school have been a nightmare for her. She has a classroom with no supplies, not even chalk. There was nothing in the room, nothing but student desks and a wooden table with splinters. She and her mother taped over it and then covered it with a cloth. There was a box of books that she was told to go through. All were years out of date. Marcy went out and bought $400 worth of supplies. She has 27 fifth graders in her class. The first days were very hard for her. The weather was hot; the classroom close. The kids threw her pattern blocks out the window. They kept hitting each other, moving around the room, refusing to listen to her. She found herself yelling. It was the only way that she could get their attention. She was shocked by what she called "their lack of respect." Once they left, she cried all afternoon. The next day was equally difficult. They are supposed to be a group of "gifted students." Marcy says that "most of them cannot complete a sentence." "They have no social skills," she says. "Lunch isn't long enough," she cries. "By the time I get the kids to the lunch room and get back to the teacher's room, I only have 25 minutes."

We get Marcy through the evening. Sara offers her number. Others offer materials and books.

Around and through Marcy's story came the stories of others in the group. A first-year teacher in Bedford Stuyvesant tells of an adorable child with the mark of an iron burn on his arm. She does not ask for help. She seems to know what to do. Andrea, a first-year teacher who is in the South Bronx, started in a classroom that was really a big closet. There was a board missing in the floor, and a broken window. She discovered that a first-grade classroom was empty. She moved from fourth grade to first grade and got a real classroom as part of the move. In her new digs, she has all the materials that she needs. Like Marcy, however, others had to buy everything, including chalk. Some had the basics but no computer. Andrea and Marcy have no peer group of new or even young teachers. Andrea is told to teach from scripted math reading programs.

That was the first night. The new teachers talked. The second-year teachers offered support and advice. The seniors and juniors sat quietly and listened.

Marcy quit her job on the fifth day of school. She began substitute teaching and visiting in the classes of her colleagues in the conversation group, and by February she had a new teaching position in a private school. Andrea continued but, though she came to every meeting of the group, she stayed quiet through most of the year, only talking when she was invited to talk. Her stories showed her struggling within a setting where her first-grade children were failing and where she perceived there to be little room for teacher initiative.

EMERGING PATTERNS AND QUESTIONS

Others joined the group over the year. Some were undergraduates. Some were first- and second-year teachers. What became clear was that the patterns of storytelling and the topics raised during these first meetings of the group varied little over the ensuing year of conversation.

After that first summer, we met over a light supper on Friday evenings every 3 to 5 weeks. The next date was always determined by the group before we broke up. Between times, I visited in some participants' classrooms and sometimes heard from them on e-mail or through phone calls. I generally sent out meeting reminders to our growing list of participants; however, when it met, the group was rarely larger than 12 people.

As a "privileged observer" (Wolcott, 1988), someone who, as Ely et al. (1991) describe it, "is known and trusted and given easy access to information about the context" (p. 45), I was able to record in writing our conversations each time we met. I did this like a running record (Goodman, Goodman, & Hood, 1989) or a script tape (Hunter, 1984), writing in a sort of shorthand notation as fully as possible what each speaker said. I chose not to use a tape recorder during that first year because I was concerned about its impact on the spontaneity of the conversation. Thus, it helped to have a colleague as a regular participant so that I could check my perceptions of the evening with her.

Later, usually the same evening, I went back over my field notes, filled in places where I'd not been able to keep up, labeled topics that had emerged in the evening's conversation, and made notations about the tone of the evening and what seemed to be the primary concern(s) of the group. Using a system of grounded theory analysis (Glaser & Strauss, 1967), I analyzed the logs of these conversations looking for recurring themes that might help me and other teacher educators understand what works in our programs and what supports our students need during the first years of teaching.

As I made "analytic memos" (Ely et al., 1991) regarding my conversation logs of the 19 meetings that were held during that first year, I began to see patterns in the ways stories emerged and were told, in the types of stories told, and in who told various types of stories. I came to realize that Christie's story, while shocking, was not unlike the stories that Sara and Sandy told and other stories that I heard from first- and second-year teachers throughout that first year. I noted, however, that the stories of the new teachers are qualitatively different from the stories told and concerns expressed by most of the preservice teachers with whom I work and who participate in the group. Quite simply, the preservice teachers don't tell stories like those that the first- and second-year teachers tell.

The First-Year Teachers

Those first-year teachers who had a "good" first year told stories about their classes in which they used words like "my class," "my kids," and "my school." Like Delpit's teacher, who gives all of her students her own last name, these successful first-year teachers were possessive about their students (Delpit, 1995). We knew their children by name. We asked after them whenever we met. Further, these new teachers took charge in their classrooms, deciding about all manner of things, from how they would teach reading to how their students would line up. The teachers also told stories about themselves. Like Diane, who had detailed her first year for them, they talked openly about their problems and their mistakes. They sought support from the group.

Some, like Christie, began their year appearing strong, sure, and as if they knew what to do. Others, like Andrea, began more tentatively, trying, it seemed to Susan and me, to please administrators and other teachers. Gradually, they moved into the "savvy" stance of their peers. For Andrea, the moment came late in January when she realized that her students were not learning to read and do math through the programs that she was required to use. "I began to say, 'No,' to the staff developers," she told us. "I pointed out that the kids weren't learning. I began to do my own thing." In a school where most first graders do not learn to read and the average teacher holds back 7 to 10 students, Andrea held back three. She *knew* that the other 25 had learned to read; she had clear evidence.

Even Marcy, for whom the year began so disastrously, found a way to salvage her first year. Marcy's time came when, after months of substitute teaching and thinking about the class that she wanted, she took a job in a private school. Despite struggling with requirements that did not coincide with her ideas about constructivist teaching, she was in a generally supportive environment and was able to articulate and act on her understandings of teaching and learning. She made up her mind to return to public school teaching.

What the stories of these "successful" first-year teachers make clear is that when they started, they were not what Berliner (1988) describes as "novices" or even "advanced beginners." The impact of their teacher education program was not "washed out" as they entered their first classrooms (Zeichner & Tabachnick, 1981). What they learned in their preservice programs did not show up as a patina that they quickly shed in the workplace (Rust, 1994). They were focused from the beginning on their students' learning and, by their own accounts, they drew heavily on the skills and knowledge that they acquired in their preservice programs. These were essential to their learning how to negotiate the system on behalf of their students.

The performance of these first-year teachers suggests that they were functioning as what Berliner (1988) calls "competent teachers":

> They make conscious choices about what they are going to do. They set priorities and decide on plans. . . . They often feel emotional about success and failure in a way that is different and more intense than that of novices or advanced beginners. And they have more vivid memories of their successes and failures as well. (p. 42)

In contrast, those first-year teachers who had "tough" first years and were not sure whether they would continue in teaching rarely told upbeat stories about their classes. They complained about their students' skills, attitudes, behavior, and families. Unlike the successful first-year teachers, they never spoke of their students as theirs. They spoke of their workplaces in ways that suggested that they had adopted the prevailing negative assessment of students and community espoused by many of the veteran teachers in their schools. They told of focusing their energies almost entirely on classroom management. Throughout the year, they taught from scripted curricula. Though they got help from the conversation group, they never asked for it. The participation of these less successful new teachers in the group was irregular. They might come two or three times in a row and then not again for several months. Still, they got through the year and they planned to continue teaching. Most were thinking about finding new settings.

The performance of these less successful first-year teachers appears to lie someplace between Berliner's (1988) novice teachers and advanced beginners. Like novices, their behavior was "very rational, relatively inflexible, and tend[ed] to conform to whatever rules and procedures they were told to follow" (p. 41). However, like advanced beginners, their progress over the year showed that they were beginning to attend to the context of the classroom, to be guided by "strategic knowledge—when to ignore or break rules and when to follow them . . ." (p. 41), and they were beginning to bring their experience together with their knowledge of teaching.

This group of first-year teachers was at that stage that Fuller and Bown (1975) describe as "survival." But they were also concerned about the teaching situation which, according to Fuller and Bown, means that they worried "about having to work with too many students or having too many non-instructional duties, about time pressures, about inflexible situations, lack of instructional materials, and so on" (p. 37). None of these first-year teachers were in settings where there was a supportive administration or colleagues who espoused a learner-centered vision of teaching; thus, the conversation group seemed to serve as a lifeline and a vehicle for professional development.

The Second-Year Teachers

The second-year teachers came less frequently as the year wore on. They were "so busy," they told me. When they did come, they seemed like elder statesmen in the group offering support and know-how to both the first-year teachers and the undergraduates. None of them were experiencing the angst that characterized the conversation of the first-year teachers. They seemed to know what they were doing. They exuded confidence. They were unhurried, not frantic.

Following Berliner's (1988) taxonomy, these second-year teachers were "proficient." "This is the stage," writes Berliner,

> at which intuition and know-how become prominent. . . . [A] holistic recognition of similarities allows the proficient individual to predict events more precisely, since he or she sees more things as alike and therefore as having been experienced before. (pp. 42–43)

By their second year, Sara and Diane had moved easily into this stage of teaching. Theirs was a fluid performance. One knew it just by listening.

The Preservice Students

The juniors and seniors listened intently to the first-year teachers, asking questions and exploring issues that revolved around finding a job and getting started. They took notes on instructional strategies and interesting curricular ideas. They asked clarifying questions about these and about classroom management. They rarely told stories about their student teaching. Instead, they would raise issues about major topics such as ebonics or parental involvement, which they discussed in general terms. The first- and second-year teachers either responded to these initiatives with stories from their classrooms or they changed the subject. At one point in the spring of her first year of teaching, Christie said, "I don't have time for consideration of big issues like that. I have to focus on whether and how my kids are learning to read and write."

As I listened to the preservice students and contrasted their stories and conversations with those of the first- and second-year teachers, what struck me was that the preservice teachers rarely talked about the students with whom they interact in the ways that Christie, Sara, Diane, and others did: They did not "own" their students. I realized that in our teacher-education program, few students are given the opportunity to know a group of children as deeply as Christie does. Despite four semesters of student teaching, they do not get it—the time, or the involvement with children as individuals, each with a story, each with a future. They do not have the opportunity to worry not only about tomorrow but also about who will work with this group next year and the following year. They do not understand the messiness of schools, the politics, the struggles to work in authentic ways in environments that militate toward the conventional.

LEARNING ABOUT TEACHING THROUGH CONVERSATION

The difference in the stories about teaching told by first- and second-year teachers when compared with those of my preservice students has made me begin to question the structure of teacher education, particularly student teaching. The fact that some first-year teachers, even in difficult circumstances, seem to thrive while others do not, has also caused me to wonder. What, I ask myself, will enable these juniors and seniors to go into their first years of teaching ready, able to move from the sheltered discourse of the preservice program to the intensely focused and expansive discourse of the "successful" first- and second-year teachers?

The answers, I know, lie in these teachers' own stories, in the ways that they have shaped themselves, and the images of teaching and learning that they carry within them (Clandinin & Connelly, 1995; Grimmet & Erickson, 1989; Schön, 1987). But the answers lie, too, in their experiences of teacher education and in the set of expectations they hold of themselves and this work that they developed there (Schubert, 1991). How their lived experience intersects with the experience of teacher education and shapes their subsequent work as teachers is what I am beginning to learn from these conversations.

Learning to teach is complex work. It is not complete in a year or 2 years or even 4 years of preservice work. Teachers' understandings of their work, I am reminded by this year of conversation, become increasingly complex and situated as teachers gain in experience (Clandinin & Connelly, 1995; Clark, 1995; Clark & Peterson, 1986; Lieberman & Miller, 1978). Thus, the lessons that the stories from the first year of this conversation group hold for teachers and teacher educators are only the beginning pieces in the construction of our group's narrative about learning to teach.

One lesson that seems pretty clear to me 2 years into this conversation is that we should promote and extend the support of teacher-education programs through something like a conversation group. There should be a number of options—all voluntary, all there and available—as supports to new teachers. Who should provide this support? Teacher educators. Teacher educators understood in the broadest sense—school teachers, university professors, clinical instructors, and peers. These were the people to whom the members of the conversation group said they turned. Such support should be a part of a program's relationship with its graduates, not something that happens by virtue of an individual professor's willingness to give additional time and support, as is the case at NYU.

A second lesson has to do with the issue of who should be engaged in this postgraduate conversation. Peer teaching, the group seems to be telling me, is a powerful tool, particularly when the coaching or mentoring that is done comes from others who know what you need to hear, perhaps because they have just been there. Thus, Diane's story of her first year's journey into calmness and Sara's descriptions of the difficult home circumstances of some of her students were timely and appropriate both as cautionary tales and lessons about learning to teach. Neither Susan nor I could have told these stories. We are too far removed from our beginnings. "You need friends who understand why you're complaining and what you need to hear," said Marcy recently.

However, there also seems to be an important role for teacher educators here. While Susan and I say very little, we are the ones who convene the group; we have seen these students develop over time; and we have developed a backlog of trust with them. Thus, our presence seems to work as a kind of glue, binding the group together and enabling the conversation across different levels and realms of experience. Additionally, we are the ones who get the phone calls about new jobs, curricular issues, and resources.

An important aspect of these conversations is that they make a space for storytelling every time we meet. As Witherell and Noddings (1991) write, "Stories invite us to come to know the world and our place in it" (p. 13). Without the space for thinking out loud about and sharing their experiences of teaching, I am convinced that many of these beginning teachers would have been quickly socialized to the anti-progressive norms of the school cultures in which they are working (Lieberman & Miller, 1978; Lortie, 1975; Zeichner & Tabachnick, 1981). As it is, I see most of those who have had good first and second years as surprisingly independent decision makers about their work. They become professionals who are confident about their choices to teach, who choose where and how they teach, and who are deeply committed to learner-centered instruction.

The awesome familiarity in their stories seems to be both comforting and challenging to them. While someone has yet to tell a story that doesn't have an analog in the experience of someone else in the group, their ability to tell these stories and to know that they are heard as important artifacts of their teaching has a tremendous power. It seems to me that it pulls their lives with children out of the dailyness that marks so much of teaching and raises it to a level of interest that encourages scrutiny and analysis . . . sometimes, even reverence.

CONCLUSION

I am only beginning to find answers to the questions sparked by my work with this group of new teachers. I am confident that teacher education can be a powerful force in shaping teachers' understandings of their craft. I am confident that it can make the difference for new teachers *if* we, teacher educators, can see beyond the often rigid structures of standards and program design and hook into and work with the personal, imaginative structures that we and our students have created out of our lived experiences.

REFERENCES

Berliner, D. C. (1988). Implications of studies of expertise in pedagogy for teacher education and evaluation. In *New directions for teacher assessment. Proceedings of the 1988 ETS Invitational Conference* (pp. 39–67). Princeton, NJ: Educational Testing Service.

Bruner, J. (1990). *Acts of meaning*. Cambridge, MA: Harvard University Press.

Clandinin, D. J., & Connelly, M. (1995). *Teachers professional knowledge landscapes*. New York: Teachers College Press.

Clark, C. M. (1995). *Thoughtful teaching*. New York: Teachers College Press.

Clark, C. M. (Ed.). (2001). *Talking shop: Authentic conversation and teacher learning*. New York: Teachers College Press.

Clark, C. M., & Peterson, P. (1986). Teachers' thought processes. In M. C. Wittrock (Ed.), *Handbook of research on teaching* (pp. 255–296). New York: Macmillan.

Cochran-Smith, M., & Lytle, S. (1992). *Inside/outside: Teacher research and knowledge*. New York: Teachers College Press.

Darling-Hammond, L., & MacDonald, M. (1997). *Where there is learning, there is hope*. New York: NCREST.

Delpit, L. (1988, Summer). The Silenced Dialogue: Power and pedagogy in educating other peoples' children. *Harvard Education Review, 58*(3), 280–298.

Delpit, L. (1995). *Other people's children: Cultural conflicts in the classroom*. New York: New Press.

Ely, M., with Anzul, M., Freidman, T., Garner, D., & Steinmetz, A. (1991). *Doing qualitative research: Circles within circles*. New York: Falmer Press.

Florio-Ruane. (1991). In C. Witherell & N. Noddings (Eds.), *Stories lives tell* (pp. 207–233). New York: Teachers College Press.

Florio-Ruane, S., & Clark, C. M. (1993, August). *Authentic conversation: A medium for research on teachers' knowledge and a context for professional development*. Paper presented to the International Study Association on Teacher Thinking, Göteborg, Sweden.

Fullan, M. G. (1991). *The new meaning of educational change*. New York: Teachers College Press.

Fuller, F., & Bown, O. (1975). Becoming a teacher. In K. Ryan (Ed.), *Teacher education: 74th yearbook of the National Society for the Study of Education, Part 2*, (pp. 35–57). Chicago: University of Chicago Press.

Glaser, B. G., & Strauss, A. L. (1967). *The discovery of grounded theory: Strategies for qualitative research*. Chicago: Aldine.

Goodman, K. S., Goodman, Y. M., & Hood, W. J. (1989). *The whole language evaluation book*. Portsmouth, NH: Heinemann.

Grimmet, P., & Erickson, G. (1989). *Reflection in teacher education*. New York: Teachers College Press.

Hunter, M. (1984). Knowing, teaching and supervising. In P. L. Hosford (Ed.), *Using what we know about teaching*. Alexandria, VA: Association for Supervision and Curriculum Development.

Lieberman, A. (Ed.). (1988). *Building a professional culture in schools*. New York: Teachers College Press.

Lieberman, A. (1995). *The work of restructuring schools: Building from the ground up*. New York: Teachers College Press.

Lieberman, A. & Miller, L. (1978, March). The social realities of teaching. *Teachers College Record, 80*(3), 54–68.

Lortie, D. L. (1975). *Schoolteacher*. Chicago: University of Chicago Press.

McDiarmid, G. W. (1990). Challenging prospective teachers' beliefs during early field experience: A quixotic undertaking? *Journal of Teacher Education, 41*(3), 12–20.

Moll, L. (1990). *Vygotsky and education: Instructional implications and applications of sociohistorical psychology*. New York: Cambridge University Press.

Rust, F. O. (1994). The first year of teaching: It's not what they expected. *Teaching and Teacher Education, 10*(2), 205–217.

Ryan, K. (1986). *Lives of first year teachers*. Paper presented at the Annual Meeting of the American Association of Teacher Educators, Washington, DC.

Schön, D. A. (1987). *Educating the reflective practitioner: Toward a new design for teaching and learning*. San Francisco: Jossey-Bass.

Schubert, W. (1991). Teacher lore: A basis for understanding praxis. In C. Witherell & N. Noddings (Eds.), *Stories lives tell* (pp. 207–233). New York: Teachers College Press.

Witherell C., & Noddings, N. (1991). *Stories lives tell*. New York: Teachers College Press.

Wolcott, H. (1988). Ethnographic Research in Education. In R. M. Jaeger (Ed.), *Complementary methods for research in education*. Washington, DC: American Educational Research Association.

Zeichner, K. M., & Tabachnick, B. R. (1981). Are the effects of university teacher education "washed out" by school experience? *Journal of Teacher Education*, 32(3), 7–11.

CHAPTER 13

In Conclusion: An Invitation

VICKI KUBLER LaBOSKEY AND NONA LYONS

In the chapters of this book the authors have presented narrative teaching practices they have used and found to be beneficial for collecting and constructing the knowledge of teaching. They have described the practices in enough detail for interested others to replicate them in other settings. They have also provided short-term, and if possible, long-term evidence for the value of the practice. They have made suggestions as to the potential uses for the practices and considered how the lives of teachers and their students might differ as a result. They have shared exemplars that vary along a number of dimensions: some are used primarily in preservice education, or in in-service education and practice, or in research; some are meant to benefit the teacher and some the students; and some are written and some are verbal. These categories are not discrete; many combine them in a variety of ways. The book, therefore, constitutes a diverse set of narrative teaching practices that can be utilized by other teachers, teacher educators, and researchers to enhance their work and their knowledge of that work in a number of ways.

More important, we believe this body of work and its mode of presentation constitute the generation of a process by which knowledge of teaching can be articulated, constructed, tested, and disseminated. We are proposing a means for practitioners, teachers, and teacher-educators to continue, and perhaps even accelerate, "the slow revolution" (Grant & Murray, 1999) in "taking charge" of their own knowledge domain. This approach to knowledge growth in teaching is similar to other recent movements in the educational arena, particularly the self-study of teacher education practices and the scholarship of teaching. In a piece constructed for the purpose of defining self-study, Loughran and Northfield (1998) state that "[s]elf-study can be considered as an extension of reflection on practice, with aspirations that go beyond professional development and move to wider communication and consideration of ideas, i.e., the generation and communication of new knowledge and understanding" (p. 15). The activity of self-study, then, is designed not only to reflect upon and improve one's own practice, but to generate knowledge. Likewise, the scholarship of teaching, according to Shulman (1998), involves "acts of mind or spirit that have been made public in some manner, have been subjected to peer review by members of one's intellectual or professional community, and can be cited, refuted, built upon, and shared among members of that community. Scholarship properly communicated and critiqued serves as the building block for knowledge growth in a field" (p. 5). The work of this volume seems to do just that and thus is comparable to both the self-study of teaching and the scholarship of teaching. However, it also makes some unique and important additional contributions to this effort. First these exemplars focus on narrative as a way of knowing in teaching, because of its particular potential to capture "the meaning of experience" (Bruner, 1986, citing Rorty) and to represent the knowledge that emerges from action (MacIntyre, 1984; Mitchell, 1981). Second, and very significantly, is the accompanying shift from considerations of validity to the testing of exemplars on the basis of trustworthiness and validation.

POTENTIAL OF THE EXEMPLARS

We suggest that the varied exemplars of reflective practice described and examined in this book and, more generally, the process of generating and testing exemplars of narrative knowing in this way can be useful for three purposes: legitimating the work that teachers do and the knowledge that they generate, thereby enhancing their political power within the profession; providing them and their students with opportunities to learn through intentional reflective activities—as a way to construct meaning; and building connections with others in situated, collaborative contexts that result in the creation of "discourse communities" (Putnam & Borko, 2000).

Legitimation

As Richert makes particularly explicit in Chapter 3, narrative teaching practices that ask teachers to tell their stories in one form or another value what teachers know. They provide teachers with the opportunity to be "acknowledged as competent knowers in the professional world." This can be very helpful to them in terms of maintaining hope and commitment. The 10th-grade English teacher whose story is told by Craig and Olson in Chapter 8 suggests that she might not have stayed in teaching if it were not for her narrative practice. In Chapter 4 Akin gives direct testimony for the role her story-writing plays in sustaining herself "intellectually and emotionally as a teacher": "Most important, through this writing I put myself back into the text of teaching in a meaningful role, as one of learner and engaged participant. In placing myself in this position I gain an important sense of ownership over my work, an increased ability to focus, and a stronger, more confident sense of myself as being in control of my teaching and learning."

Rath's Deirdre and Claire (Chapter 10) gain confidence in articulating their knowledge in ways that can challenge and transform the system in which they work. Anderson-Patton and Bass (Chapter 7) provide evidence that a similar benefit can accrue to the students of teachers who use narrative practices. The students' individuality is acknowledged and self-confidence boosted.

In addition to legitimating what they know, teacher narratives make what they know more accessible to others. Their stories make visible the sophisticated nature of the undertaking; in Richert's words, "It would be impossible to read them and not have an enriched image of how complex the work of teaching is and how vast the knowledge base must be to do the work well." The teachers who told their stories of reform to Freidus and her colleagues (Chapter 11) not only provided the researchers with a more complete picture of the enterprise, including the very emotional aspects of the struggle; they also felt respected and supported. As Freidus notes, such an environment encourages risk-taking and promotes professional growth. Likewise, Lyons found that her portfolio narratives (Chapter 6) could "affirm, disconfirm, or redirect the teacher intern in the process of identity formation, the identities of both personal self and the emerging professional person." Thus, these narrative practices could affirm teacher expertise, grant them greater political power, and lead to transformation.

Opportunities to Construct Knowledge

All of the chapter authors make clear that the narrative practices not only provide opportunities to share what teachers, prospective teachers, and teacher educators know; they also furnish the means and the incentives for changing and developing that knowledge. Indeed, argue Anderson-Patton and Bass, the bringing to consciousness of one's knowledge through narrative practice is only a beginning. As Rust points out in Chapter 12, when new teachers tell their stories they are engaged in "'acts of meaning' (Bruner, 1990) through which they are making sense of the work of teaching." In Chapter 9 Clandinin and Connelly stress the need for narrative inquirers to learn "to think narratively."

Freidus found that the group conversations helped "teachers to gain insight into their own practices and those of their colleagues," and that "[t]ogether, the individual stories narrated a sequence of events that brought to life what Sarason (1982) called the 'prehistory' of the people involved. The composite retelling of this prehistory . . . enabled both researchers and teachers to look at current experiences in more complex ways."

LaBoskey found that stories can also help teachers come to know what they do not know and need to know about teaching and learning (Chapter 2). She suggests that this is especially important for "preservice teachers at the outset of their credential programs . . . [because they] are individuals who are at the stage in their careers when they need to call into question much of what they 'know' about teaching as a result of their previous 'apprenticeship of observation' (Lortie, 1975)." The writing and discussing of stories helped the novices to determine that they needed to know "not only specific curricular and instructional strategies and techniques, but also the attitudes and skills of reflective practice." All of the authors in the book agree with LaBoskey that reflection is a critical aspect of teaching well and that narrative practices can promote and scaffold this process.

Lyons, too, is affirmed in her perception of "narrative as a way of knowing in teaching." She argues that the portfolio narrative provides a structure whereby the student teacher can engage in "intentional reflection." This "explicit performance experience as a self-directed, reflective learner, interrogating one's practice, and ultimately authoring one's own learning" benefits the teachers in the moment and provides them with "a potential model for lifelong professional development." Rath suggests "that narrative may be the one way that teachers enter wholeheartedly into the learning process."

Richert also stresses the value of narrative practice in the fostering of reflection. The quotes from her teacher writers make clear that they gained new insights about their teaching through individual and group analysis of their stories. This actually led them to make changes in their practice, which was true for Freidus's teachers as well, who acknowledged that the narrative conversations helped them to be more reflective about and attentive to the implementation of the new curriculum. As a result of their participation in the focus groups, they acquired "new skills and new ways of being in the classroom." In other words, as several authors suggest, narrative practices help teachers to construct and reconstruct their "personal practical knowledge" (Clandinin, 1986).

Akin, too, speaks about how the writing, reading, and sharing of her narratives of teaching allow her to reconceptualize her practice. Indeed, her stories have enabled her to gain a greater sense of ownership over her work and encouraged her to discover ways to improve an institutional context that she finds hostile to herself and her students. Cardwell (Chapter 5) claims that one way to work toward equity, to help urban students learn, is by telling them stories that can make the curriculum more personally meaningful to them. Craig and Olson also found narratives to be beneficial in efforts to work against the social injustice inherent in our educational systems. Their students make a beginning by examining and revising their own taken-for-granted assumptions. One of the structures that help them to do so is the interaction with others in their group who come with different experiences and perspectives.

Building Connections

Rath identifies the creation of "a community of inquirers" as foundational to the process of knowledge development through action research. Clandinin and Connelly speak about opportunities to tell and then to live new stories. This comes about primarily through interaction with colleagues—by listening to and learning from the stories of others, as well as one's own. All of the authors agree that narrative helps us to do that— to build connections with others in ways that both allow and encourage the joint construction of knowledge.

Some, especially Anderson-Patton and Bass, Akin, and Lyons, focus upon the need to articulate one's views for an audience as a factor in the promotion of self-awareness and growth. Indeed, as one of Lyons's students notes, in going public with one's philosophy, you not only have to be more conscious of what you are doing and why, you have to take responsibility for it: "So just the act of binding yourself to those ideas was a very educational experience."

Some, including Cardwell and Freidus, consider the important role that narratives can play in fostering relationships among members of an educational community so that it will be more conducive to learning for all its constituencies. In Cardwell's words, "The unscripted, spontaneous stories teachers tell invite children to make connections, creating shared meaning and culture across the boundaries of race, class, gender, and ability/disability, which allows everyone the gift of stretching academically and emotionally to understand the lives of others beyond their experiences." The sharing of stories thus sets the stage for group learning, as it also provides the means.

In fact, many of the contributors to this book found that one of the reasons social interaction is a necessary condition of narrative practice is that it provides a "check for narcissism" (Anderson-Patton and Bass). That is, as LaBoskey notes, sharing can help teachers and learners to both hear and acknowledge multiple perspectives on an experience or idea. They come to recognize that their view is only one among many and that it may even be inaccurate and possibly detrimental. Olson's students comment very explicitly on how much they learned from their narrative practices of the need to "work on [their] own preconceived views and judgments of others."

Rust's discussion group worked so well as a learning environment for the participants because they were at different stages in their development as teachers. The mix of experiences allowed for "broad learning" and yet the limited 4-year range made it possible to capitalize on the power of peer teaching. Richert's teacher researcher group used their narratives to create a "culture of shared inquiry" where questions were raised of one another that pushed both the writers and the listeners to deeper levels of understanding.

The exemplars of narrative knowing in teaching described in this book have been tried in particular contexts, with certain constituencies, and for clearly articulated purposes. The teachers and teacher educators who have used them have found them to be beneficial. They have garnered evidence demonstrating that these practices can be useful for legitimating the work that teachers do, providing them and their students with opportunities to construct meaning, and creating communities of discourse engaged in the social construction of knowledge.

BEYOND THE EXEMPLARS

Most books of this genre would stop here. The presentation of a collection of possible "best practices" would be sufficient. But this text is different in two notable ways: 1) the authors make explicit the potential limitations of their strategies—they enumerate their cautions and caveats, and 2) most remarkably, the authors admit that their experiences and self-studies are not enough to establish the validity of the practices they describe. Instead, the approaches are offered not as ideals but as prospects. Readers are therefore encouraged to move beyond the exemplars by engaging in active inquiry into their potential.

Possible Limitations

First, we need to consider the limitations previously identified by the authors. We need to ask questions about whether or not these potential problems are insurmountable or subject to amelioration.

One of the most basic problems with narrative practice is that it can be very time-consuming. It takes time to both construct the narratives and to respond to them; it also takes time to develop the relationships that need to surround and support these efforts. Some authors describe strategies they have utilized to reduce the demands, as did Olson, who had her students respond to one another's work so that she did not have to do it all. Though such efforts are encouraged, all authors agree that we may need to accept the fact that additional time will be necessary. If our contexts do not acknowledge and support us in this regard, we may have to reconstruct them so that they do.

This, of course, is no simple task, which leads to our second and more significant caveat. Narrative practices can be very inconsistent with the prevailing epistemology of our educational institutions—the structures, orientations, and practices of our work environments. In some instances, as Akin notes, this may actually put narrative practitioners at risk of censure or even dismissal. At the very least, as Craig and Olson point out, the individual may feel alienated from her circumstances: "In this work . . . evidence of individual change—and change within small groups— prevails. Because large systems, whether they be school districts or networks of white privilege, are embedded within more positivistic and hierarchical ways of knowing, there are transitional periods where individuals may no longer fit comfortably in a conventional system but may be living a story that is yet to be or is in competition with stories of 'the way things are.'"

The additional problem with this is that for narrative practices such as those presented in this volume to have their full benefit, they need to be consistently practiced and supported, which is harder to do in unfriendly contexts.

Therefore, the third caution has to do with the need to provide adequate support mechanisms. The potential of these approaches can only be realized if they are engaged with consistency and are not isolated instances of reflective practice. As Rath notes, if teachers do not have adequate professional resources, including "access to reading, discourse communities, reflective time and space," they "may be left within their own frame." Similarly, Lyons has warned, there can be wide variations in definitions of reflection and we need to be explicit about our meanings and monitor congruence. The narratives generated by teachers and their students need to be heard by understanding colleagues and mentors who will both legitimate and advance their stories in meaningful and coherent ways. The more such circumstances prevail, the more likely a positive outcome will result from these exemplars.

Even if these conditions can be provided and narrative practices fully instituted, there are still other cautions to be considered. Most significantly, we need to remember that stories are limited interpretations; they carry with them our assumptions and biases. Listeners process the stories through their own experiential lenses. There is danger, as Hargreaves (1994) has posited, of "romanticizing" the stories educators and their students tell. Indeed, some can be such distortions—are so "cynical, elitist, sexist, or racist" (Hargreaves, 1994)—that they are potentially very harmful. We need, therefore, as the authors of this book have emphasized, to raise questions about the stories we hear and the stories we tell, especially when they are intentionally employed to influence learners, as in Cardwell's exemplar. We must, as Bleakley (2000) proposes, move beyond the current genre of the "personal-confessional" to ensure that our stories are "ethically sensitive" and principled.

In a similar vein, we need to ameliorate the tendency for stories that are presentational, like the Anderson-Patton and Bass portfolios, to be mere "showmanship." Some of the authors have built-in strategies for strengthening a reflective orientation, as did LaBoskey with her guiding questions and Richert with the self and group analyses. But all who attempt to use these exemplars should make a conscious effort to include structures that will ensure a principled interrogation of the knowledge claims represented by and in the resulting narratives. And we do hope that you will employ these strategies in your own contexts since it is only in that way that their validity can actually be determined.

Validity Through Validation

Unlike most other texts of this sort, we do not expect you to just take our word for it. Instead we consider this book to be an invitation to our readers to join with the authors in an exploration of narrative teaching and research practices as a way of constructing meaning and of gathering up the knowledge and understanding of practice. As we explained in the introduction, the premise for this volume is derived from Mishler's (1990) notion of the testing of validity by employing the exemplars in new contexts and engaging in an "ongoing discourse among researchers" and, in this case, practitioners as well. We hope that you have, and will continue, to examine the trustworthiness of the exemplars we have provided by considering the adequacy of our descriptions of the practices and their contexts, as well as of our evidence, both short-term and long-term. But more than that, we hope you will try for yourselves these practices, with appropriate modification for your circumstances.

Some of us have already begun the process of validation in earnest. Freidus (1999), LaBoskey (1999), and Lyons (1999) presented their exemplars of narrative practice at a session of the annual meeting of the American Educational Research Association. After that presentation, each author solicited a colleague to test her respective exemplar in a different context. The results of this process have been undergoing careful analysis (Freidus, 2000; Freidus & Rust, 2001; LaBoskey & Henderson, 2000, 2001; Lyons, 2000; Lyons & Mulligan, 2001; Mulligan, 2000). In essence, what we found in all three partnerships is that the narrative exemplars were beneficial in the trial situations. However, the benefits were not always the same. For instance, in the case of LaBoskey and Henderson (2000), Henderson found, in the initial trial, that the positive effects were neither as consistent nor as strong for her students as they were for LaBoskey's. This difference seemed due in part to an incomplete implementation of the original strategy, and in part to a difference in context that was not adequately accommodated. As subsequent adaptations were made based upon that information, the results improved (LaBoskey & Henderson, 2001). Thus, the validity for these narrative teaching practices has increased through validation in the practice of others.

An especially powerful aspect of the above collaboration involved our direct communication with one another. All partners were able to answer each other's logistical questions and deliberate together about the meaning of the outcomes. We believe that such interchange is especially consistent with Mishler's (1990) notion of "validation as the social construction of knowledge." Our hope, therefore, is that as you, the readers, will engage in the practices described in this book and share your results with us and with the public. We believe that such an approach has tremendous potential for advancing the field in authentic ways. Teaching involves the active engagement of human beings with one another in the interest of learning. It is therefore complex by nature, unpredictable and context-specific. We cannot aim to discover final answers or magic recipes. We can endeavor to develop exemplars that can provide frameworks for meaningful interchange and thereby make powerful knowledge construction more possible.

The authors of this volume have found that narrative teaching practices in general are particularly consistent with this perspective because they can help us to articulate what we know and construct new meanings ever more consistent with our ethical aims. Thus, they hold great promise for making a positive contribution to the lives of teachers and their students. The specific strategies we have designed and implemented seem to be good starting places. We offer them to you as just that—a beginning.

We hope you will join our community of narrative practitioners and researchers in the development and validation of trustworthy exemplars of practice.

More important, we are inviting you to engage in the more fundamental deliberation about the place of narrative teaching practices in the profession. Our argument and our discovery in examining this set of exemplars is that narrative teaching practices like these are especially trustworthy because they are intentional reflective activities that are socially and contextually situated and involve the identities of those involved; they are a way of constructing meaning—a way of knowing.

REFERENCES

Bleakley, A. (2000). Writing with invisible ink. *Reflective Practice, 1*(1), 11–24.

Bruner, J. (1986). *Actual minds, possible worlds.* Cambridge, MA: Harvard University Press.

Bruner, J. (1990). *Acts of meaning.* Cambridge, MA: Harvard University Press.

Clandinin, D. J. (1986). *Classroom practice: Teacher images in action.* Philadelphia: Falmer Press.

Freidus, H. (1999). *Narrative research and teacher education: New questions, new practices.* Paper presented at the annual meeting of the American Educational Research Association, Montreal, Canada.

Freidus, H. (2000). *Narrative research and teacher education: A quest for new insights.* Paper presented at the Third International Conference on Self-study of Teacher Education Practices, East Sussex, UK.

Freidus, H., & Rust, F. (2001). *Narrative practices—Teacher education, professional development and the conduct of educational research.* Paper presented at the annual meeting of the American Educational Research Association, Seattle.

Grant, G., & Murray, C. (1999). *Teaching in America: The slow revolution.* Cambridge, MA: Harvard University Press.

Hargreaves, A. (1994). *Dissonant voices: Teachers and the multiple realities of restructuring.* Paper presented at the annual meeting of the American Educational Research Association, New Orleans, LA.

LaBoskey, V. K. (1999). *Stories as a way to learn both practical and reflective orientations.* Paper presented at the annual meeting of the American Educational Research Association, Montreal, Canada.

LaBoskey, V. K., & Henderson, B. (2000). *Stories as a way to join practice and reflection.* Paper presented at the Third International Conference on Self-study of Teacher Education Practices, East Sussex, UK.

LaBoskey, V. K., & Henderson, B. (2001). *Examining the trustworthiness of narrative practices in teaching and teacher education: Stories as a way to learn both practical and reflective orientations.* Paper presented at the annual meeting of the American Educational Research Association, Seattle, WA.

Lortie, D. C. (1975). *Schoolteacher: A sociological study*. Chicago: University of Chicago Press.

Loughran, J., & Northfield, J. (1998). A framework for the development of self-study practice. In M. L. Hamilton (Ed.), *Reconceptualizing teaching practice: Self-study in teacher education* (pp. 7–18). London: Falmer Press.

Lyons, N. (1999). *Toward the creation of exemplars for professional development: Narrative teaching practices*. Paper presented at the annual meeting of the American Educational Research Association, Montreal, Canada.

Lyons, N. (2000). *Developing exemplars of narrative teaching practices through self-study partnerships: The reflective portfolio narrative*. Paper presented at the Third International Conference on Self-study of Teacher Education Practices, East Sussex, UK.

Lyons, N., & Mulligan, C. W. (2001). *Using reflective portfolio narratives to scaffold meaning and the construction of knowledge*. Paper presented at the annual meeting of the American Educational Research Association, Seattle, WA.

MacIntyre, A. (1984). *After virtue: A study in moral theory* (2nd ed.). Notre Dame, IN: University of Notre Dame Press.

Mishler, E. G. (1990). Validation in inquiry-guided research: The role of exemplars in narrative studies. *Harvard Educational Review*, *60*(4), 415–442.

Mitchell, W. T. J. (1981). *On narrative*. Chicago: University of Chicago Press.

Mulligan, C. W. (2000). *Portfolio narrative practices at Colby-Sawyer College*. Paper presented at the Third International Conference on Self-study of Teacher Education Practices, East Sussex, UK.

Putnam, R. T., & Borko, H. (2000). What do new views of knowledge and thinking have to say about research on teacher learning? *Educational Researcher*, *29*(1), 4–15.

Sarason, S. (1982). *The culture of the school and the problem of change* (2nd ed.). Boston: Allyn & Bacon.

Shulman, L. S. (1998). Course anatomy: The dissection and analysis of knowledge through teaching. In P. Hutchings (Ed.), *The course portfolio: How faculty can examine their teaching to advance practice and improve student learning* (pp. 5–12). Washington, DC: American Association for Higher Education.

About the Editors and the Contributors

Rebecca Akin teaches elementary school in the Oakland Unified School District in California. She received both her teaching credential and master's degree from Mills College, where she first began to do teacher inquiry. Her classroom research has been supported by the Bay Region IV Professional Development Consortium, and by the Carnegie Academy for the Scholarship of Teaching and Learning, where she is a fellow. She cofacilitates the Mills Teacher Scholars Project, an inquiry group for teachers in the Oakland area.

Vicky Anderson-Patton has been an adjunct professor in elementary education at West Chester University, Pennsylvania for 9 years. Vicky moved to Philadelphia from New Zealand to earn her doctorate in psychoeducational processes at Temple University. Her current research investigates engaging educators in self-study to enhance their awareness of utilizing creativity in the classroom.

Elisabeth Bass is associate professor and chair of the remedial English department at Camden County College in New Jersey and an adjunct professor at Rutgers University in Camden, New Jersey. She received her doctorate in psychoeducational processes at Temple University. She is involved in diversity work, self-study, and composition studies.

Nancy M. Cardwell is a member of the graduate faculty at Bank Street College of Education. Before joining that faculty, she worked as a public school teacher in central Harlem. Her research interests include narrative teaching practices in urban public schools, interactions between black women teachers and black girls in urban public school classrooms, and urban teachers' beliefs about effective teaching strategies.

Elaine Chan is a doctoral candidate in the Centre for Teacher Development at the Ontario Institute for Studies in Education at the University of Toronto. Her dissertation is on the ethnic identity of first-generation Chinese Canadians in particular, and multicultural education in general. Under the supervision of Professor Michael Connelly, she is conducting her research in a multicultural school context using a narrative approach. This work is embedded in a grant-supported research project examining the diverse cultural stories of experience that parents, teachers, and students bring to the professional landscape of a school. Interest in this area developed through her experience growing up in a Chinese Canadian family, teaching English in the Japanese education system, and working with the children of recent immigrants in the Canadian education system.

D. Jean Clandinin is professor and director of the Centre for Research for Teacher Education and Development at the University of Alberta. She has been involved with innovative programs of teacher education and with graduate studies programs. Professor Clandinin was the recipient of AERA's 1993 Early Career Award, the 1999 Canadian Education Association Whitworth Award, and the 2001 University of Alberta Kaplan Award for Outstanding Research. She was vice president of Division B of AERA from 1995 to 1997. She can be e-mailed at: jean.clandinin@ualberta.ca.

F. Michael Connelly is professor and director at the Centre for Teacher Development, Ontario Institute for Studies in Education at the University of Toronto (OISE/UT). He is also director of the Hong Kong Institute of Education/OISE/UT doctoral program. He is the founder and editor of *Curriculum Inquiry*. Professor Connelly was the recipient of the 1987 Outstanding Canadian Curriculum Scholar Award of the Canadian Society for the Study of Education, the 1991 Canadian Education Association/ Whitworth award for Educational Research, the 1995 Ontario Confederation of University Faculty Associations Outstanding Teaching Award, and the 1999 Lifetime Achievement Award from the American Educational Research Association. He can be e-mailed at: mconnelly@oise.utoronto.edu.

Professors Connelly and Clandinin worked together for many years on studies of teacher knowledge, classroom practice, and narrative inquiry. They began their work in 1978, and in 1980 began to work on their longstanding narrative inquiry with Bay Street School. Professors Connelly and Clandinin are pioneers in narrative inquiry and have spent 26 years collaborating on the study of teachers' personal practical knowledge and teachers' professional knowledge landscapes. They founded the Among Teachers Community in 1990. They are coauthors of *Teachers as Curriculum Planners: Narratives of Experience, Teachers' Professional Knowledge Landscapes,* and *Shaping a Professional Identity: Stories of Educational Practice,* as well as numerous articles and chapters in contributed volumes.

Cheryl J. Craig is an associate professor in the Department of Curriculum and Instruction, University of Houston. Her research interests involve narrative inquiry and the contextualization of teachers' knowledge. Craig's research has appeared in such journals as *Curriculum Inquiry, Journal of Curriculum and Supervision, Journal of Teacher Education, Reflective Practice, Teaching and Teacher Education,* and *Teachers and Teaching: Theory and Practice.* She has also authored a number of chapters in edited books.

Helen Freidus is codirector of the Reading and Literacy Program at Bank Street College, where she has been a faculty member since 1991. Her recent publications include *Guiding School Change: The Role and Work of Change Agents* (coedited with Frances Rust) and several chapters in contributed volumes.

Vicki Kubler LaBoskey (Editor) is a professor of education at Mills College in Oakland, California, where she codirects the Teachers for Tomorrow's Schools Credential Program, as well as the Master of Arts in Education with an Emphasis on Teaching (MEET). Last year she was named the college's Trefethen Professor. She received her Ph.D. from Stanford University in curriculum and teacher education. She is president elect of the California Council on Teacher Education and chair elect of the American Education Research Association's special interest group Self-Study of Teacher Education Practices. LaBoskey is actively involved in many groups and projects intent on supporting both preservice and in-service teachers in the transformation of their practice and their institutions according to the goals of equity and social justice. She has had numerous publications on the topics of reflective teaching, narrative knowing and practice, and self-study, including the book *Development of Reflective Practice*.

Nona Lyons (Editor) is a visiting research scholar at University College Cork in Ireland and has been involved with teaching and teacher education, most recently at Dartmouth College and previously at the Harvard Graduate School of Education, at Brown University, and at the University of Southern Maine. At University College Cork she is engaged in a new collegewide initiative working with faculty across disciplines on documenting their teaching for the Scholarship of Teaching Project. Lyons's current research includes the study of reflective development across professions, a project looking at the ethical and epistemological dimensions of the work of professionals for which she received a Spencer Fellowship, and a project examining narrative ways of knowing and their connection to institutional epistemologies. In 1996–97 Lyons was a visiting research scholar at the Wellesley College Center for Research on Women, where she extended her work on narrative. She is the editor of *With Portfolio in Hand: Validating the New Teacher Professionalism* and a coauthor of *Making Connections: the Education and Development of Adolescent Girls at Emma Willard School*. She can be e-mailed at: nonalyons@hotmail.com.

Margaret R. Olson is an associate professor at St. Francis Xavier University in Antigonish, Nova Scotia. She received her doctorate from the University of Alberta. Her research interests are narrative inquiry and the personal, professional knowledge development of teachers in preservice and in-service contexts. Olson's work has been published in the *Canadian Journal of Education*, *Teaching and Teacher Education*, and several contributed books.

Anne Rath is a teacher educator at University College Cork, Ireland. Her primary interest is in understanding how change and transformation are supported in formal educational settings. Her research is informed by her own experiences as a classroom teacher, guidance counselor, teacher educator, community worker, and consultant to groups interested and committed to developing and building a more inclusive, critical, and expansive world in education.

Anna Ershler Richert is a professor of education at Mills College in Oakland, California. She received a Ph.D. in curriculum and teacher education from Stanford University, an M.A. in education from Syracuse University, and a B.S. from Skidmore College. She directs the single subjects component in English and social studies for the Teachers for Tomorrow's Schools Program at Mills College. Dr. Richert is a national leader in the school reform movement, emphasizing pedagogy and the professional development of teachers as learners and leaders in today's changing schools. She is a board member of the Coalition for Essential Schools. She recently served as codirector of the Bay Area School Reform Collaborative's School/University Partnerships initiative. Dr. Richert has written numerous articles and chapters on her areas of research interest: school reform, teacher learning, teacher knowledge, and teacher research.

Frances O'Connell Rust is professor and coordinator of Early Childhood and Elementary Education Curricula in the Department of Teaching and Learning at New York University. She is the winner of the 1985 AERA Outstanding Dissertation Award, the recipient of the Teachers College Outstanding Alumni Award (1998), and the recipient of the Association of Teacher Educators 2001 Award for Distinguished Research in Teacher Education. Her research and teaching focus on teacher education and teachers' research. Her most recent books are *Guiding School Change: New Understandings of the Role and Work of Change Agents* (coedited with Helen Freidus), *Changing Teaching, Changing Schools: Bringing Early Childhood Practice into Public Education*, and *What Matters Most: Improving Student Achievement*, a volume of teacher research coedited with Ellen Meyers as part of her work as advisor to the Teachers Network Policy Institute.

Index

Academic success, role of narrative in, 83–84
Achebe, C., 102
Action research, 146–59, 193
Agency, 150–53
Akin, Rebecca, 8, 63–75, 191, 192–93, 195
Allender, Jerry, 102
American Association of Higher Education (AAHE), 9
American Educational Research Association (AERA), 197
American Psychological Association (APA), 15
Analysis
  grounded theory, 180
  and limitations of narratives, 196
  as making sense of narratives, 166
  See also Self-study
Anderson, G., 17, 18
Anderson, Ms. (teacher), 77–80
Anderson-Patton, Vicky, 8, 101–14, 191, 193, 196
Andrea (first-year teacher), 179, 180, 181
Antler, J., 171
Aristotle, 4
Artifacts, teaching, and self-study, 102–3, 104, 105, 106–11
Artistic forms, 111–12, 114
Australia, narrative research practices about literacy instruction in, 161–72
Authority, 92, 115–30, 153, 170
Axline, Virginia, 83
Ayers, W., 171

Baker, E., 20
Bakhtin, M. M., 76
Bank Street College, 80, 162, 169, 178
Bass, Elisabeth, 8, 101–14, 191, 193, 196
Belenky, Mary, 22, 169

Berliner, D. C., 182, 183
Bernstein, R., 3, 22, 134
Bleakley, Alan, 23, 99, 151, 196
Bloom, B., 133
Border crossing, action research as, 146–59
Borko, H., 4, 18, 21, 190
Bowen, O., 183
Boyer, Ernest, 1, 5, 9, 20, 24, 131
Britzman, D., 79, 85
Bronx, New York, teaching in Catholic school in, 80–82
Brown Foundation, Inc., 128
Bruner, Jerome, 3, 15, 16, 18, 22, 34, 90, 176, 190, 191
Brunner, D. D., 83

Cardwell, Nancy M., 8, 76–86, 193, 196
Caring, 32, 147, 176
Carter, Kathy, 3, 16, 21
Casey, K., 4
Catholic school, teaching in, 80–82
Centre for Teacher Development (OISE/UT), 136–45
Challenged students, 13–14
Chan, Elaine, 8, 133–45
Christie (first-year teacher), 173–75, 181, 184
Claire (teacher), 157–58, 191
Clandinin, D. Jean, 3, 4, 8, 16, 34, 44, 45, 69–71, 115, 116, 124, 133–45, 151, 161, 184, 185, 191, 192, 193
Clark, C. M., 175–76, 177, 185
Class issues, and sharing narratives, 80–82
Clinchy, Blythe, 22
Cochran-Smith, M., 4, 16, 17, 18, 176
Collaboration
  and action research, 149, 151–52, 153, 155
  building, 149
  and characteristics of narratives, 29

Collaboration (*continued*)
  and narrative as mode of inquiry, 4
  and narrative authority in knowledge
    communities, 128
  and narrative practices as exemplars of
    inquiry, 21
  and narrative research practices, 160–72
  and portfolio presentation narrative, 92,
    93, 99
  and potential of exemplars, 190
  and problems with narratives, 23
  and reflective restorying, 44
  and self-study, 101, 104, 105, 114
  See also Colleagues/collegiality;
    Connections; Discourse community;
    Team teaching
Colleagues/collegiality
  and building connections, 193
  and conversations, 176–77
  and defining teaching, 65–66
  and dissertation presentation, 135
  lack of time for, 65
  and narrative authority in knowledge
    communities, 128
  and narrative research practices, 169
  and portfolio presentation narrative, 92
  and potential of exemplars, 193
  and sharing of narratives, 60–61
  and teaching as collegial act, 32
  See also Conversations; Sharing of
    narratives
Collective narratives, narrative research
  practices as, 161–72
Commitment, 150–51, 154, 158–59, 170
Community
  creating/building, 148–49, 163, 190
  discourse, 148–49, 151, 152, 158, 159, 190
  importance of, 158
  and narrative research practices, 163,
    167–68, 169
  and potential of exemplars, 190, 193
  teachers' narrative authority in
    knowledge communities, 115–30
"Confessionalism," 23, 99, 196
Connections
  and action research, 159
  making/building, 71–72, 77–85, 106,
    190, 193–94
  and potential of exemplars, 190, 193–94

Connelly, F. Michael, 3, 4, 8, 16, 34, 44, 69–
  71, 116, 124, 133–45, 151, 161, 184,
  185, 191, 193
Conscious awareness, 91, 95–96, 98, 191
Context
  and adaptation of exemplars, 46
  institutional epistemologies as, 534
  "it depends," 16, 34
  and limitations of narratives, 195
  meaning in, 148–49
  and narrative as mode of inquiry, 3, 4
  narratives as situated in, 21
  and teacher-researcher relationship, 1
  unfriendly, 195
  and validity/validation, 197
Conversations
  "authentic," 176
  as means for learning about teaching,
    184–86
  of new teachers, 173–88
  patterns of, 180–84
  and potential of exemplars, 192
  and scaffolding of portfolio process, 2
Copeland, W. D., 99
Coppola, E., 126, 127
Craig, Cheryl J., 8, 115–29, 190–91, 193, 195
Cronbach, L., 19
Cuban, L., 101
"Culture of dependency," 157
Culture of shared inquiry, 194
Cultures, differing, 53–56
Curriculum, and action research as border
  crossing, 146–59

Darling-Hammond, L., 176
Day, C., 153
Deirdre (Irish teacher), 148, 156–57, 191
Delgado-Gaitan, C., 154
Delpit, L., 82, 181
Denzen, N., 18
Developmental Continuum, 165
Dewey, John, 14, 20, 29, 57, 123, 151
Dialogue
  internal, 50
  with mentors, 45–46
  and narrative authority in knowledge
    communities, 127
  and self-study, 102, 103–6
  See also Conversations

Diane (first-year teacher), 178, 181, 183, 184, 185
Discourse community, 148–49, 151, 152, 158, 159, 190
Dissertation presentation, 134–45
Diversity, and action research, 154–56
Doyle, W., 21
Duckworth, E., 18
Dyson, A., 84

Egan, K., 4, 23
Eisenmann, L., 17
Elbaz, F., 3
Ely, M., 180
Emma (student intern), 97
Engagement
    and action research, 150–51, 158
    and dissertation presentation, 144
    and narrative research practices, 163, 170
    and validity/validation, 197
English Language Development (ELD) program, 53–61
Environment
    adaptation of, for meeting needs of students, 155
    creation of safe, 151–52, 191
    suppressed teaching, 64–66
Epistemology, 1–2, 5, 11, 23, 24, 195
Erickson, G., 184
Erikson, E. H., 81
Ethical issues, 22–23, 32
Exemplars
    beyond, 194–98
    definition of, 6
    helpfulness of, 31–46
    implementation of and debate about, 46
    introduction of idea of, 6
    Kuhn's promotion of, 19–20
    and narratives as candidate, 1, 5, 21–22
    and new forms of scholarship, 5
    possible problems with, 22–24
    potential of, 190–94
    and validation process, 6, 19–21, 196–98
    as way of learning practical and reflective orientations, 31–37
Extended Reflective Narrative, 91

Facts, 141, 142
Feedback, 90, 103, 112–13, 114, 149

Fenstermacher, G., 16, 34
Florio-Ruane, S., 176, 177
Focus groups. *See* Conversations
Formalism, 134, 135, 142
Frames of reference, 136, 137
Freidus, Helen, 8, 160–72, 191, 192, 193, 197
Freire, P., 22
Friends, good/"critical," 148, 149, 151, 152, 153
Fullan, M., 169, 176
Fuller, F., 183

Gender issues, 17
Genishi, C., 84
Gilligan, Carol, 77, 81
Glaser, B. G., 180
Gleeson, J., 146
Goldstein, L., 113
Goodman, K. S., 180
Goodman, Y. M., 180
"Grand narratives," 69, 73, 133, 134
Grant, Gerald, 4–5, 17, 18, 102, 189
Greene, Maxine, 71, 150
Greeno, J. G., 18, 21
Grimmet, P., 184
Grounded theory analysis, 180
Guba, E. G., 162, 166
Gudmundsdottir, S., 3, 21

Hamilton, M. L., 101
Hanmer, T. J., 77
Hardy, Barbara, 3
Hargreaves, A., 162, 169, 196
Harvard University, 1, 124
Hatch, T., 126
Haver, Susan, 177, 181, 185
He, Ming Fang, 136, 138, 140, 142, 143–44
Helen (teacher), 154–56
Henderson, Barbara, 46, 197
Herr, K., 17, 18
Hiley, D. R., 3
Hood, W. J., 180
Hopedale Elementary School (New York City), 77–80
Humanities Research Council of Canada, 128
Hunter, M., 180

Identity
  and action research, 154
  and dissertation presentation, 136–44
  and narrative practices as exemplars of
    inquiry, 22
  and portfolio presentation narratives,
    96–97, 98
  and potential of exemplars, 191
  and reconceptualizing teaching, 64–65
  validation of professional, 167
In-service teacher education
  and conversations, 175
  journaling in, 123–27
  See also Teachers: first-year; Teachers:
    second-year
Inquiry
  and characteristics of inquiry-guided
    research, 19
  culture of shared, 194
  narratives as exemplars of, 21–22
  narratives as mode of, 1, 2–4, 21–22, 95,
    190
  teaching as act of, 32
Intentional narrative practices, 2–3, 6, 90,
  91, 92–98, 99, 190, 192
Interview narrative, 45–46
Ireland, 146–59

James (preservice teacher), 177–78
John (physics teacher), 87–89, 96–97
Journal writing, 99, 104, 123–27

Kegan, R., 151
Kellaghan, T., 146
Kelly, Ms. (teacher), 80–82
Kingsolver, Barbara, 161
Knowledge
  and action, 190
  and action research, 156–58
  and building connections, 193
  and characteristics of narratives, 29
  communities of inquirers as essential to
    construction of, 193
  conscious awareness of, 91, 95–96, 98, 191
  fluidity of, 66
  formal/practical dualism of, 15–17, 34
  "it depends" context of, 16, 34
  and justification of professions, 4–5
  and learning and storying of experience,
    66

  modes/types of, 15–17, 34
  and narrative authority in knowledge
    communities, 115–29
  and narratives as mode of inquiry, 1, 2–
    3, 4, 21–22, 190
  personal practical, 34, 115–30, 192
  and potential of exemplars, 191–93
  and principles of Mills College program,
    32
  researcher-practitioner coconstruction
    of, 171
  role of narrative in, 11–28
  scholarship as building block of, 190
  scientific, 2, 3
  as social construction, 18, 32
  and students as constructors of
    knowledge, 156
  subject matter, 32
  teachers' lack of, 54–55, 122–23, 192
  of teaching, 17–19
  teaching as, 3
  teaching for acquisition of, 32
  validity/validation of, 6, 156–58, 197, 198
  what counts as teacher, 4–5
Kuhn, Thomas, 6, 19–20

Laboskey, Vicki Kubler, 2, 7, 9, 11–28, 31–
  47, 192, 193–94, 196, 197
Lagemann, E. C., 133
Lampert, M., 4, 18
Lane, B. C., 116
Language development, 52–61, 68–69
Learning
  about teaching from stories teachers tell,
    48–62
  and action research, 149, 150
  to ask right questions, 154–56
  and conscious awareness, 95–96
  constructivist view of, 32, 66
  conversations as means of, 184–86
  feedback as part of, 149
  forging explicit performance of self-
    directed, 98
  group/shared, 193
  and knowledge as social construction,
    18
  and narrative as mode of inquiry, 4
  and narratives that teach, 48–62
  and portfolio presentation narrative, 90,
    91, 92, 96, 98

and potential of exemplars, 192, 193
presentations as key to, 150
and reconceptualization of teaching, 66–67
responsibility and agency as central to, 151
and self-study, 102
situated, 148
social and active nature of, 76, 148
and storying, 66–67
and teachers as learners, 53–56, 61, 62, 63–75, 150–51
to think narratively, 133–34, 138, 191
Lee (first-year teacher), 178
Legitimation, of teachers' work, 2, 190–91
Leibowitz, H., 140
Leitch, R., 153
Leonard, D., 146
Lieberman, A., 176, 185, 186
Lincoln, Y., 18, 162, 166
Linn, R., 20
Literacy instruction, narrative research practices about, 161–72
Logical-scientific mode (paradigmatic), 3, 15, 16, 34, 41
Lortie, D., 169, 186, 192
Loughran, J., 101, 189–90
Lyons, Nona, 2, 3, 8, 9, 11–28, 45–46, 77, 87–100, 101, 102, 113, 152, 191, 192, 193, 195, 197
Lytle, S., 4, 16, 17, 18, 176

MacDonald, M., 176
MacEwan, H., 23
MacIntosh, Peggy, 119
MacIntyre, Alasdair, 3, 15, 190
Marcy (first-year teacher), 178–80, 181, 185
Martha (case), 45
Maura (Irish teacher), 148, 151–52
McDiarmid, G. W., 176
McDonald, J., 51
McEwan, H., 4
McLaughlin, M. W., 163
Meaning
  and action research, 148–49, 152
  acts of, 176, 191
  and building connections, 193
  and characteristics of narratives, 29
  construction of, 4, 6, 22, 190, 198
  in context, 148–49

and knowledge as social construction, 18
and knowledge communities, 117
and modes of knowing, 15
and narrative as mode of inquiry, 4
and narrative authority, 116
and narrative practices as exemplars of inquiry, 22
and narrative research practices, 161
and portfolio presentation narrative, 90, 95
and potential of exemplars, 190, 193
reconstruction of, 135, 136–37, 138, 139, 141–42, 144
recovery of, 135, 136, 138–39, 140–41, 144
shared, 161
and storytelling, 77
and students as meaning makers, 156
and teachers as meaning makers, 153
and validity/validation, 6, 198
Memories, 138, 139, 140
Mentoring, 45–46, 92
Miller, L., 185, 186
Mills College/Bay Region IV teacher research projects, 48–62, 66–67, 69
Mills College Credential Program, 31–46
Mishler, Eliot, 6–7, 8–9, 11, 18–19, 20, 21, 99, 124, 196, 197
Mitchell, W., 3, 15, 190
Moll, L., 176
Morrison, Toni, 90
Moss, Pamela, 20
Mulligan, C. W., 197
Multiculturalism, 148, 156–58
Munby, H., 116
Murray, Christine, 4–5, 17, 18, 189

Nager, N., 80, 171
Narrative inquiry, definition of, 138–39, 151
Narrative practices
  adaptation of, 46
  alternative representations of, 111–12, 114
  benefits/helpfulness of, 22–24, 31, 33–46, 84–85, 127–28, 190–91
  cautions and caveats about, 15–16, 22–24, 44–46, 84–85, 127–28, 170–71, 194–96

Narrative practices (*continued*)
  characteristics of, 21–22, 29
  and claims of narrative knowing, 15–17
  creating text of, 49–50
  current research about, 6–7
  definition of, 4, 6
  as exemplars of inquiry, 1, 21–22
  exploring feelings in, 57–58
  focus of, 51, 56, 69–71, 72
  functions/purposes of, 3, 4, 6, 12, 15, 21,
    23, 48–49, 50, 61–62, 67, 90, 91, 128,
    159
  incentives to do, 61
  "internal dialogue" in, 50
  and learning about teaching, 48–62
  making sense of, 166
  methodology for, 49–52
  as mode of inquiry, 1, 2–4, 11, 95
  outcomes of, 52–62, 63, 68, 98
  perspective of, 68–69
  questions about, 4–5, 22–24
  reading, 58–59
  and reconceptualization of teaching, 1–
    2, 9, 13–14, 63–75
  and research, 160–72
  role in sustaining academic success of,
    83–84
  as socially and contextually situated, 21
  using narratives to teach about, 133–45
  value of, 37–46, 68
  and writing narratives, 67–74
  See also Exemplars; Reflection; Stories/
    storying; *type of narrative or story*
National Board for Professional Teaching
  Standards, 1, 2
Noddings, N., 3, 176, 177, 185
Northfield, J., 101, 189–90
Nova Scotia, 117–23
Nussbaum, Martha, 4, 14

Objectivity, 15, 20, 141, 142
Olson, Margaret R., 8, 115–29, 190–91, 193,
  194, 195
"One model fits all" approach, 156
Organization for Economic Co-operation
  and Development Review of National
  Educational Policies, 146, 147

Paley, Vivian, 11–13, 24
Paradigmatic mode, 3, 15, 16, 34, 41

Pendlebury, S., 16
Perry, William, 22
Personal practical knowledge, 34, 115–30,
  192
Peterson, Penelope, 160, 185
Piaget, J., 76, 81, 84
Polanyi, M., 136, 137
Politics, 4, 32, 190, 191
Portfolio Conferences, 1, 6, 124
Portfolios, 1, 2, 3, 45–46, 87–100, 191, 192,
  196
Positivism, 3, 18–19, 116, 142
Power, 4, 5, 23, 190, 191
Presentations
  and action research, 150
  dissertation, 134–45
  as key to learning, 150
  and knowledge communities, 117
  and limitations of narratives, 196
  portfolio, 2, 87–100
  public, 92, 93, 112–13, 117
  and self-study, 112–13
Preservice teacher education
  and action research as border crossing,
    146–59
  conference groups as core of, 171
  and conversations, 175, 177–81, 182,
    183–84, 185, 186
  and Martha's dialogues with mentor,
    45–46
  and narrative authority in knowledge
    communities, 117–23
  as narrative inquiry, 44
  narrative research in, 160–72
  as ongoing process of inquiry, 45
  and portfolios, 1–2, 87–100
  and potential of exemplars, 192, 193
  reading response and base groups for,
    117–23
  and "setting the tone" assignment, 33–46
"Problem" students, 154–56
Professional development
  and action research, 146–59
  and conversations, 175, 176, 183
  and learning about teaching from stories
    of teachers, 61
  narrative research practices as tools for,
    160–72
  and portfolios for self-study, 91
  and potential of exemplars, 191, 192

Professional Development and Inquiry
Groups, 175–76
Professors, teachers' contest with, 17
Puckett, Abbie, 123–27
Putnam, R. T., 4, 18, 21, 190
Putney, L., 162

Quiet, thoughts about, 35–37

Rabinow, P., 3
Race, and sharing narratives, 77–80, 82–84
Rath, Anne, 8, 146–59, 191, 192, 193, 195
Reading at the boundaries, 136, 137–38,
140, 142, 144
Reading response groups, in preservice
teacher education, 117–20
Real life/authenticity, and self-study, 105
Rebecca (preservice teacher), 178
Reconstruction of meaning, 135, 136–37,
138, 139, 141–42, 144
Recovery of meaning, 135, 136, 140–41,
144
Reductionism, 133–34, 135, 142
Reflection
and action research, 149, 150, 152–53,
155
and conversations, 176–77
and definition of narrative practices, 6
definitions of, 99, 152–53, 195
Dewey's views about, 14
essential dispositions of, 151
and Extended Reflective Narrative, 91
intentional, 190, 192
and learning about teaching from stories
teachers tell, 49
and learning to think narratively, 133–
34
and limitations/problems of narratives,
23, 195
and narrative authority in knowledge
communities, 123–27, 128
and narrative research practices, 163,
168, 169, 170
and narratives as exemplars of inquiry,
21
and narratives as mode of inquiry, 2–3
and outcomes of narratives, 52, 58–59
and portfolios, 1, 2, 89, 90, 92, 95, 96, 97,
98–99
and potential of exemplars, 192

and principles of Mills College program,
32
and purpose of narratives, 67
and reading responses as narrative
practice, 118–20
reflecting on, 90
and reflecting on text, 50–51
as self-deception, 23
as self-discovery, 23
and self-study, 102, 103, 105, 106–11,
189–90
and "setting the tone" assignment, 33–
46
and teacher-student relationships, 155
teaching as act of, 32
and what is reflective development, 99
Relationships
and action research, 154–56
building, 154–56
and limitations of narratives, 195
and potential of exemplars, 193
power, 23
subject-researcher, 162–63, 164
teacher-researcher, 1
teacher-student, 154–56
teaching through, 76–86
Reliability, 18–19, 20
Research
caveats about narratives in, 170–71
characteristics of inquiry-guided, 19
and exemplar idea, 6
"grand narrative" of, 133, 134
influence on teachers and policy makers
of, 160
and narrative research practices, 160–72
and novice researchers, 133–45
and paradigmatic mode, 3, 15, 16, 34, 41
and potential of exemplars, 194
and questions about narratives, 5
and reconstructing another researcher's
journey, 134–45
split between practitioners and
educational, 15–19
and subject-researcher relationship, 162–
63, 164
in teacher education, 1–2, 160–72
university, 1–2
validity of, 160
as "works in progress," 149
Responsibility, 14, 150–53

Revised Curriculum for Primary Schools
(1999), 146, 148, 156
Rich, Emma, 13–14, 24
Richert, Anna Ershler, 7–8, 48–62, 64, 66,
67, 68, 74, 190, 191, 192, 194, 196
Ricoeur, P., 22
Ritchie, J., 68, 74
Rivera, Mr. (teacher), 82–84
Role models, 79, 81, 84
Ron (teacher intern), 93–95
Rorty, Richard, 15, 190
Russell, T., 116
Rust, Frances O'Connell, 8, 173–88, 191,
194, 197

Sadker, Myra and David, 119
Sara (first-year teacher), 178, 179, 181, 183,
184, 185
Sarah (learning support teacher), 149
Sarason, S. B., 61, 161, 169, 192
Scaffolding, 2–4, 90, 91, 95, 98, 101, 114, 192
Scholarship
and characteristics of narratives, 29
new forms of, 5
of teaching, 1–2, 9, 20, 24, 29, 190
Scholarship of Teaching project, 24
Schön, Donald, 5, 18–19, 20, 24, 102, 117,
123, 170, 184
Schools
culture of, 154
and isolation of teachers, 169
as stifling and painful, 152
Schubert, W., 176, 184
Schwager, Sally, 17
Self-concept, 77
Self-deception, 23
Self-discovery, 23, 77–80, 191
Self-study, 101–14, 189–90, 196
Self-Study Conference (Herstmonceux,
England, 2000), 103, 112
Serena (teacher), 48–49, 51, 52–57, 58–59,
60–61, 62
"Setting the tone" assignment, 7, 33–46
"Settling in," 154–56
Shapiro, E. K., 80, 171
Sharing of narratives
and action research, 149, 159
and building connections, 193–94
and culture of shared inquiry, 194

and dissertation presentation, 135, 144
and learning about teaching from stories
of teachers, 50, 51–52, 59, 60–61
and narrative research practices, 161–72
and potential of exemplars, 191, 192,
193–94
and reconceptualizing teaching, 69
and teaching through relationships and
stories, 77–85
See also Conversations; Dialogue;
Stories/storying
Shulman, Lee, 9, 20, 92, 113, 190
"Speaking the truth," 49
Stories/storying
Bruner's views about, 90
interactive, 45–46
and learning, 66–67
as limited interpretations, 196
and Martha's dialogues with mentor,
45–46
and narratives as exemplars of inquiry,
21–22
and outcomes of narratives, 56–58
and portfolio process, 2
purposes of, 76–77
and reconceptualization of teaching, 66–
67
retelling of, 161
romanticization of, 196
selection of, 142
as self-discovery, 77–80
and "setting the tone" assignment, 34–
46
sharing of, 77–85
teaching through, 76–86
telling, 56–58
truth in, 49
See also Conversations; Narratives
Strauss, A. L., 180
Student teaching, 184
Students
and building connections, 193
as meaning makers, 156
and potential of exemplars, 193
Subject matter, 32
Sullivan, W., 3
Support mechanisms, 169, 195
Sustainable Teacher Learning and
Research Network Project, 175–76

Tabachnick, B. R., 182, 186
Tan, Amy, 161
Tanya (teacher), 49, 52–58, 60, 62
Taxy, Cara (teacher), 37
Teacher education program. *See* Preservice
    teacher education
Teachers
    "advanced beginning," 182–83
    backgrounds of, 53–54
    as caring facilitators, 147
    "competent," 182
    dismissal, demeaning of, 15, 16, 17
    emotions/frustrations of, 53–55, 57, 59,
        71, 76, 84
    first-year, 173–75, 177–80, 181–84, 186
    gender of, 17
    lack of knowledge of, 54–55, 122–23,
        192
    as learners, 53–56, 61, 62, 63–75, 150–51
    as meaning makers, 153
    as model of inquirers, 12
    novice, 182, 192
    professors' contest with, 17
    "proficient," 183
    as role models, 79, 81, 84
    second-year, 183–84, 186
    students' relationships with, 77–85, 154–
        56
    as supports, 169
    as taking charge of practice and
        profession, 18
    vulnerability of, 51–52, 60, 74, 111–12,
        114, 138, 170
    See also specific person or topic
Teachers for Tomorrow's Schools (Mills
    College Credential Program), 31–46
Teaching
    for acquisition and construction of
        subject matter knowledge, 32
    as act of inquiry and reflection, 32
    as collegial act, 32
    as construction of knowledge, 3
    conversations as means of learning
        about, 184–86
    culture of, 154
    defining, 65–66, 150
    emotional and interpersonal aspects of,
        40, 57–58
    and ethical issues, 32
    "grand narrative" of, 69, 73
    knowledge of, as contested domain, 17–
        19
    narratives/stories as means for learning
        about, 48–62
    peer, 185
    as political act, 32
    and real life and work life, 64–65
    reconceptualization of, 1–2, 9, 13–14,
        63–75
    team, 148, 149
    through relationships and stories, 76–86
    and using narratives to teach about
        narratives, 133–45
Team teaching, 148, 149
Technical rationality, 1–2, 5, 20, 24, 133–34
Thinking narratively, 133–34, 138, 191
Trust/trustworthiness, 6–7, 11, 19–21, 60,
    99, 176, 190, 196
Truth, 15, 20, 49, 141

Validity/validation
    and action research, 156–58
    and beyond exemplars, 196–98
    characteristics of, 20
    and characteristics of narratives, 29
    consequential, 20
    definition of, 6
    of educational research, 160
    essential criterion for, 19
    and exemplars, 19–21
    expansion of alternative approaches to,
        11
    and knowledge of teaching as contested
        domain, 18–19
    and narrative as way of knowing, 190
    and narrative research practices, 167
    and new forms of scholarship, 5
    and portfolios, 91, 98–99
    as process of validation, 11
    as social construction of knowledge,
        197
    and trustworthiness, 6–7, 19–21
    vignettes about, 11–14
Voice, 150–53
Vygotsky, Lev, 72, 76

Warren, D., 17
Wasserman, S., 51

White, H., 21
Whitehead, J., 102
"Wide-awakeness," 150
Wilson, D., 68, 74
Wilson, S., 163
Winterson, J., 63
Witherell, C., 3, 176, 177, 185

Wolcott, H., 180
Writing, and reconceptualization of
   teaching, 67–74
"Writing myself into," 67–68, 73–74

Zachariou, P., 50
Zeichner, K. M., 17, 182, 186

DATE DUE
